GOD'S
OFFSPRING

Robert Goeringer

authorHOUSE®

AuthorHouse™
1663 Liberty Drive
Bloomington, IN 47403
www.authorhouse.com
Phone: 1 (800) 839-8640

Published by AuthorHouse 09/25/2018

ISBN: 978-1-5462-4939-9 (sc)
ISBN: 978-1-5462-4937-5 (hc)
ISBN: 978-1-5462-4938-2 (e)

Library of Congress Control Number: 2018907720

Print information available on the last page.

CONTENTS

PREFACE

these words shall allow understanding Spirits thus humans and weather: learn why specifics have occurred throughout history and where humans shall proceed within the near future for chosen humans/**God's** offspring.

when spoken, **God's** quotes shall remain in bold type: here is your first,

'I am the beginning, there is no end and life becomes Our pleasure. in genesis 1:26 God spoke: We shall create human beings that will be like Us and resemble Us. We, Us and Our are God as well as the Spirit.'

'The lower case bold me, mine, our, us and yours remain Christ speaking: the upper case words from God within regular print remain the chosen as well as elected.'

You shall become revealed why all living creatures feel, think and behave as they do. when **God** first spoke for his writer to slate offspring in 2009, earth's weather was volatile and there remained significant hurricanes and tornado deaths in **America.** over time, **God** asked for specific prayers and the alleviation of storms, where he chose. a few years passed and **God** asked your writer to pray for the decrease of weather anomalies globally.

were these correlations or from prayers? irrelevant, goodness occurred.

through your writer's life, the **Spirit** revealed answers from specific as well as broad questions: his words remain slated within your book for chosen humans to receive heightened awareness of what shall occur in the future.

'Write, move and speak continuously what You hear My anointed one.' one month into book, **God** said, '**Return to the beginning, modifying any reference of I, Me, My and Mine from your perspective. also, use refrain rather than** negative **verbiage: Our readers shall understand when reading latter chapters. I created and live within and through every human.** if You are christian, muslim, buddhist, agnostic or atheist, all receive good thought processes, feelings, direction and otherwise. **listen to Me, You shall learn to receive only good: when You listen and adhere to My plain words slated herein, life is good.'**

'**I asked Robert to write this book and spoke what to title, names and order of the chapters, as well as, every word within for a reason, You the reader. My writer is a vessel who remains aware of his illusion of giving My gentle goodness: he receives continuous information from Me and I spoke when and where to slate historical truth. everything has occurred for a reason upon earth and your enlightenment shall as well. please, read from the beginning to the end: I have a wonderful plan and numerous shall receive My perfect direction, thus, wellness.'**

what remains written in offspring shall allow your understanding: future, depends on praising and prayers; how **You** rear offspring and work **God's** will through **You** transcends all boundaries. from **God**, through hope, love and peace, many shall prevail into good futures. **God**, has worked well through writer's soul, however, disallowed final editing because time's come: **God's** offspring shall receive his favor. please read while understanding these general, as well as, specific ideas, feelings and words from **God**, rather than induced fleshly, focused upon incorrect syntax or grammatical composition—**God**, works well through your soul, thus, heart and mind.

'**Enlighten Yourself from My absolute truth: when asking and doing My will, your perspective and perceptions modify well: one question, why do humans focus upon the unchangeable past for others** grief?'

'Within this blessed book, You too shall receive information regarding healing others, as well as, Yourself from any inequity received through humanism. I am God, have a plan and You remain blessed further.'

'Within your book, I shall reveal humanism, spirits and weather for your hope filled awareness. learn why global negativity remains steadily declining through whom I choose and how, You too, shall receive numerous blessings continuously, within your favored life.'

'I shall continue enveloping souls of whom are chosen, You are invited. follow My suggestions and become a part of the wonderful solution.'

'Numerous parables shall be written and I remain speaking through Robert: humans receive the illusion of power, as well as, control while unaware why specifics occur well and unwell. is humanism spiritually driven? yes, and your awareness shall heighten perfectly with Me.'

'I shall bless individual readers, You shall feel My presence from and through all of these words and parables spoken revealing God's mystery: a spiritual paradigm shift remains occurring globally- I created everyone and have a wonderful plan through You as well. My goodness shall prevail: life remains good within My thinking, perspective, perceptions, ideas and feelings within your blessed soul.'

'The present remains the best time to live throughout human history for numerous blessed further and We love one another perfectly well.'

'Relevant information spoken within the bible remains slated within this book for the future: I shall simplify everything for your reason.'

'Slate colossians 4:3-4 from My quoted words—connect the bible with the present and future: write what remains spoken from Me for all humans.'

'Withal praying also for You, that God would open unto You one door of utterance and speak the mystery of God, which all of the writers of the bible and religious documents remained unaware: I shall regard humanism, spirits and weather.'

'The present and future remains the time God has decided for the truth of everything to be revealed within many: slated for humans awareness, My and your book, God's offspring remains the door, thus, book of utterance spoken for whom I choose to learn regarding earth's calm.'

'Every specific moment throughout history shall remain understood within this book for one reason: future generations to be revealed My perfect ideology regarding everything and future historical truth.'

Chapter

GREETINGS

'Please, relax and receive spiritual awareness from God's perspective, absent distortion within human minds through past written religious doctrines globally. human thoughts and feelings remain energy: I erased My writer's negative energy and spoke for him to slate the answers for life upon the following pages for future generations perfected awareness. My writer receives continual goodness, however, shall reveal reality upon these pages. I am and shall remain continual goodness, anyone alive whom follows My suggestions within this historical book shall receive continual goodness, as well. numerous humans shall become aware of Their perfect direction received from Me.'

all within this book shall remain dictated from **God** for a good reason: your soul, heart and mind becoming enveloped with calm awareness. remain unashamedly aware, **God**, is privileged knowing all good and bad thought processes through all of **Our** wonderful minds and specific behaviors throughout **Our** bodies. numerous viably wonderful and sustaining occurrences shall transpire and various unpleasant ones remain present through your information filled following pages. humans past, present and future are **God's** offspring; writings allow insight within **Our** complex minds and **You** shall receive various solutions for living blessed.

allow **God**, painting **You** upon life's canvas and negativity decreases through and around You. receive higher awareness for thinking and behaviors of everyone living on earth. **God**, allows everything good upon earth through **Our** calmness, joy, as well as, love. sharing correct information accordingly, **God's** continual desire remains assisting difficult times, love through pleasurable and your fullness shall be achieved. there are two requirements to receive a blessed life: praise and ask for **God** to bless others globally. when **You** do this, calmness, harmony and contentedness envelop your soul, thus, heart and mind throughout life.

following writings encompass numerous specifics for thinking, as well as, living: spiritual, generational and physiological with common sense as your foundation. offspring, shall reference humans good common sense as **God's** sense, for this is. title was chosen from **God**, for all offspring maturing through a sometimes uncertain world. **God** works through offspring well: sometimes overwhelmed souls shall receive a calming discernment of truth. all information remains good and bad, true and false. learn continual truth.

'**Preceding My writer's age of two, I have spoken and heightened his awareness of what shall occur around him. over time, he was revealed the consciousness of humans and the process of receiving continual goodness through thoughts and behaviors. following his enlightenment, I instructed him to write this book to share with whom desire My blessings as well. he remains My humble messenger: My wonderful plan has been slated within him for human awareness.'**

before proceeding further into offspring, **God**, is referenced as him: however, humans remain aware, **God**, encompasses male, female, thus, everything good that remains seen and unseen. please, receive parables throughout writings. individuals who are discontented in life or desire increased calmness through **Their** present spiritual, thus, psychological, emotional, intellectual, mental and physical realms shall receive **God's** good historical truth.

your vacillating consciousness, determines the progression and digression within your persona. through continuous feelings, as well as, thoughts occurring through your three faceted self (soul, heart and mind), this book shall reveal the process of alleviating negativity within. from **God**, with your awareness and implementation of the numerous suggestions within this book; anxieties, impulsiveness, anger and impatience shall be replaced with a blessed mindfulness of love, thoughtfulness, patience, peace, focus and an optimistic drive living certainly perfect within your soul.

'I have revealed complexities to My writer regarding human interaction, chemicals within the human body, as well as, atmospheric specificities within the earth's weather; You shall receive what I desire, continuous certainty through your gently blessed journey. I have a plan through your soul, as well.'

progress further, knowing your life shall proceed more wonderfully through every new miraculous sunrise: with heightened faith, hope, love and peace **God** shall prevail. implement consistent calm, love and optimism from **God**, through **You** forever. writer shall discuss feelings and emotions first, they are intrinsic for **Our** personas through everyday occurrences transpiring within **Our** lives and continuously apparent. navigating through these pages, **You** shall remain copiously aware how prevalent emotions have occurred and shall remain within **God's** present, thus, future societies.

where do these continual emotions, feelings, thoughts and your behaviors derive?

throughout life, **God**, has taken your writer on one spiritual journey after another.

God desires quoted, **'your writer's life experiences occurred to write this book for others and for Them understanding all of Their or others**

bad **occurrences are from the** bad **spirit,** negative **energy or as** satan **has spoken,** satan **through humanism and weather, rather than Me.'**

numerous chosen shall become well aware: **God** has revealed information regarding why bees and mosquitoes bother You, why others cut **You** off in traffic and why everything flows perfectly one moment then zero thrives upon next through work and private.

why there are bad occurrences for good people, why good occurs for bad. why **You** remain sometimes annoyed easily and upon the next completely calmed. why numerous of global human populations lose the illusion of control of themselves and yell. why animals attack anything and why people remain nonobjective and intolerant.

reading chapters, **You** shall receive many good answers from **God**, through and within your writer regarding humans meaning of life and the reason **You** sometimes think, communicate and behave impulsively inappropriate, yet, unaware why: short answer- humanism remains spiritually predicated.

reading book, **You** too shall learn, **God** has been and remains only good. plagues, infections and negative physical inequities remain from satan.

Your writer has received three significant spiritual rebirthings over life: each one, occurred for reasons understood following the last intense one on july 19th 2009. over a broad lifetime and living in the spirit, **God** proceeded working through his writer in continual stages, revealing how **God's** good direction flows perfectly within offspring desiring wellness.

Your heart remains significantly relevant and related throughout your life: all of **God's** offspring, globally have received spiritually recurrent lessons in life, thus, good essences and numerous feelings of faith, hope and love. when blessings occur repetitiously, **You** desire assisting other families whom remain presently overwhelmed and are needing calmness within: **God** chooses many for his agenda. when assisting others, **God**, gave **You** these thoughts, therefore, remains perfectly aware and reciprocates through those involved affecting optimistically You, Them, offspring and others, thus, future generations directed well upon an enlightened earth.

'I, am God, who loves and cares for You through all good thought processes, wonderful feelings, functional behaviors and consistent love through your heart. My goodness, through numerous individuals encompassing masses, remains reasoning why good paradigm shifts occur, perfectly well. life remains spiritual: I choose individuals continuously as well as envelop Their ideas, feelings, perspectives, perceptions, senses and thoughts well. humans remain aware of great distances within this infinite universe. all vastness encompassed within remains void of life, however, My good energy upon earth teems with life for a reason, your love for Me and love for others, then My potential flows perfectly through You. life is good, remain further blessed from the divine will, through your frictionless splendor in My perfect timing. You shall receive awareness of why oceanic weather anomalies have decreased significantly in 2013, 2014, 2015 and shall into the future. I remain the originator of all goodness, alleviate negativity and have a gentle plan within your consciousness as well.'

Chapter

FEELINGS AND EMOTIONS

philosophizing three decades from **God**, your writer's conclusion remains: fleshly, feelings and emotions predicate why **You** think, behaviorally move and verbalize as **You** have. every thought process and behavior **You** receive remains formed, acted and reacted upon because of your conscious and subconscious feelings, as well as, emotions. how **You** feel determines your actions and behaviors and these determine others reactions towards **You** or otherwise. here lies one palpable example: your stuck in a traffic jam, late for a seminar, meeting, work deadline or receiving offspring from school. what are your multitude of feelings, emotions, thoughts, actions, thus, reactions? are **You** calm and collected or overwhelmed and anxiety ridden beyond rational sometimes? dependent upon spiritual, thus, temporal specifics, humans vacillate between spectrums. how **You** act and react within any given situation remains relevant from spiritually induced correlations inscribed within your thoughts and feelings occurring continuously and accordingly manifests within and through numerous.

naturally occurring bodily functions: sneezes, coughs, feeling the need to urinate or stomach growling are released because of feelings, emotions and thoughts: something heard, viewed, touched, smelled, tasted or thought a millisecond earlier differed from the good and bad energy within You. next time **You** sneeze, contemplate thought process a millisecond before particles were expelled: **You** also are physiologically aware, all humans sneeze because they have pollen or dust within. why do they? emotional discharges occur because **You** remain disagreeing and uncomfortable: observing what was heard, spoken, smelled, thought, touched or seen remains riveting or powerful within your mind. often times, they remain subconsciously triggered from a latent former memory, rather than awareness of the pollen count, psychosomatically induced through your mind. here remain a few general questions related with your persona, generationally speaking. upon early childhood, were your innate needs received? more than likely they were if **You** love well and are reading these words. secondly, what optimistic and pessimistic behavioral predispositions had your parents internalized in **Their** rearing process? thirdly, were parents patient or impatient? hereditarily predisposed behavioral characteristics remains inherently significant, thus, profound specifics within life. remaining as humans nature/nurture debate, it is both and shall become discussed further in one following chapter. understanding **Yourself** remains most significant fleshly factor for resolving your generational inequities as self respect, worth and image depicted inwardly and out. modifying generational issues, creates healthier and absolutely more self sufficient offspring, families, thus, **God's** future offspring. calm parents contribute rearing healthy offspring and many societally, over time. your spiritually conscious and subconscious mind remains very powerful and **You** shall understand an abundance traversing through these pages why **You** spiritually, then behaviorally, psychologically, thus, fleshly feel, think and behave as **You** are directed.

from **God, You** shall become a light of strength, self worth and love with others: from **God**, through hopefulness and faithfulness, **You** shall have a more wonderful future filled with contentment through Yourself, thus, enmesh calmly into others. loving **Yourself** wonderfully transcends, especially into your family and offspring. presently, humans throughout industrialized, technologically and informationally overloaded societies, numerous remain overwhelmed through and within a distortion filled living. placing socioeconomic status aside, every individual human who has conversations with others, accesses internet, drives a vehicle, lives, works with others, reads newspapers and listens are profoundly aware: individuals remain needing something more sustaining than emotional fixes, via, materialistic purchases, medications, as well as, many other durationally short term remedies for **Their** incompleteness within.

what numerous presently desire remains inherent, free and shall last throughout life. conscious awareness of **God** s continual love and apparent wellness through Them. human lives are becoming exacerbated: others overflowing agendas and a plethora of demands of humanism feeling **You** must adhere, **God**, becomes shunned or placed aside for the sunday service or zero for countless encompassing societies masses. humans societally desire working together towards purposes common, however, many place **God** figuratively near the back of the line through **Their** daily progression.

pardon, looks as if countless have forgotten who created You, why **You** are here and what shall become societies when most are intertwined receiving self serving needs and placing **God**, secondarily, thirdly or nil. first, for those whom believe, remain faithful, praising, as well as, praying to **God** throughout **Their** day, bravo! **You** are completely aware, **God** is good. second, for countless others whom are overwhelmed currently and refrain from receiving solace through **God** s embrace and love through Them, there are suggestions and information of hope throughout your blessed book.

continue reading further: if zero improvements remain needed for family, friends, spiritual, personal, professional, as well as, your offspring's lives appropriately becoming calmed, contented and enlightened, please return your book where **You** purchased.

when finished traversing through **God's** offspring, become aware of why there remain numerous humans whom remain completely calm and placated within themselves and desire abundantly more for humanism.

many reading remain unaware why they develop contentedness then figuratively fall upon **Their** faces again and again. preceding statements remain very relevant. individuals societally furthering themselves from **God**, rather than embracing his assistance and calm, sadly continue digressing through soul, thus, heart and mind. subtle and significant digressions proliferate further within offspring and future generations, **You** are aware. **God**, has revealed through writer's soul, progressive and positive views how he feels, loves and thinks through every human and absolutely You.

shall close with another quote from **God's** request when writing your book:

'**I am the good energy who raised Jesus into heaven: all healing and goodness globally has and shall continue to occur from Me alone and through human minds/hands. I am God and live in chosen human hearts and minds for progress and peace within My elite on earth.**'

3

WRITER'S REARING

'Leave unedited: I have relieved your negative memories, thoughts and feelings for life, however, desire past personal inequities slated for a reason: others to relate and realize I have a plan for Them as well.' writings occurred following rebirth: all good words remain directed from God, through writer: asking repeatedly if this was what he desired. taken upon a journey that proceeds presently; for now, shall discuss your writer's childhood, many may empathize or relate through personal discountings.

born in Tulsa, Oklahoma, united states of America- february 11th of 1969 within st. francis hospital; parents, Eva and Gary Goeringer remained unaware what was in store for Their offspring: blue collar and reared in mid west, We struggled with life. Father's vocation was a route man, whom picked up soiled diapers for Our living: discontented, was wanting more for his family. working his way up with abc uniform a promotion came; working in washroom entailed back breaking work. generational and spiritual issues hindered him further, through anxieties, anger and control amongst many other discountings. generationally was demeaned and belittled as a child from Father as more than likely You. please, receive parables. scarred deeply, his desires for betterment were a quest, thus, work ethic remained strong and resolute. persevering, **We** needed **Our** Fathers monetary contributions. although poor, **Our** Father was very aware through his hard work, anything could become achieved: this is America, land of the free and home for numerous brave.

working 80 + hour weeks was taxing mentally and physically, however, looking back two generations his grandFather worked this and more on a farm establishing homestead, thus, bettering his spouse and 16 offspring. forward two generations: writer's Mother, comparable with 90% of females in 1970's, nurtured offspring. sister, Cara Lynn, remains two years, three months and eleven days older: learned running by eight months and said alphabet forward and backwards before age two.

writer was youngest and male, enabled, belittled and demeaned often from Father, because of these generational discountings: **God** said, 'all inequities **instilled in childhood are spiritual and then generational.**' growing up poor, life was trying for **Our** family, thus, built character and **We** appreciated rather than anticipated life. generationally, **Father** was taught from his Father, love your offspring, family and spouse with all your heart, however, take out much of your generational, personal and societal insecurities upon those who love **You** most, your family. sound familiar? retiring at age forty nine, monetarily, his hard work and perseverance paid off, however, much unresolved anger remains apparent through numerous inequities. insecurities, became latent with actions and reactions for others. his generational inequities of anger, impulsivity, inappropriate behaviors, impatience and chemical abuse remain a hand book for self mutilation, figuratively speaking: **You** comprehend.

spring became summer and summer was soon fall: proceeded throughout every evening, dependent how Father's day transpired. on numerous specific moments, were enveloped within his presence, his conscious and subconscious control was completely paramount: mind **You** he was and is **Our** Father, **We** knew no other way. upon his generation as numerous today, his behaviors towards family remained most influential, Mother knew how She should act, react, thus, what behaviorally should become accomplished meeting his expectations: remain complacent while attending **Our** home and offspring: sadly, many females currently behave comparably. many females reading, proceed throughout **Their** day walking on eggshells and are attempting to keep conflict minimal while sustaining **Their** self esteem and worth. back to story. from a prior generation, thus, learned life was a males Kingdom; heightening internal pressures were apparent for him and overwhelming because throughout adult life, always was making things happen rather than allowed **God's** good presence working through him. meaning, absolutely, humans shall remain focused, work and proceed through day, performing **Their** vocational tasks assisted from **God's** calm, efficient, generous, patient and loving persona within everyone desiring.

once receiving an ability of letting go and allowing **God's** calming love and peace through Us, **We** proceed viewing less overwhelmedness and function progressing Yourself, family and society from **God**. fleshly, parents are ultimately responsible for **Their** offspring's emotional, mental, as well as, psychological progression.

aware or unaware, telekinesis remains implemented amongst numerous families globally for well or unwell. within humanism, all goodness occurring through **Us** remains from **God** and negative perceived control remains an illusion from otherwise. **God** remains a gentle goodness through **You** and everything alive. please, allow for further delving.

maturing consequentially because of **Our** Fathers behaviors over Us, he stated, 'created character' and many resentments, as unwell. before proceeding, writer's **Father** is caring, loving, good natured and passionate through respects, from **God** : beliefs, feelings, thoughts and behaviors experienced optimistically and pessimistically through rearing process, consciously and subconsciously are fleshly why humans lives transpire as they do.

typically through life, Mothers truly instilled wonderful qualities in **Our** behaviors, outwardly expressed for others, however, Mothers were scarred from **Their** Fathers perverse anger and power issues, generationally instilled in themselves and so on: **God** said, **'began spiritually through males**

preceding numerous generations.' females, attempt keeping relative peace within families, thus, homes and females are wonderful with most respects, especially how they care for others intuitively, while placing **Their** needs secondarily of **Their** offspring: specific remains respected because females whom are calm and work in societies most important vocation, rearing offspring, remain great examples for wonderful following generations. back to story, evening to evening became dependent upon **Our** Father's emotions, feelings, thus, angry, bitter, harsh words, thoughts and behaviors: what **Father** had conveyed was rather dissimilar of facade society portrayed and emitted for an abundance of youths.

instrumental progressing family forward monetarily: verbally, awaited calmness in response with decisions throughout **Our** days. before proceeding further, again remain aware, picture painted of **Father** remains undeniably harsh: he also is good and loves others intensely, completely and passionately, as well. yen and yang or good and bad as probably **You** and your families thinking: why does your writer rationalize? love.

although life was difficult, numerous wonderful, thus, joyous moments occurred: unstated now, nonetheless, reading deeper in book shall your awareness heighten.

what occurs maturing into adulthood remains intrinsically relevant with how **You** were reared: **You** remain aware. generationally, responsibility lies through what's learned, discarding less functional while modifying to appropriate, thus, offspring receive **Their** functionality from rearing and have better lives or skips a generation. why? in your book, **God**, revealed numerous answers from deep specific questions.

every human on earth remains influenced from predecessors more greatly than many are aware, thus, think before **You** act, this takes one millisecond and remains why **God** gave **You** cognitive reasoning in the first place. allowing further, loving **God** first, then **You** desire love for family and **Yourself** second, life becomes wonderful. **You** may be thinking, **Yourself** second? answering this question. if a relationship with **God**, becomes first, your return, meaning, every facet for your life especially good human interactions and business transactions become amazingly heightened.

God and **You** together, remain the only ones whom have intimate awareness of how **You** feel and think upon every occasion through life. existing, remaining in states of limbo or contributing further, **Our** spiritual progressions are extremely relevant related through self esteem, worth and happiness. **God**, entirely views your good deeds through contributions within societies, thus, blesses **You** accordingly. **God**, views power or control completely against his offspring's historic objective. **God**, placed **Adam** and **Eve** into the garden loving another unconditionally, while living comfortably, with an abundance of fruit for healthy nourishment of body. a perfect life, your aware what transpires biblically and shall clarify zero further: **God** desired **Them** listening to a good and simple instruction, though, life is fragile.

why had they resisted listening? one of numerous parables. satan, distorted **Their** perceptions and spoke cunningly through one bad tangible serpent into eves soul: **Adam** was unaware and unable to resist temptation, as unwell. both were directed well and unwell.

progression occurs in family units relying on mortal intuitions, **You** also are aware the bad choices affect individual family digression and societal digression throughout.

believing most in fleshly life, over time, in fact throughout human history among populations what has transpired? significantly what remains occurring presently? more than likely, one shall consider modifying beliefs and thinking. throughout book, **We** shall vacillate between humanism and spirits because they remain **Our** lives and your writer is directed well.

with this stated, every discounting within your current persona remains predicated from your inner persona, spiritually, then generationally instilled through Yourself. traversing through life, numerous view incompleteness from the fault of others. blame and egocentric behavior are human nature: are they **Our** choice or deeper? outward egocentric accountability occurs for positive and great occurrences rather than negative ones, thus, very biased **We** remain through **Our** internal progression.

You are well aware, this exactly has become societies behaviors currently, in fact, with heightened cognizant awareness of self, numerous remain apparently in tune with themselves rather than others around Them. industrialized societies have internalized almost everything, therefore, remain thwarting **God**, for culmination of reasons that shall become delved further through your following pages. related with those who are shunning **God**, weaknesses or lacking sufficient faith shall be known as falling deeper into satan's grasp: it wants this. typically, individuals have become enmeshed with humanism and overlook **Their** obvious reasoning remains absolutely spiritual.

factual statement remains, look around You; many are aware, elderly generations understand good and bad entities power, however, many youths believe otherwise. why have many vacillated away from faith, especially over the last few centuries? proceeding through book, **You** shall understand more related from prevalence of **God's** positive and how unwell a negative satan are throughout earths humanism, weather and more, thus, life remains absolutely from **Our** good energy **God** or otherwise.

'I desire to assist You further, ask Me to direct your eyes, focus, feelings, thoughts and your behaviors shall be directed well because You asked and living within My Spirit omits negativity. negative **memories and thoughts remain directed** unwell **and shall, in time, be directed well. writer remains aware where** negativity **derives and hears to write truth.'**

Chapter 4

LETTER TO OUR PASTOR

present chapter remains relevant with personal affiliations with **Our** church. writings are unedited and written only a few months post spiritual rebirthing: was emotionally youthful on specific stage and egocentric, however, **God** was working through soul, thus, mind and received an ability while typing to pray for others, have continual conversations with **God**, think how next sentence shall be written and was aware preceding cars, joggers or walkers passed outside and to pray for Them, upon same moment.

since conception in 1985 within pastor Eugene Moll's residence, **Our** family remain members of this wonderful church, contributing fully with many specific aspects. **You** see, **Our** congregation remains one family, assisting functionally, therefore, working harmoniously well, together. following acquiring sufficient monetary funds constructing new church, **God** blessed all members within **Our** congregation, as well as, new location. 1993, was year and perfectly located for growth, 15400 north western, Edmond, Oklahoma, remained extremely significant landmark for numerous children of **God**, as well as, a blessed new place through **Our** worship.

learning construction, thus, entailing having structure withstand elements, over time, your writer, was 21, with a femoral nail within right fractured femur from a high diving accident july 23rd 1990 while working with great escape theme park, within lake George, New York. built **Our** church with a group of retired lutheran mission builders primarily residing within central to north central U.S.A., was extremely enlightening: for one, they were elder and wiser and, two: they were people united with similar beliefs of **God** and desired constructing building within the same wonderful and conservative denomination of christianity, lutheranism.

likewise, **We** were of same minds, as well as, having similar views with society thus, remained conservative and viewed **God** and family first with all endeavors. presently, **God** said, '**job was given to You from Me, through other humans because this was good for maturation and coming out of self.**' **You** see, previous one half decade your writer had been in horrific car accident forever altering two families lives comparable through **Our** faith filled view of **God**. specifics related with car accident shall become deeply delved further in the book from spirits within writer.

following letter was written for **Our** female pastor and letter transpired one month following significant profound rebirthing from **God**. further, this letter as others in book, shall remain unedited, thus, showing accuracy, egocentricity, immaturity, as well as, tangentialness within writer's overwhelmed, racing, blessed and increasingly favored mind: as readings progress **You** shall observe from **God's** direction, through concluding writings how much clearer **God** has acquiesced progression of thought processes. throughout and following letter, **God**, directed every thought and movement through stages, thus, molded one individual with calmed persona, heightened faithfulness, focus, pure thoughts and very powerfully instilled drive. remember, your fast thoughts remain from **God** and shows his power within You. all **You** need remains corrected information, negative energy denounced, faith, slowed movements, focus and a perfect direction.

God? **'yes.'** do many profound human minds think fast sometimes? **'yes.'**

'Scientists have labeled My new age of humans the era anthropocene: who do You think provides Their ideas for heightening earth's clean and renewable energy, thus, decreasing carbon emissions upon earth?'

'Why are religions, spirituality as well as science enmeshing presently?

Why are numerous globally focused on solutions/progress rather than remaining stagnantly complacent? **patience, over My time living is good within whom are directed well: why do You listen upon the** negativity?

Why do many believe what they have received from humans is truth?'

'The spirits within Robert remain on the following pages for humans.'

sent: wednesday, august 19, 2009 10:17:35 pm
subject: **God's** presence

pastor dawn,

reading your monday memo this evening, felt inclined to proceed with this letter. therefore, it is a jumbled and disorganized and very tangential, bear with. allow Me to get past the small talk, please. since the most recent calling to **God** ; july 19th, subtle and profound miracles continue occurring without being asked for. these transformations have occurred before, two times since mid 1988. first was after getting out of the hospital, something came over Me. this was **God**. soon thereafter, parents were overjoyed **Their** Son had lived, they enabled continuously. staying dependent almost two decades thereafter had grown anticipating behavior. a transformation was occurring through full time cognitive/neurological/physical rehabilitation, observing professionals assisting with recovery/cognitive retraining, it became a quest emulating **Their** mental and physical actions. while physically moving slowly, this mind was in a continuous mania. they were psychologists, medical doctors and other cognitive retraining specialists. moreover, My physical actions and demeanor became methodical and was aware how others would move, what would be said and aware how specifics, as well as, societally, how things would occur before they did.

life before accident was, go fast, be efficient, show everyone what **You** can do, go go go! also, as **You** are aware, My Mother and **Father** are great people and the most loving parents anyone could wish for. furthermore, 90 percent of friends in high school and college were envious of **Their** love for one another. they have taken My friends snow and water skiing, the list goes on and on. although, **Their** faith is strong and they care for others as zero met before; they, as society can not slow down. as stated in the previous email, persona modification remains more difficult for Mother and Father. explain to Them, this is why elderly, generally, have figured life out. **God** speaks, **'life refrains being about** control **or impressing another, life's about love and calm compassion for others.'**

'I, speak through Robert's mind and have given much information over life, when receiving good thoughts in You, it is Me.' God is good.

many elderly, as self's Father, have high blood pressure because they worried entire lives about making things happen instead of letting go and allowing **God**, work through Them. additionally, am surmising this may be one significant factor as to why, generally, females have lived longer than males. pastor, zero of the writings sent have been expressed to My parents. finally, if needing anything done at church, please ask. in closing, please, digest and understand, letter is from **God**, within heart and mind.

* just have proofed this document, was leery of sending this to You. My **Father** says I am not unique, am well aware he is wrong. am I incorrect or more in tune than most? could this be **God** working through Me? know the writings are latter.

peace and love,
Robert Goeringer

very well, refraining from critiquing letter, however, shall allow your awareness: what transpired one month prior from **God**, through david, via, facebook in tenth chapter, remained **God**, showing repetitiously numerous miraculous occurrences. preceding writing book for others, remained perplexed: why were wonderful then horrible occurrences transpiring through **Our** lives? with answers in mind making zero sense, had asked **God**, why. his answer was profound, thus, extremely clear. please, receive parables through your life.

'All of You have gone through good and bad **throughout your lives, these are teachings for the present and future; past is past, let it go, move forward through optimistic thinking and faithfulness helping others find Me. there remains one God who gives You all your good thoughts, feelings, perspectives, perceptions, as well as, wonderful behaviors.'**

immediately following hearing statement began to cry and tremble uncontrollably. falling to knees and looking up to heaven, thought, **God**, am giving up, please, show your way and your will. **God** spoke, **'I, placed the words 'show your way and your will into your enlightening soul.'**

your writer had become a child again and **God** spoke to ask him what to do and where to go upon every moment when awake: with an immediate reply, sometimes preceding asking question, was directed well and received discernment of human history and creation of the universe over millisecond clips/visions.

following several months of conversing continuously with **God** and hearing only optimistic and progressive blissful information, satan abruptly stepped in seeking writer's demise with continuous negative information, thoughts, feelings, perceptions, depression and paranoia. voice became dangerous, proceeded crossing street without looking either way. peripherally had observed vehicles coming from the right, thus, stopped in a three foot flat median in the center of one major four lane road in Edmond. vehicles traveled on both sides at 45 m.p.h., a foot from writer. uncomfortable, **God** spoke, **'remain still, I, shall direct Them: zero shall honk. pray for each of Them as they pass.'** returning home, asked **God**, what would become permitted for your writer to think or pray. mind You, **God**, was showing repetitiously miracle after miracle through humanism and the weather.

voice said, 'You're going to die tonight.' ravens flew in and sky became clouded. trembling, asked **God**, if he was present? he said, **'yes My son, I am here.'** clouds vanished, ravens flew away and the song birds returned. **God** had spoken, 'negative **voice and thought processes are** satan **attempting to hold You back from proceeding in life, thus, giving in and up which has occurred several times previously My loving son.'**

'I am God and dwell through your soul: I taught My writer and now You—when desiring alleviation of any emotional inequity **such as** anger, impatience **and** anxiousness, **simply pray this following specific prayer—before, ask Me who or what needs a blessing? I yield your answer through a thought, vision, word or feeling of a person or place. when qualified and living in the spirit, You shall receive blessings of continual wellness and assist others revealed within your consciousness.'**

ergo:

God, will **You** bless (person or place) further? **(I reply yes or remain silent.) God**, will **You** denounce satan from (Them or there) and pray **God** envelops **Their** soul, thus, heart and mind further? **(I reply yes or remain**

silent, all is well.) then pray God heals the inequity. believe, remain blessed further from Me.'

'Everyone receives relief, good enmeshments spread perfectly and You are implementing My desire, reliance on Me, rather than humanism.' 'remember, your book remains parables for life. I am God and your awareness shall heighten for a reason: the presently wonderful future.'

'Throughout Robert's life, I have instructed him over milliseconds for awareness, what to do for others and My desires regarding recovery from tornadoes and hurricanes affecting the united states. following his final rebirth and over a short time, I taught him to live within My good Spirit with Me and for the dissipation of hurricanes and tornadoes following forming. all of your goodness, awareness, prayers and alleviation of negativity, remains from Me. into the future, the present shall be remembered as a significant decrease of hurricanes and tornado deaths for America, as well as, typhoons and tsunamis affecting other places around the earth. further in your book, You shall receive specific prayers for You to pray from Me to alleviate badness through humanism and weather, as well. My spiritual revolution remains upon all of humanism: remain confident and blessed further because I have a marvelous plan for those who respect Me and live within My goodness. there remain zero coincidences and You shall live peacefully favored: I am God and You are Mine forever.'

ending chapter four, God, desires implementing another specific quote for all readers, 'I spoke for Robert to write My book God's offspring for a reason: You—to receive My ability of denouncing boundaries of negativity throughout life, alleviate irrelevant distortions and receive My joyful peace, embraced alone and perfectly with others loved. dissimilar from other religious doctrines globally, your book remains absent negativity from satan's voice regarding Me through the writer's minds and shall teach countless, historical truth from My only good perspective/direction. I am God and have a wonderful plan.'

Chapter

5

YOUTHFUL ACHIEVEMENTS AND FATHER

while age nine through eleven and living in Jenks, Oklahoma outside of Tulsa; writer was performing with an elite boys choir and comparable with vienna boys choir located in western Europe. practicing three days per week and performing formal concerts within Tulsa, Dallas, Houston, Nashville, Graceland (elvis's residence) and through south eastern united states, in Georgia and Cape Canaveral, Florida. performances intertwined one popular play Oliver twist. receiving the opportunity of playing the lead, Oliver, was memorable: loved being directed well as every reader. involvement within Tulsa boys singers remained wonderful, reserving numerous exciting occurrences while keeping writer very busy. mowing yard was two and a half acres, attended school, swam, constructed forts and riding bicycle, remained continually doing and thinking of something, comparable with probably Yourself.

was an ordinary child, living life having fun, however, life refrained from continuous fun for writer had to return home for dinner in Father's presence: dependent upon how his day was, vocability and behaviors shown to family remained comparable. toddler through present day, **You** had better be prepared for consequences, thus, yelled at, demeaned or belittled behaving outside his control, power and thinking. also was very kind, completely giving anything and everything possessed in body, mind or possession for whoever needed. loving within his whole heart, however, generational baggage would fill an oil tanker. his unresolved anger was apparent through inappropriate behaviors. again. yen and yang, as well as, good and bad.

irrationally inappropriate, he sadly behaved similarly with both of his offspring and remained incapable of proceeding patiently or calmly in his mind because of numerous latent insecurities from satan wanting **Our** failure: therefore, he imposed negative generationally deficient behaviors learned throughout rearing, as unwell.

related for all, human behavior remain fleshly authenticated for those around You; consciously acting and reacting within positive and negative thoughts, internally then externally expressed, ultimately remains spiritual, thus, from **God** or otherwise.

back within story. writer's **Father** cares zero what people think about him or his behaviors, thus, this thinking remains good in many respects, however, speaking preceding thinking caused his foot needing removed from mouth countless times. respecting others, remains significantly functional and relative for those who are empathetic and appreciate others. having good intentions with his thoughts and words, however, was incapable curtailing feelings, thoughts or ideas from others, because his were egocentrically best in one negative and optimistically induced mind.

moving forward: another escape was athletics. **Father** purchased trampoline when writer was four years of age and was hurt numerous times learning difficult tricks. specific apparatus became influential progressing forward physical agility through bodily movements and soccer became favorite sport: learning unity with others on team and working together, thus, winning. in Tulsa, eight years of age attended lee elementary and on one wonderful team: in fact, Pele' came congratulating **Us** and signed a personal soccer ball. remains humorous how upon specific juncture in life, who Pele was and what his life was associated with soccer was irrelevant and played with ball often: name withered, becoming flat and was placed in trash. second, moving to Edmond when 12 years of age, naturally began playing soccer: position was striker, offense go, go, go! played on under 12 and 14 classic teams.

previous paragraphs focus remained with team unity, the following page remains attributed within athletics as well, however, now individually. springboard diving with extensive agility within early age became very natural. trampoline work had prepared your writer through a ballet of focus and flowing movements within an arena of high difficulty.

God spoke, '**your accomplishments remained from Me, working well through every individual good feeling, thought, as well as, movement.**'

loving water sports, springboard diving was becoming one athletic forte. aside from wearing speedo swim suit, loved everything regarding sport, specifically females wearing swim suits, as well. hmmm. sport was completely attributed with focus from **God** speaking continuously. won the state championship attending Edmond high school and two time all american when freshmen in college: then 20 months post car accident began high diving in north east U.S.A., where femur was broken near hip in lake George, New York, year 1990. step before end of springboard, voice in mind said, 'take a hurdle.' thought it was **God**, should have refrained. had gone too far, half out of cement tank and breaking femur near hip. had this occurred because of tangential thinking and bad entity distracting thoughts? throughout life, did what the voice spoke. apologizing, when reading again feel sad rather than proud because referencing negative entity, shall close the chapter soon. writings occurred two weeks following third spiritual rebirth from **God** ; he spoke continuously in mind: here remains one of thousands of specific sentences spoken.

'My calm son, bless and pray for others rather than Yourself, I, shall envelop and work through your feelings and thought processes well.'

hearing sentence, remained unaware; was becoming aware of **God's** plan: humans alive shall receive reliance upon **God** rather than only themselves. regarding and respecting neighbors (humans) shall heighten significantly. live in spirit, often, **You** receive the answer preceding asking the question.

at times, when You're receiving negative through your heart and thinking, **God** denounces negative energy within from praising/praying **God** blesses others, as well as, denounces negative energy within, thus, envelopes **Their** soul, heart, mind as well as perspective, perceptions, thought and feelings. over **God's** time **You** receive a perfectly blessed consciousness and health.

the uncertain chemicals (energy) within your mind and body modify well, your chemicals, thus, thoughts, as well as, health become certainly stable.

'Well spoken, proceed into next chapter: I through My writer shall discuss psychosomatic influences within your soul, heart and mind.'

PSYCHOSOMATIC LABELS

parables follow in second paragraph.

once hearing something auditorilly from parents and others repetitively, **You** proceed believing Them. psychosomatically, positive, as well as, negative information are internalized. many fleshly factors culminate producing **Our** personas. genetic predispositions instilled are physiological, however, when these physiological behavioral traits are expressed verbally, they become psychosomatically compounded. here lies several examples.

angered internally came from **Our** German heritage. untrue, psychosomatic label. Father, was labeled manic-depressant or bi-polar, writer would become, as unwell. untrue, psychosomatic label. observed, life was an emotional struggle for Father, therefore, inevitably anticipated life would be difficult. spiritually proven untrue. also, please refrain from telling offspring of illness or disease **Their** former lineage had—this is psychosomatic, negative and past.

chemically dependent, impulsive, obsessive-compulsive, perfectionist, risk taker, sex addict and more were labels placed on writer from other mortals educated and trained to understand why **We** behave and think in certain ways within humanism. they received knowledge and thinking from professors or former teachers, thus, **Their** teachings of generalities in group settings of patients, thus, seeking return on investment rather than curtailing individually for those who have a most different interpretation and perception than instructor, as well as, the person next to Them. **We** egocentrically believe **Our** perceptions remain how all perceive: dependent upon numerous variables intertwined, via, spirituality thus humanism and discussed through book, your awareness shall be heightened. having an ability constructing compassion, love and optimism for one another or otherwise; spirituality through humanism remains why good and bad occurs for everyone throughout **Their** consciousness. the scientific community, from **God**, has figured out the most intricate details of why and how humans are, however, **Our** consciousness or where **Our** thinking and feelings derive, remains a mystery and shall be revealed in this book.

everything living has a consciousness: humans specific feelings and thought processes determines **Their** spiritual origination. closing this chapter, **You** shall be revealed two examples of how there is a fine line determining the spiritual origination of thoughts and feelings.

receiving a thought yielding intimacy remains from **God** because the thought process and feeling yields good and pleasure: however, the thought and feeling of receiving intimacy without the other parties consent remains from bad entity because the feelings with hold consent. appropriateness and inappropriateness differs individually: empathize. second, regarding athletics: intention of thoughts and feelings towards an opponent determines where origination derives: if competitive, functional and good, they are from **God** ; if your feelings and thought processes are filled with anger and negative, they remain from otherwise. finally, as **You** are well aware, lack of sleep, use of chemicals, nourishment and personal contentment affects your consciousness significantly: living in the spirit, alleviates all distorted negativity: then **You** desire to receive the perfected desire to receive good nourishment within your consciousness (soul, heart, mind) over time.

'Thoughts and feelings, as well as, dreams remain good and bad energy. in Our book, You shall learn how to receive continual goodness. I direct My writer to silently ask Me to bless individuals and sometimes masses further, denounce satan throughout Their souls and allow My goodness to envelop Their thoughts and feelings further, this occurs. he asks My desires and follows every perfect suggestion: a parable.'

Chapter

DENOUNCING LABELS FOR OUR OFFSPRING

current writings attribute how, from **God**, **You** may denounce negative behavioral predispositions within **Yourself** and offspring through meditation, prayer, positive beliefs and thinking. from **God** through those whom adhere with these simple suggestions within this book shall be directed very well individually and shall receive what is desired most, peace through your mind.

all offspring and your writer's son's birth were from **God**, as everything seen and unseen and life became modified upon this wonderful juncture. Evon, remains his **Fathers** and Mothers offspring and shall receive an absolute peaceful course from birth. rather than believing he was his Father, filled with anxieties, sadness, impatience at times and other times, filled with mania, perfectionism and praying for others before himself, would learn he could do anything without negative psychosomatic labels instilled through his wonderful mind: his course through life shall become filled with consistent encouragement, focus and optimism for Evon's chosen soul.

withholding spiritual, thus, generational psychosomatic predispositions verbally and behaviorally expressed, life, for him remains generously anticipated. infancy through age six years of life, Evon was calm and placated because **God**, expressed through writer's mind, correct nurturing and maintained personal calm demeanor for his good example. **God** spoke what specific silent prayers to pray for Evon the great, thus, all of these negative emotional predispositions were effectively denounced for his future well: intrinsically had received the greatest honor of rearing one Son with zero negative instilled boundaries of psychosomatic and generational inequities from humanism. stating **You** are your **Father** or Mother remains factual, however, within societies past, present and assuredly in the future **God** chooses many exceptions through Us. encompassing humanism— **You** have an influx of information from birth forward, regarding how **You** shall behave and think relating family and societal criterion.

upon specific occurrences, your offspring experience behavioral and generational inequities within nurturing, however, believe they shall become all dreams, hopes and strengths through optimistic generational instilments, as well. **God's** Spirit is always good.

You, have learned wonderful lessons from your rearing and loving offspring with calmness and happiness remain consequential for **Their** lives and many following. consciousness remains induced spiritually and vacillates through life: living blessed, contented, joyous, optimistic, patient and emitting abundant love for **Yourself** and others around You. if your desired emulated image is filled with the optimistic Spirit through You, life is good. praising **God**, caring for neighbors, fulfilling needs and reproaching ego significantly remains his blessing.

You remain well aware numerous humans live deceptive facades, therefore, often times, difficult perceiving **Their** true selves. **Their** facades may work well, they may have or had an internalized saying, 'fake it till **You** make it,' while youthful. portraying image rather different from who **You** are may fool others, leaving **Them** misunderstanding who **You** really are and most importantly deep inside your heart, mind and soul: living untruths, **You** receive subtle spiritual repercussions through your feelings and thinking.

fleshly, generational nurturing becomes significantly relative with progressing optimistically forward functionally or otherwise, therefore, understanding **Yourself** remains a significant factor regarding how your behaviors affects all interpersonal relationship through life. resolving generational issues, as low self respect, worth and image becomes handbook through functional healthy thinking and behaviors; thus, modifying generational and psychosomatic labels, over time, creates healthy offspring, thus, ultimately more productive individuals encompassing the masses.

example: john is alcoholic, his **Father** and grandFather were alcoholics, as unwell. behaviorally john observed his **Father** taking edge off following a hard days work. John may be labeled alcoholic, however, what was learned from his **Father** was behavioral rather than genetics: if john was reared in a tribe in Africa from birth, he would have zero hindrances regarding alcohol. humans, are born behaviorally perfect, free of generationally observed negativity; these learned traits from birth forward, fleshly are placed on **Us** generationally then societally through humanism.

through life, **You** consciously decide ingesting alcohol or shooting dope in body: because someone who counsels through chemical dependency setting says, '**You** are alcoholic or drug addict.' **You** have one pertinent decision to make, believe, following advice or resolve what underlies your inappropriate thinking, feelings and behaviors. spiritual, then fleshly instilled generational pain over a lifetime. modifying self and people **You** are enmeshing with, bad places **You** attend and things **You** do resolves labels: regarding other isms this applies, as well. readers, your writer neither condones nor desires **You** refraining attending alcoholic anonymous meetings, for this works well for millions. people need people, enveloping **Yourself** similarly with others, working 12 step programs wonderfully has modified countless lives well globally: your writer remains well aware, countless families receive zero negative affects from alcohol use. living in the Spirit relieves temptation.

proceed reading and understand writings: deeper in book, a plethora of realizations shall come to a light and **You** shall receive inner calmness.

regard discussions of negative behavioral and generational observances as profound storms before **God** blesses your enlightened calmness further.

finishing your seventh chapter, **God**, desires to complete this chapter perfectly. please note this quote within your mind if alcohol causes any friction through **Yourself** or into others.

'I, am clean, good and sober within your soul, thus, heart and brilliant mind for your functional peace: We shall work well together as one: I am God and You are Mine forever.'

Chapter

RELATIONSHIPS

knowing persons from all socioeconomic levels: Albeit, LaToya an aspiring fitness trainer, Kimberli and Sean Brownlee who are close personal friends, Dr. Jeffrey Auth, one best friend and chiropractor, Douglas Stussi, chief financial officer of a national corporation, Randall Robinson, prominent lawyer in hometown: his **Father** retired chief executive officer of Exxon Venezuela and Paulo Jacuzzi, one best friend in college, his **Father** remo jacuzzi, retired chief executive officer of Jacuzzi north America. one significant notation, regarding differential treatment of one to the other remains zero, they are all humans and put on **Their** pants the same way, one leg at a time. all of **Them** have calmness and wonderful intellect as You, and sometimes receive many unpleasant emotions, generational pain, pessimistic influences, as well as, distortions in life. **You** see, pain remains relative and painful. what differentiates one human from another and succeeding in life contentedly desiring more, remains controlling mania and becoming calmly contented with your three faceted self: from **God** through body, mind and soul, **You** receive hope, love and calmness, then shall receive a propensity of consciously dismissing past pessimistic improprieties, then focusing on the present and thinking of the future.

Douglas: one leg at a time? aware or becoming aware, **God** is directing **Our** good ideas, suggestions, humor and gentle communication within others.

on the other hand, a minority have become perverse through hidden agendas, pessimistic media, as unwell as, numerous believe humanism shall end soon. negative belief and thinking are incorrect and ludicrous: through this spiritual journey, **God**, has revealed generally when. second, remember psychosomatic? when numerous humans believe untrue information through senses and think negatively through **Their** minds, persona enmeshment occurs and negatively infectious individuals become societies. if **God**, were human and had shoulders, would shrug **Them** and wonder why sometimes pessimistic, pompous humans have gone awry? **God**, knows why and shall be revealed in this book through You.

going awry remains exact point where **God**, observes **You** franticly looking for the car keys when **You** remain late for work, angered because c.p.u. refrains working correctly or looking for the remote control because **You** arrive home late watching television show because one of your offspring was caught fighting at **Their** school, skipping class, using drugs or behaving inappropriately with others: why were **You** late for work? why do children fight, use drugs and behave inappropriately? this is because of thinking and feelings within **Yourself** and Them. this may have been your favorite show and one of the few escapes from life. escapes from life?

God, remains quoted per his powerful and calm request, **'why are many concerned with all this temporal and trivial data? remain contented You live, have faith in Me, thus, calmness while loving others, well: when allowed from Me, I shall direct your thinking and feelings well: when You are faithful with Me, life flows frictionless within You.'**

'I have observed many created within My perfect image traversing through Their day having sometime depressed **and** overwhelmed **souls: continually, I shall love and patiently await Our faith filled embrace.'**

humans are products of **Their** environment: when visually or auditorilly, ingesting good stimulation or communication, through other humans regarding optimism or discussing pleasurable emotions, feelings, as well as, thoughts, life remains good. receiving repetitively, stimulation in mind through media and societal influences, regarding global economic conditions, negatively and infectious this may become You. similarly, observing information related with catastrophic specifics through nature and internalizing views regarding **Our** younger generations having unexplainable anxieties, associated with brilliancy, are overwhelmed and hysterically irrational. across societies, through all socioeconomic levels, global anger remains apparent within numerous: from the parent into offspring, silent and verbal enmeshments fleshly occur. offspring, consciously and subconsciously feel what remains occurring within your words and Yourself.

also, remain aware regarding specific children who have calm parents, however, child remains unexplainably anxiety ridden. within humanism, **You** remain aware why, however, if zero answers have been received from medications and counseling, the emotional, as well as, mental afflictions lie significantly deeper than humanism attempts unnaturally resolving. there remains reasoning why psychiatrists, psychologists and counselors are unable to implement **God** within **Their** sessions, however, most have a personal relationship with **Their** maker. **God**, remains solution, pray and seek a priest, pastor or find a blessed mortal, there are many whom have innate blessings of faith healing through meditation, thought and prayers from **God**, through Them.

proceeding with humanism: herein lies pertinent question please answer honestly. have **You** been somewhere in public and hear another speaking within deep tone? first, tone and calmness becomes enticing, in fact entrancing: **You** listen earnestly, few moments pass, suddenly realizing why **You** are there in first place, proceeding with higher priorities related with your life: **You** may think, yes this occurred, zero time available listening to someone inconsequential or irrelevant with My life, had too much to do and received a little time to listen, thus, had to hurry. go, go, go!

possibly remains where **You** should have listened to the speaker, sharing calmness and information benefiting your life, as well. please remember, from **God**, 'there are zero coincidences. consciously slow Yourself down, ask Me what shall occur and confidently allow the occurrences to transpire rather than making Them, life becomes wonderful.'

grandparents said, 'wake up and smell the coffee and admire the beautiful roses.'

numerous euphemisms expressed back then had purposes true today, if **You** allow. meaning- slow down and enjoy your day, calmly refrain becoming overwhelmed, appreciating small stuff and it's all, small stuff. life, remains too short, ignoring small things **You** take for granted every day. praise **God**, love others and live life knowing family and society awaits your calmed, magnificent and optimistic glow.

'**Why do numerous free climbers traverse vertical mountains withholding ropes or numerous globally feel confident within life? is Me through Them: boldness remains from Me,** arrogance **is otherwise.**'

over the past numerous decades, your writer, has observed a plethora of humans seeking solutions for such a paradoxical society. America, as well as, numerous countries globally continue searching for functional resolutions within **Their** societies. earths solution for problems within humanism are spiritual through silent prayer. related with cohesion, fluidity and unity amongst different cultures, educations, governments, religions and **Their** numerous economic levels: **God**, desires quoted upon editing, 07.04.11. and independence day for the blessed united states of America.

'**My offspring, understand everyone upon earth prays to the same God : faithful human souls and significant weather** anomalies **shall calm well through My profoundly gentle plan. I'm always available, You shall be given an abundance of good direction when asking and following My good suggestions that shall flow within this blessed book, your mind and within Our future offspring's gracious living.**'

receive parables, **God** spoke, december of 2011.

following writing this book for **God** and his offspring, became perplexed. why **God**, will **You** deny allowing to send your verbiage and book for others to publish?

'**Remember son, Our book is basically completed, however, I, shall teach You patience, as well as, instruct You to pray and ask Me to bless countless through your day. do You know who You are?**' zero without You. '**You are everything with Me.**'

thank **You God**, love **You**. he replied, '**thank You, I, love You and shall speak through Our words: in book, We shall show why emotions, thought processes, human behavior, electronics, mechanical, weather and all of the past, present and future remains spiritually driven.**'

CYCLIC AND FLESHLY ARE OUR BEHAVIORS

humans remain cyclical sheep, with souls enmeshing subconsciously through one another, having <u>optimistic</u> and pessimistic lives with whom they desire or do they? **God** desires humans on earth enmeshing **Their** living through the underlined word. industrialized or high technological societies, **God**, remains aware how many humans have become: more than ever, life has become extremely egocentrically dysfunctional. impulsively wanting items now and if available yesterday, many would want then. wants are wants and needs are needs: **We** may be wanting new shoes, car or home, however, need food, shelter and a relationship with a power greater than Ourselves. **God**, has always desired humans view life, as a **You** place of loving others while denouncing inner anger, control, impatience, pessimistic thinking and numerous other inequities sometimes occurring through **Their** spiritually induced souls.

human behaviors and thinking are cyclical, **We** do what **We** do, consciously and subconsciously from what was behaviorally observed through life from senses and physiologically predisposed minimally through genetics. personas are obtained observing human behaviors and most importantly your parents. **You** know this. if **You** are a parent, look in a mirror. good or bad, parents are whom offspring most emulate, consciously and subconsciously upon rearing process: **Our** parents persona's remained what was internalized consciously and subconsciously, as well. your offspring live vicariously through You, over much time, **You** shall live vicariously through **Them** and **Their** offspring.

a marvelous world **God**, gave all to respect and cherish perfectly and loving for **Our** desired future filled with peace from prayers and **God's** favor filled blessings: all negative perspectives and perceptions remain modifiable from receiving **God's** perfect awareness, continue reading further, this book is intended for You. your writer has been revealed an abundance of information regarding the process of how **God** can heal others, calm winds and cease significant weather anomalies occurring globally through **Our** prayers. this global goodness has occurred and shall continue to occur into the future for a reason, others to receive heightened awareness of **God's** spiritual truth. your writer has refrained from initiating any of these miracles through humanism and weather, they are all directed from **God**.

here remains philippians 4:8–9; ephesians 5:18—6:4

'**By relying on the holy spirit's indwelling power, the believer can reject** foolishness. **his thoughts please the lord, and can make decisions that glorify God as he enriches his life and the lives of those around him.**'

he spoke after relieving negativity and revealing the truth for human awareness, '**continually ask Me what shall occur and follow only good suggestions: I shall show You how every** inequity **through humanism and weather shall be healed and alleviated. there is a reason You receive the propensity to think upon one specific and receive My information upon the same moment. the truth has been revealed to You My son, You are teaching historical truth for others so they also shall receive favor and blessings. life is spiritual, everything alive remain spiritually induced. for humans, Their consciousness, thus,** thought processes and feelings remain from Me when good, as well as, all goodness. when observing everything good from the inside rather than the outside, You receive knowledge and understanding (wisdom) from your creator within You. does your faith remain for humans or God? when your faith is for God, life remains a pleasure and You are becoming aware of the perfecting plan for the future.'

10

LIFE CHANGING OCCURRENCE FROM GOD

july 19th 2009.

following electronic transmission with david, always referenced him as Davis, regards one life changing occurrence and finding **God** again. having zero contact for a quarter century, preceding specific evening, **God**, worked through Davis, via, facebook and alleviated anxieties, depression, discontentedness, overwhelmedness and all other inequities received. following unedited transmission, **God**, thus, holy Spirit arrived within writers life, more intensely than every preceding occurrence, replenishing faith, hope and peace within. following was the beginning of the last and absolute spiritual rebirthing from **God**, through faithful humbled writer.

ergo:

19:39 Robert

Davis, **You** are loved by many, and want to know more, in time....enjoy your evening with your wife and family and thank **You** for taking the time to give hope.

19:40David

We are too accepting of others pushing a perverse agenda down **Our** throats and need to fight back. just as Jesus would.

do **You** go to church every sunday?

19:41Robert

only when Evon is here and Jesus wouldn't fight.

19:41David

does he enjoy it?

19:41Robert

he doesnt and have expressed My feelings to him last sunday

19:42David

do **You** keep him in the big service or does he go to the childrens

19:42Robert

he is in the former

19:42David

big?

19:42Robert

yes

19:42David

good.

19:43Robert

but it is very boring, equates to nothing of the present

19:43David

all of **Our** kids have always stayed in the big service. then **We** discuss on the way home.

19:44Robert

am aware the past is the best predictor of the future

19:44David

2500 predictions are in the bible. 2000 have already been fulfilled, 80% in the last 200 years

19:45robert

whos interpretation is this?

have to let go and let **God**?

am aware of this

19:46David

I am currently reading "in the revolution", about the rise of radical islam and the increased use of terrorism.

19:46Robert

but am trying to discount

19:46David

to discount what?

19:46Robert

God

dont know why, may be subconscious from atheist college profs.

19:47David

You are not a salmon and this is not a stream **You** can swim up

19:47Robert

am saddened, with My discountings

19:48David

My opinion on why **You** are trying to discount him is that possibly **You** feel like **You** will have to do without somehow in life.

19:48Robert

I know I am wrong

yes, was told 20 years ago that **God** is a crutch for the weak by an atheist girlfriend

19:48David

You are not neccesarily wrong but vulnerable to satan distorting your perceptions

19:49David

of course. but what proof did they offer?

19:50Robert

intellectually, I understand both sides, am still confused have talked with a pastor rob, one on one he was baffled

19:50David

why was he baffled?

19:50Robert

am guessing he had no answer for My questions asked him, who was correct, buddhism, christianity, hinduism, judaism?

thinking these are all correct, just interpretations from different cultures.

God, encompasses all of **Them** perplexed, maybe?

Davis?

19:51 David

give him My fb account info and i'll let **God** work through Me to help him too

:):)

You still there

19:52Robert

apologies Davis, Juliet sent a message. thank **You** Juliet.

You are of a higher calling Davis, than your earthly body

19:53David

I am not always this dialed in

I would love to finish a degree in christian theology and travel the country as an evangelist.

will **You** be around this evening?

19:54Robert

enjoy your evening with family, and contact when **You** have more time

yes

am staying home, the world is hurting My thoughts

I am, rather

19:55 David

continually will ask **God** to make himself more visible to You. continually.

will be back soon.

19:55Robert

no one knows this other than **You** Davis.

19:55 David

God knows

19:55Robert

thank You

19:56David

:):)

19:56Robert

more than **You** shall ever know am crying, trembling and weak now

19:57 David

it is his business anyway. he will allow **You** to grow in your own time.

be back soon.

19:57 Robert

thank You, Davis

love You

19:57David

most welcome. love **You** too.

God, worked through Davis's soul effectively and then Davis through technology. adapting and modifying for **Us** through all generations and centuries, **God** is good. those believing **God** created cosmos, earth and humans in past only, are incorrect. remaining apparent, orchestrating everything seen and unseen good in life, **God's** unending love and peace remains present through all of You. following electronic communication, complete body was tingling; nearly weightless, stood and humbly asked **God**, relieving all former discountings transgressed upon others lives. was drunk and depressed, **God** spoke, **'You shall be sober and speak with Me.'** became immediately sober and lucid, then had began rigorous training for others. awakened three days and nights without caffeine continuously spoke with **God**. upon juncture, **God**, directed writers thinking, behaviors with higher awareness: every moment, revealed plethora of relevant general and specific current and past, global information understanding human behaviors, as well as, the earth's weather.

speaking with **God** over 40 years, let go of negative memories from earlier in life. over time, **God**, revealed your writers life became anew for several reasons, most importantly, **'I shall work through My writer and the chosen to restore individual calm and hope within whom need.'**

from **God's** blessing and conversing continuously with him, became willing and able to refrain from thinking negatively or using negative words and behaviors, spiritually instilled through humanism, thus, assisting numerous people societally. replacing satan's bad negativity with optimism, from **God**, through your emotions, feelings, thoughts and behaviors regards your eminent and obtainable future: **God**, remains present, longingly awaiting **You** and your offspring perfectly as well.

upon specific juncture, **God** released all negative feelings, emotions, insecurities, labels and thoughts. from **God's** enlightenment, became fleshly aware deficits were because many want egocentric control, power and correctness over others, is humanism, however, unhealthy and zero of **God's** desires through **You** and others.

You know this, writer has known this several decades, however, feeling powerless as previously had felt, vanished: attained a higher linear plane allowing *God's* good power in and praying for denouncement of bad, anything becomes achieved. believe and have faith: your desires shall follow from him through **Yourself** and various others.

letting go of will, **God**, asked writer what specific discountings within mind had desired vanished: instantaneously, they were and the most wonderful feeling ever! rising to feet, had zero emotional or physical pain and rest of evening proceeded into sunrise, living and thinking in Spirit from continual communication with **God**. from **God**, prayed for others, desired assisting and caring for **Them** has been what life regarded through your writer. awakening every morning thereafter, **God** spoke,

'good morning, ask and follow My good suggestions: I shall reveal countless specifics regarding humanism, spirits as well as weather.' august 1st 2009, **God** said, **'walk around your neighborhood.'** this remained two weeks following the third spiritual rebirthing, thus, praying and thinking of others as instructed, **God** said, **'look up,'** 16 doves soared above unified within a gentle breeze. floating directly above for 2000 yards, these birds of his peace were profoundly **God's** symbol, signifying wonderful missions lying ahead of helping others find **God**, and reiterate your faith within writers experience, strength and hope throughout book. decade previously, **God**, had twelve doves float in breeze following son's baptism. these gorgeous doves following writers rebirthing from **God**, were showing peace encompassed within writers soul, thus, heart and mind implementing **God's** calm.

forward to unedited writings on october 19th 2009:

on rebirthing process, double vision ceased: instantaneously, thoughts or desires escaping life, via, alcohol, chemicals or other unhealthy negative venues vanished: **God's** good direction through peace and solace within oneself becomes achieved. speak **God's** constant good presence and **You** shall receive calm and hopeful love.

remains a magnificent feeling saying, '**God** bless You,' to anyone in society then watching **Their** sad eyes immediately lighting up! when **God's** Spirit envelopes your soul, wonderful and modifiable life occurrences transpire: load lifts, anything becomes possible when sharing and praising his unending love. others feel your good energy: good enmeshments occur well.

time is of an essence, however, **Our** patience remains virtuous. if aware of **God's** presence through You, wonderful: however, if unaware here is some good advice. once **You** desire less overwhelmedness, thus, contented through every facet of life and a spiritual awakening transpires, turn off distortions and proceed somewhere still and quiet and listen to what **God** speaks, absent questioning, unless negative. life becomes peacefully wonderful: in fact, focus intensifies, perspective alters and **You** receive a heightened awareness of miracles occurring continuously around You.

please, remember this process occurred for heightening your faithfulness in **God**, and he has known of **You** preceding earth's continental drift, throughout life, thus, this wonderful experience remains his and your enmeshed wills together as one: **God**, dwells inside yielding significantly less friction when choosing his will above Yours and others. **God**, directs perfectly every moment occurring through your loving and good grace.

his universe, milky way galaxy, as well as, every single optimistic and functional process through your wonderful soul, thus, mind remain choreographed from **God**.

revealed first quarter of 2010. '**do You understand why solar** storms **occur? I made earth's star:** bad **energy, thus, solar** storms disrupting **communication and direction of g.p.s. are** negative **energy:** negative **energy affects as** unwell **as** distorts **communications and human life. all whom breathe are spiritually trumped.**'

preceding writing this book, **God** spoke and had shown throughout history, he has been and yields only goodness. proceeding through book, **You** too, shall learn an abundance what has been spoken through writer's soul from **God**, concerning humanism, spirits and weather upon **God's** magnificent and gloriously perfecting earth that was given for his offspring to cherish, love and respect for several following generations whom shall live well.

'**I told My writer where to write all words and what shall be spoken throughout this blessed book for You. through your willingness, sometimes immediately, Our communications heighten perfectly: when You live within and through My good spirit, I answer questions and keep You safe: when all** negative **memories, thoughts and feelings are denounced from Me, the duration of the day remains perfect and flows smoothly. life remains good and You are further blessed for Me.**'

'**When My Son learned how I heal anyone anywhere upon any moment, he asked and I suggested he play backgammon. directed to a specific website, he asked many questions and I gave him perfect suggestions. I spoke, one female shall sit across from You in three seconds and did. they began playing and I spoke for him to ask, where Her country was? She replied Malta. I said for him to ask God to bless Malta further and denounce** satan's negative **energy from humans and Their atmosphere. he did and I said She shall speak of an** inequity. he asked Me what Her inequity was and I said, remain patient, She will reveal the information: Camille said She had sciatica: as taught, he asked Me what shall occur? I said, ask God to bless Camille further, denounce the negative energy within Her and envelop Her soul, thus, heart and mind further: he did. then I spoke: ask if I will heal heal Her of sciatica? he thought, God will You heal Her of sciatica? I replied yes: now tell Her, She shall be healed in one week: he did and healed Camille contacted Robert in one week: She said thank You to Robert: he asked and said from Me: God is who healed You, please give God the praise rather than his humble vessel.'

Chapter

GOOD AND BAD SPIRIT

receiving life, contributing progressively for others rather than stagnantly existing within **Yourself** remains where achievement and fulfillment derive. in life, there is good energy, functionally yielding your faith, happiness, hope, love, optimism, peace and stamina that envelops your soul, heart and mind. following the final rebirth mid-2009, **God** revealed profound occurrences that transpired throughout history through visions and sentences explaining the spiritual origination of thoughts and feelings. over milliseconds, received questions to ask, as well as, awareness of countless specifics at once, with an amazing focus. wondering how this was occurring, asked **God**. his reply,

'I can do anything within anyone upon any moment, I am God and your perfect enlightenment occurred for My reason, to teach others future historical truth through what I have spoken and shall speak.'

overtime, most thoughts and answers remained negative. uncertainty was showing itself. your writer was unknowingly becoming prepared for writing parables and instructions for your alleviation of negativity as well.

God? 'yes My son?' can this negativity be stopped? 'yes.' how? 'ask who needs a blessing?' who needs a blessing? 'I shall reply through a thought, word or vision.' God? 'yes.' will You bless who You revealed? 'yes, now ask Me to denounce satan within Their soul and weather around Them.' God, will You denounce satan within Their soul and weather around Them? 'yes, now thank Me.' thank You God. 'You're welcome, now proceed with confidence, optimism, patience, peace and love.'

that is all, after some practice this becomes habitual and You receive an ability of feeling negativity and stopping before it occurs through your mind: over God's time, negativity becomes omitted from your thoughts and feelings forever. life becomes only good and filled with an optimistically peaceful perspective overflowing with God's perfect blessings.

directed well from God, all that remains slated within these pages occurred because the information was spoken for You. your writer rarely does anything without asking God first because when living in and with the spirit, every single facet of life becomes pleasureful.

now We shall return to the story. your writer desires zero more information to be slated regarding satan, however, God spoke and shall for a reason, please bear with your writer.

ergo:

You remain completely aware where We are proceeding, thus, shall remain abrupt. satan is reasoning why anger, discontentedness, irritableness and restlessness occurs fleshly apparent among all spiritually instilled individuals. numerous humans are aware, however, many more think only of themselves and numerous fleshly others. bad entity, is reasoning individuals, as well as, societies remain negative, thus, sad. looming as the creator of pain, whom causes confusion, suffering, depression and overwhelmed negative thoughts, through your heart, mind and soul, thus, persona. viable negative entity shall become discussed throughout your book. for now, please allow proceeding fleshly with a questionable power through humanism presently.

following paragraphs allow deeper understanding of questionable psychological and psychosomatically induced medications adults, as well as, offspring globally, consume for purpose of controlling mania and depression remains unneeded. from **God**, through your writer, following information was received and asked to be slated first quarter of 2010.

ergo:

presently, through technologically unified lands there live and work psychiatrists. psychiatrists, naming only a few locations of origin were reared in Asia or India. these psychiatrists were aware of America, Western Europe and Australia, among others when small children. parents, desired **Them** traveling to distant lands where they have received heightened options for success: receiving a degree here or there, remained working in America, western Europe and becoming wealthy afterward. doctors prescribing psychological medications or mood stabilizers, suppress **You** and your offspring's generationally learned persona ultimately from **God** or otherwise. rather than spending unnecessary amounts of your time and monetary sufficiency, suppressing your feelings from medications and becoming entirely different from your persona, proceed with free and continuously available relief from **God** who can do anything for anyone.

before proceeding, numerous think they are unable controlling generationally then societally instilled behaviors and thoughts, however, if numerous parents viewed themselves through **Their** thoughts, thus, behaviors first and foremost modifying accordingly, **Their** offspring would most likely need zero medication in first place. fleshly and first, youth and adult personas are dependent most from rearing, birth through age six and what was observed through the senses. 'secondly, **personas enmesh through nurturers, coworkers, teachers and peers, You feel others.**' consciously and subconsciously with or without conscious awareness, **We** are one. third, most important and an absolutely integral cog within every facet of first two examples, lives are positive and negative entities influences. disbelieve? observe profound good and bad individuals throughout societies past, present and Yourself.

'All remain spiritually directed.'

further remain quotes from **God** through the christian bible.

another observance. regarding all of his earth's fleshly societies: north America, Europe, Asia, Australia, South America Africa: shall name individuals sheep. **God?** '**yes.**' why does the bible refer to all humans as sheep? '**You remain aware: humans remain directed from how taught.**' does this remain negative? '**depends upon your individual perspective: when You slated God's offspring in 2010** satan **spoke and abundance of information within your mind. you've learned to discern thinking: truth remains, heightened peace has increased significantly in Europe and America following the age of reason within the 16th century. if humans consciousness were the same within 20th century as biblical times in Europe/America there would have been two billion** deceased **rather than 100 million: figures include both of world** wars **combined. what the media as well as numerous humans believe remains** untrue.'

You awaken, shower and eat within time consistent manner then travel frictionless following where vehicle in front of **You** travels or your own path as an individual who has friction filled differential advantage, thus, makes own decisions good and bad, accelerating ahead of pack causing accidents, thus, disturbing flow for others.

pasture or destination comes into view and **You** wait, then proceed further, pin bottlenecks, unable traveling further, patiently await for congestion minimizing. please, here are additional observances, expounding on few sentences previously. navigating congested roads, with numerous stop lights, one youthful motorist proceeds out of control, speeding and cutting off, other motorists for purpose of becoming front of herd upon next stop light, thus, three directions may observe how cool and beautiful he and his car remains. calmly, as well as, obeying laws, **You** smoothly flow past him and sometimes, achieve more, comparative with his racing, unfocused mind. with age, experience and offspring, hopefully he learns, using steadiness allows others arriving to **Their** destination safely and frictionless. remember aesop's fable as a child related with tortoise and hare? very true.

back within story. humans perform similarly when working or living in a larger city with a million people and highways: commuting becomes difficult when your a sheep so to speak. reasoning why **You** are a tortoise or hare remains extremely relative, how or what **You** fleshly ingest within your consciousness from nurtures and life determines everything. imagining through wonderful mind, traveling in Tulsa, Oklahoma City, Dallas, St. Louis, New York City, Los Angeles, Paris, London, Amsterdam, Japan, Tokyo, Beijing, Sydney, Auckland and Christ church. all cities, on **God's** technologically unified world are cluttered with external distractions. albeit, advertisements, cell phones or the angry motorists attempting arriving to **Their** destinations efficiently. finishing your stress filled day working, then **You** have a stress filled drive home: people honking horns and others decide running red lights, for this shall help **Them** to arrive home faster? living and working on farm or mountain, seems enticingly less stressful and many youth living on mountains wished they lived within cities.

do **You** get it? **We** return home with the ones who **We** love, having energy to play, or read with children then take a hot bath or shower and relax with good book or proceed to bed where **Our** least distortions flow. getting into night clothes and brew some green tea and then turn on news: oops, that was a mistake, thinking soothing child of Yours has something wonderful to share regarding **Their** day. would rather ask John or Amanda, naming five good specifics they learned in school that day. 'this is My desire.' turning off distortions in life: televisions, computers, cell phone, ipods, black berries and spend quality time with family, constructing one puzzle together or look upon another silently with contented approval on your face. remember, quality time given and remaining a good behavioral role model when children are young, determines all facets with **Their** behaviors and thinking for life. whom they enmesh with, grades, how strong **Their** focus, becoming calm or hyper, if strong or diminish weakly to peer pressure, who they date, marry, if they become risk takers, how fast they drive, if they are doers, thinkers, hard workers, slackers and plethora of definable ways of thinking and behaving.

observing **God's** blessings through **Our** calmness remains what **Our** children need. within humanism, there absolutely remains zero better interaction than calming human interactions. your writer was reared within a family where physical tasks remained related with behavioral speeding, thus, who became fastest completing a task was the winner: parents constantly said 'hurry!' the voice was saying, **'slow down.'** had to do what parents said or was in trouble. performing efficiently and thinking fast, type 'a' personality, wonderfully became instilled for future achievements, however, mind continued thinking on three other specifics when teacher was teaching, thus, unable slowing mind for schoolwork. having heightened public stimulation then returning home, extreme high becomes often times generationally low, fleshly instilled through many of your wonderful offspring.

roller coaster lives remain extremely inconsistent and children observe peaks and valleys through every sense, thus, offspring are peaking and racing within **Their** minds through days: when bed time arrives stimulation has overloaded, adhd and manic/depressant labels occur. please awaken, bad Spirit is negativity within, thoughts and prayer alleviates negativity.

consciously and subconsciously, with persona enmeshment instilled in children: your feeling overwhelmed yields overwhelmed feelings through Them, disengaged yields disengaged and pessimism yields pessimism with numerous consequences. with this being stated, your calmness yields calmness, optimism yields optimism, loving yields loving, respect yields respectfulness and yes, societies need further instillations of optimism and respect through **Our** offspring. your optimistic enmeshment spreads; your enmeshed negative thinking and behaviors diminish, thus, negative consequences diminish, as well. individuals within society become more healthy. individuals who are viewing societies human conditions, presently remain feeling powerless, however, when numerous individuals, homesteads and global societies remain part of the solution rather than feeling overwhelmed and powerless, **God's** world progresses rather than digress further. remember, when feeling, hearing and seeing optimism repetitiously, psychosomatically **You** act and think optimistically.

optimistic persona enmeshment occurs throughout individuals who have physical contact through others, thus, behaviors and thinking of individuals, families and communities proceed feeling functionally optimistic, also: and this remains why when attending a wedding or graduation, people feel joyous and are smiling, thus, happiness perfectly enmeshes, spreading wonderfully well through human souls.

rather than individuals thinking of **Them** self and **You** thinking of Yourself, **We** all begin thinking externally together. through a wonderful heightened awareness of **God's** peace and love, calmness and happiness reverberates for others through **Us** and within neighbors, friends or a random human **You** may meet anywhere. once perception and perspective of **Yourself** living well optimistically modifies, then **You** feel many joyous desires and receive solace externally from helping others. feeling is **God.**

'What a wonderful world. I, remain calm, good and patience through all humans.'

'Pastor rob came to Robert in 1989 and said, from Me, numerous christians gathered in a stadium in Canada. offering communion, they gave a small loaf to receive this symbol of Christ's body, they took one pinch and passed this loaf upon to the next person throughout the vast stadium: I regenerated the loaf for everyone. this information refrained becoming known to the masses through media because they whom received remained faithfully aware and media unaware.'

God through Jesus speaks in john 16: **'I tell You truth; it's expedient for You that I go away: for if I not go away, the Comforter will not come unto You; but if I depart, I will send him unto You. I have yet many things to say unto You, but ye** cannot **bear Them presently. howbeit when he, the Spirit of truth, shall come, he will guide You into all truth: for he shall not speak of himself; but whatsoever he shall hear, that shall he speak: and shew You things to come. he shall glorify God : for he shall receive of Mine: therefore said I, that he shall take of Mine, and shall shew it unto You. 16 a little while, and ye shall not see Me: and again, a little while, and ye shall see Me, because I go to**

the Father. 20 verily, verily, I say unto You, that You shall weep and lament, but the world shall rejoice: and ye shall be sorrowful, but your sorrow shall be turned into joy. 25 these things have I spoken to You in proverbs: but the time cometh, when I shall no more speak to You in proverbs, but shall shew You plainly of the Father.'

'Jesus used the name disciple rather than christian. early church had other names for themselves: they used 'disciples', 'saints' 'brothers.' the holy Spirit remains God's word within an Advocate.'

'You're reading the Advocate's words in your book, God's offspring. the word means 'one called alongside,' but the gospel emphasizes that the holy spirit, as parakletos [paravklhto'] 'sent' from the Father remains the chosen one revealing the perfected truth of every good everywhere.'

'God's word was the Spirit spoken to Abraham preceding Jesus birth: within your book You shall receive information regarding all truth. I remain well aware of everything that shall occur within many chosen. within book, learn briefly of the past and much regarding solutions: why do humans spend 100's of billions seeking a cancer 'cure' when the solution shall remain free and learned: follow a perfected plan.'

'Finishing the chapter, here remains another helpful suggestion: when You are in private or public, silently ask Me to bless others. this takes one second through your blessed mind and most importantly, You asked: living within My continuously good spirit, spiritual enmeshments occur and humans connect well.'

Chapter

SLOWING DOWN

chapter relates how to modify mania behaviorally through non verbal movements. first and foremost, **You** profoundly need a relationship with **God** of understanding; following **God's** will, every task perfectly becomes more obtainable through You. move slowly, think well.

1997 was year and july 23rd month and day. was saturday, specifically 7:00 pm. molly and writers first date was proceeding: meeting within flips for dinner, She brought Her cousin john f. for plethora of reasons learned later. She, had recently broken up with one male whom was Her mate for nine years, he was stalking Her and behaving completely inappropriate. thinking of his name for five minutes, still remains blank for **God** desires self and Yours letting go of past negativity and consciously remember good occurrences, thus, shall joyously leave this one alone.

without further ado, was 29 years of age when writer had a wonderful date with his lovely future wife, molly. molly's Father's name remains john; although **God**, introduced numerous persons within writers life whom remained patient and calm, zero affected non verbally the way john luther has. through life writer observed thousands upon thousands of successful men in movies, television, businessmen, successful **Fathers** of friends, Father's friends and appropriately desired mirroring physical demeanor of those whom self desired becoming. upon young adulthood, behaviorally through private or public and within casual or formal settings received propensity consciously and methodically slowing non verbal physical movements:

his influence remains most influential, thank **You God**, through john. successful with life, thus, emulating or mirroring his demeanor and disposition was fervent becoming what had always dreamed of: calm, patient and soft spoken: a thinker rather than doer if **You** will. enmeshing personas, he was becoming the important role model with specific respects. **You** may obtain anything, following suggested behaviors anywhere: consciously and methodically desire to slow your movement, repetitiously and focusing on praying for others, thus, thinking of progression for family and others rather than what **You** receive, **God**, reciprocates through You.

having your gate slowed allows increased focus, imperative thinking, heightened awareness of the surroundings, as well as, your confidence increases significantly: through slowing physical movements your mind focuses from **God's** good love. remaining still and quiet, pray for **God** allowing peace of mind and contentedness through You, then when speaking with someone, speak slowly and softly with a gentle tone which people desire listening and they shall lean towards You; most significantly, be aware of information **You** speak of: subtle and calming functional love remains from **God** through your good. from **God**, through your remaining optimistic, life yields positive occurrences for **You** and a wonderful example for all of those who remain present. **We** have learned go faster and be more efficient. what hurries your and numerous others unfocused minds, thus, behaviors sometimes throughout societies globally?

You see, upon former generations, numerous learned from parents and societally, life was almost as egocentric as present, thus, 'do unto others before they do unto You,' 'life sucks then **You** die,' 'life is a bitch and then **You** marry one,' 'take what **You** can get before someone else does,' 'kill or be killed,' upon thousands of negative others. preceding processing further, what has this temporal negativity fleshly instilled in present societies? anger, depression, hostility, isolation, lack of empathy, aggression, thus, numerous negative souls. yes, writer remains well aware these negative statements are words, likewise, coupled with numerous other definable behaviors and thoughts introduced within this book, your comprehension shall heighten: when **You** understand why humans are negatively where they remain, shall **You** desire to allow and receive an optimistically driven differential advantage flowing through your three faceted self.

'**What is My great universe comprised of? energy. preachers, priests, clergy, scientist, theologians, agnostics and atheists remain aware.**' '**encompassing every atom, cell, molecule, organism, consciousness and physical realm, My good energy oscillates, reverberates and vibrates continuously.** negative **energy occurs,** distorts **and remains less frequent through some and modifiable through everyone. your life receives emotional, mental, as well as, physical certainty and** uncertainty: **both are spiritually provided. life remains simple and blessed further, You are safe, calm, happy and peaceful when living in the Spirit with Me rather than within My humans rumor of free will.**'

'**Soon after My writer's rebirth, I would have him watch the local and international news: I taught him to always ask, what shall occur? he became aware that one infant was** abducted **within oklahoma city. immediately, he thought from Me,** what shall occur? **I simply spoke that he should ask Me to bless the child and keep Her safe. he did. then I said for him to pray that I denounce satan from the abductors thought processes and feelings: he followed the suggestion perfectly. I asked him to pray that God works through Their souls and they drop the child off safely at a church. he did as spoken. I said good, continue to ask and do My will and all shall be well. the news came on that evening and he prayed, 'God** will **You** denounce satan from the specific badness.' **he did as suggested and an emergency update occurred, they reported the child had safely been dropped off at a church and returned to Her parents. robert thought,** thank **You God** and I spoke, You're welcome: My peaceful prayers within You yields peace for others.'

'This specific illustration is one representation of thousands from the previous few years. what You shall contemplate remains this question. did the goodness occur from his prayer or was the good outcome going to occur and God correlated his mind and soul? your answer remains, what is the relevance? all good remains freely given from Me.'

'I have zero jealousy: does jealousy remain confident and full of your faith? the good assistance I have through any human and anything remains slated: continue reading for earth's graciously anticipated future that shall occur. I remain joyous anticipating what shall reside perfectly within your heart.'

Chapter

13

MACRO RELIGION

unedited. slated first quarter of 2010.

preceding writing chapter from **God**, asked, how he desired writings and he spoke,_'I am God, thus, goodness within all optimism in humans and religious doctrines, globally; in a latter chapter, I, shall work through your soul and reveal more information.'

'Throughout your current chapter, You shall clearly be refreshed and understand how God encompasses everything living through thought processes, love, good energy, nutrients on earth and the atmosphere.'

spiritually: control, power, distorted religious interpretation or generational issues are why there remains friction between humans, thus, nations. **You** know this. **God** spoke, 'why is robert slating these pages? allowing your insight of how differing religious interpretations throughout history, shall proceed unified and increasingly more well understood. proceed within your perfect source, Me, God of everything good.'

from **God**, through his writer shall expound upon religion generally then specific.

through **Our** plethora of oppositional beliefs, shall humans work together as one? yes, a good paradigm shift remains occurring and numerous are becoming globally compassionate. **You** are aware there remains one **God**, now and forever through goodness in humans, animals, weather and things seen and unseen: remains fact and empirically proven true later. regarding muslims, many living outside **Their** beliefs or culture label **Them** badly, however, all are **God's** children. islam remains similar to christian: overwhelming majority are wonderful people. islam teaches **Them** to praise **God**, love humans, as well as, nature: sound familiar?

absolutely yes, excluding spiritually downtrodden extremists, believing **God**, remains speaking to Them, however, who they hear through thoughts remains satan. Abraham, remains founding **Father** of **Our** christian, jewish, and islamic religions. christian bible within genesis states the nation of Israel descended from Abraham through second Son isaac; in new testament, Abraham, is mentioned prominently as a man of faith who obeyed everything, **God**, had spoken to him. (hebrews 11).

many authors of **Our** new testament reported Jesus had cited Abraham supporting belief with resurrection of the dead. **'concerning the dead they all shall rise.'** have **You** read the bible? **God**, through the burning bush passage spoke to Moses, **'I, remain God of Abraham, God of isaac and God of jacob: I remain a God of goodness within everything living.'** (mark 12:26-27) traditional observances through christianity remain chief promises made to Abraham: genesis 12:3 from **God**, to Abraham, **'all families on earth shall be blessed,'** God, spoke february 11th 2010, **'all of My people remain blessed: if christian, jewish, muslim and others whom believe in Me and follow My suggested good ideas, beliefs and teachings You shall receive a wonderful flesh, then a perfect eternal life: in heaven,** satan **remains gone from every occurrence, thought process and feeling, everyone remains directed perfectly well.'**

christianity remains open for all rather than a limited few, as many religions, thus, christianity encompasses every geographic region, globally. many living in the middle east, indonesia and others, view christianity through Jesus as hope, love, thus, **Their** eternal salvation. **God**, chose global prophets from numerous cultures originally, they were mortal and male with spiritual discountings, thus, thought with **God**, speaking through Them, of course, believed egocentrically **Their** way, was only correct and definable path. regarding overwhelming majority of **Us** amongst every society through numerous socioeconomic tiers, pondered some time in life who **God** is and why **We** remain here. remains irrelevant how **You** believe, as long as **You** believe and love all: then through You, he, gives joy, love, patience and calm: all **You** need remains delighting through **God's** will and traversing along his path. christian clergy are aware, **God**, blesses all christians, muslims, buddhists and others who praise him while loving others: then life is perfectly underwhelmed and more loving than **You** may have anticipated on planet earth.

regarding brutal dictators, past and present, perverse extremists and those praying to 12th imam, maude, isis dysfunction and numerous individuals who are inhumane because satan has power over human souls seeking its negative agenda, thus, chaos, confusion, dysfunction and societal demise. however, **God**, restores hope, faith, love and calm shining bright in humans functionally united, upon his, beautiful, glorious and plentiful earth.

following soon after rebirth, over two days, **God** spoke for his writer to lie down and let go of everything. then, he enveloped all thoughts within mind and visions occurred over milliseconds: he placed your writer within the days of Abraham, Moses, jesus, buddha and even mohammed. he revealed what was spoken to **Them** from **God** and otherwise. **God** revealed humanism, spirits and weather generally and then specifically over the following four years: 1000's of questions and answers occurred for You. finally, **God** reveals spiritual truth for humans enlightenment. directed to live in the spirit, **God** spoke to ask what he desired? he suggested countless prayers to think and miracles were occurring from his writer's prayers through the weather as well as healing known and unknown globally.

'Over millisecond clips/words, I revealed the complexities of humans consciousness, weather and where the thought processes spiritually derived: 2002, his Son was two, they had gone on vacation to the white river within arkansas. enveloping your writer's consciousness, as life, I regarded what shall occur through the weather and many humans preceding Them transpiring. directed to one tall bridge with his Son from Me: the voice vacillated in same sentence: satan spoke.' 'throw your Son off the bridge if You love Me.' My messenger remained confused and thought, he would die: upon that moment I spoke for him to refrain and My good words spared his Son as well as negative to refrain from occurring.'

'Following his rebirth and for your book, he was revealed what occurred within Abraham's vacillating consciousness and how I spared his Son issac as well: humans shall learn the truth, where Their negative feelings, voices, thought processes, thus, consciousness derive. life is blessed, I have a plan.'

'Here remains john 14:16-17 from jesus' love, power as well as spirit: 16 I will ask the Father and he will give You another helper who will stay with You forever.17 <u>he is the Spirit who reveals the truth of God.</u>'

'Jesus repeated what was spoken through his favored consciousness and added words when regarding himself because he was told it was him healing and denouncing satan's negative energy within nature: everyone observing was unaware of what God, who is the comforter, spirit, helper and originator of every goodness was speaking within. following looking at trees and the wind calmed and healing humans, robert was told the miracles were from him: he learned truth in time.'

'Regarding the present, humans whom say when You're speaking with the fleshly deceased is demonic remains untrue: all true information remains from Me. My and your writer shall allow for your awareness. following My chosen writer's final rebirth, he was revealed the truth of everything: when directed to watch preachers, speakers and other humans anywhere, from Me, he asks countless questions and learns if what they are speaking is the truth: if specific words within sentences are true or otherwise, he receives My truth and remains highly aware.'

'You too, may silently ask Me questions and receive the perfect truth: specific prayers have been slated further for You to receive a perfect consciousness, as well. remain My significance within the solution.'

'Perfect health shall occur for My future chosen offspring upon earth because of My gentle favor, love, patience, peace and your guidance.'

'Global nuclear war shall refrain from occurring: I have a perfecting plan.'

Chapter 14

GOD'S GUIDANCE

these writings factually are one story, transcending boundaries from **God** through divine spiritual intervention following one wonderful rebirthing from your creator.

was a november morning, 2009, **God** said, **'pray for calm winds in edmond,'** had appointments with two chairmans and one professor at university of central oklahoma in edmond. arriving to old north, realized, had absolutely forgotten directions where appointments were and with whom. remember, these meetings remained subconsciously transfigured by **God** through writer, thus, was speaking, thinking and walking completely in his spirit: with eyes wide open, continually communicated with/from **God** through mind and arriving without appointments, **God**, was silent: becoming anxiety ridden, was unsure what should occur. immediately and calmly for reasons orchestrated from **God**, had given up entirely. **God** spoke, **'feel the wind.'** followed accordingly, thus, did exactly. eyes focused forward, slightly upward in spirit, felt gentle breeze and proceeded where he was directing.

moving across campus, **God**, directed all steps through his gentle breeze, turning left upon specific junctures and then right on others: feeling spiritually interwoven and completely connected was calmly told, **'pray silently for all in sight,'** whom would be approaching, how many leaves would fall directly in front and a higher awareness of humanism from milliseconds and understanding all that was spoken. then was taken to a building, in fact, specific doorway. letting go of self will, control and ego, **God**, said door shall open before it had. went through entrance. finding zero wind inside, let go further. **God**, was directing every thought process and behavior, saying, **'pray for all in sight and others spoken for You to pray for in city, country and continents, because i'm aware what they're needing.'**

proceeded with eyes focused forward: looked upon zero others, mind was on **God** and his will flowing within: walked up stairways, around corridors, through hallways with zero conscious movement from self, almost floating. peripherally was aware others were watching entranced writer, however, focus was upon what **God** spoke. arriving upon one door **God** said, **'open door.'** opening door, this was exactly where first appointment was. soon, chairman of genetics walked in waiting room: She said, 'hello robert, please walk to My chambers.' baffled, for this was **Our** first contact, how did She know My name? focused and having zero emotional or verbal response, proceeded to office then asked questions related within Her forte, genetics. **God**, was saying when She would speak, what She would say, as well as, what to reply. following 30 minutes of intense discussion, **God** said, **'time was finished and I, shall work through You when asking final question.'** therefore, 'why are psychosomatic learned pessimistic behavioral predispositions more imperative through human personas than physiological, thus, **Our** genetics?' with zero response, She immediately directed writer to sociological department, which coincidentally was exactly where following appointment remained located. thanking Her, for Her time and knowledge, proceeded across campus following direction of **God's** wonderfully gentle wind within following two appointments, sociology and other with chairman of theology. complete wonderfully surreal occurrence was orchestrated from **God**, would have been somewhere other than u.c.o. in first place: through continuous stages, **God** was preparing your writer for writing book **God's** offspring: please, remember, preceding writing for You, finished only one book as an adult because of receiving a different direction. good occurrences through humanism are from **God**, through **Us** and remains discussed deeper in your book. every day brings miracles from **God** : may your faith permanently be restored from his will throughout your future. restoring everything for anyone desiring his calmness, confidence, happiness and love, therefore, everyone living; **God**, remains goodness through all his faithful offspring.

PSYCHOSOMATIC VERBAL INSTILLATIONS

present writings explain how negative verbal instillations ingested through humanism, psychosomatically affects your mind, offspring, as well as, all others.

ergo:

You hear and see negativity all around: purchase paper, read internet, watch world news, local news, communications with others and much music remains negative. **You** know this. media implements optimistic stories, however, overwhelming are negative, exacerbating feelings and thoughts, compounding throughout a lifetime. feelings and thoughts enmeshed in **You** and your offspring's senses, generationally and environmentally remain what holds relationships, thus, communities together or otherwise. faith and praise from **God** through **Us** are keys for **Our** good living.

God, had writer slate in previous writings and shall deeply within latter chapters: '**spiritually, You remain directed well or** unwell.' we're influenced saying positive or negative words. examples: **You** will do great! You're extremely beautiful today! that was a wonderful job! on other hand, **You** also express negativity. I, don't like that. that's not what **You** were told. bad job, your wrong or use your brain. why are **You** so ignorant? negative words were freely expressed in the home where writer was reared, **You** relate upon some level. pessimistic words, at times were what all have learned: negative thinking and words, thus, behaviors are life generationally speaking. hmmm, '**My favored and chosen shall become enlightened.**'

delving deeper.

life learned from nurturers and others vacillates your thinking throughout life. positive or negative remains significant temporal reasons **You** receive as **You** do. all of **Our** offspring desire receiving optimism through senses from parents then societally, however, throughout societies past and present, sometimes nurturers behave oppositionally from one bad Spirit through fleshly negative learning souls. shall attempt justifying briefly parents pessimistic words and behaviors for Them. first- they remain unaware because this was how **Their** rearing occurred. sporadic negativity were consciously encoded within **Their** generationally influenced souls. second- spiritually, throughout history upon specific moments, all individuals are discontented and overwhelmed sometimes receiving numerous negative thoughts. third- many heard bad words, thus, behaviors creates character, yet, resentments trumped character, (friction), teaching **Them** cyclical generational dysfunction forever. negative behaviors are apparent with all generations, however, upon what specific juncture shall **God** denounce these dysfunctional thoughts and behaviors occurring through You?

what about now, this evening or this specifically profound and healthy moment? '**when finished enmeshing with this book, all shall become well within You and over time others around You for You: good remains Me.**'

from **God**, through writer will attempt to progress your soul and thinking, thus, increasing your faith, yields **You** more calmness, optimism and lessens pessimism. listening to body and denouncing negativity, naming only a couple: then proceed placing your good thoughts, feelings and life forward. having **God** as your central and profound reason for living shall **You** progress complete, as well as, contented.

would **You** like one current text book, palpably assisting forward with solutions, from **God's** unending love, optimism and peace? continue reading, **You** shall find what **You** desire, perfectly placed upon these wonderfully information filled pages: the bible shall continue as the most read book, globally: this book's intention remains revealing current truth for humans globally from **God** for countless alive and future generations.

HUMAN LABELS TWO

following writings remain attributed with labeling again, however, this time shall bring together two examples of functional obsessive and compulsive livelihoods of colleagues because this works well for numerous people and possibly Yourself.

ergo:

labeling individuals pessimistically hinders; disorders remain negative views how humans manage daily life. here remains two good examples. first, paulo jacuzzi, one friend while attending college, would walk through his residence picking up minute pieces of debris from carpet. forward two decades, bumper sticker on his vehicle says, 'c.d.o. alphabetically correct, as it should be.' **You** see, humans behaving compulsively and obsessively throughout life, fleshly, remain emulating behavioral observations from parent and on the deepest level, spiritually, shall be understood throughout book. what occurred for paulo, generationally from **Father** remo, retired c.e.o. jacuzzi north America, presently jason international, shall become understood one paragraph further on following page. secondly, another personal friend, attending **Our** good church, douglas stussi, has functional o.c.d., as well. compulsiveness works perfectly for him, he remains wonderful with his family, professionally and church accountant. douglas and your writer worked intimately together, moving his family into **Their** new residence here; his organizational skills are more than appropriate: having specific items boxed, alphabetized and labeled, for specific rooms was organizationally perfect, thus, the move went perfectly as well.

absolutely zero confusion from either, suzie his wife, nor Us: minds were one and personas enmeshed, calmly and silently from **God**, through your writer's prayers. douglas, remains chief financial officer of love's country stores, one nationally recognized company in America doing well within distorted economic conditions occurring through numerous.

over time personas were observed, writer learned reasoning feeling obsessive and compulsive remains this: first, **Their** Fathers had instilled organizational behaviors, thus, emulated organized **Fathers** functional behavior. **You** see, numerous males and females across societies presently and throughout history, having everything perfect, subconsciously they were ascertaining Fathers, would remain more calm and patient when they had come home for dinner that evening, as well as, learned constructive organizational behaviors benefits entire family structure for everyone. writer and numerous individuals in all societies, globally perform exact behaviors emulating **Fathers** and Mothers and clean or organized lives yield organized minds: with less clutter your family feels good and organized, thus, receives significantly less stress: negative energy yields negative energy.

with a great responsibility comes relief or tension instilled in offspring from birth. dependent on a couple of spiritual then manifested fleshly factors, **You** learn what is needed for proceeding through life by age six. upon this juncture, hopefully, **You** have learned how to relate with other living things through your lovingness: show love, compassion, patience and respect for **Yourself** and others, thus, receive correct deductive and abstract reasoning, as well as, visual spatial assessment. learning instinctual propensities of becoming great, greater or influential: **God**, is reasoning for each wonderful occurrence through **Us** all. optimism, honesty, unity and loss of ego are great places to begin: then peace through **You** shall come while negative labels shall become replaced with positive examples for all **Our** offspring.

through your faith, as well as, praise with **God** and prayers for others, life is good.

finishing your chapter, **God** desires quoted, **'religions remain cultural interpretations of spirituality. follow My direction and life is good.'**

Chapter

IMPULSIVITY AND POOR JUDGMENT YIELD DIRE CONSEQUENCES

God, spoke to write these chapters order following third rebirth and your current chapter was written, august and september 2009: chapter shall remain unedited because **God** was asked and this remains what was spoken.

current chapter reveals, believing **You** are bullet proof when young and all ages, may result with catastrophic life changing occurrences. most significant profound occurrence in writer's life, was meeting one female, which only dreams are made of then taking Her life preceding Her blooming. shannon lee albright and writer knew one another for one month. She asked for **Us** to attend riverfest together: annually party on arkansas river in little rock, were young and in love. further; may 28th, 1988 was month, day and year. Shannon, absolutely was the one, **We** attended Hendrix college near accidents occurrence, as well. Shannon was a senior, virtually prepared beginning professional life. **You** see, She and your writer met following Her winning the title of miss Conway, where Hendrix remains located: although She had won pageants throughout state, most formidable achievements were miss teen little rock, miss teen Arkansas and competed in miss teen U.S.A.

shannon was real, refraining boasting of Her beauty and outstanding disposition: She loved everyone, who crossed Her path. one person whom stands out was one male confined within wheelchair: john, had spinal bifida: She explained he would never walk and he needed a friend. john, came over, many times to see Her during **Our** month long courtship: he would push and glide one mile, to see Her awaiting arms and smile, speaking volumes of Her class and elegance instilled from **God**, through Her chosen Mother linda's, loving, glowing and wonderful disposition.

allow proceeding post accident first because **God**, has spoken. shannon's Mother linda, present for writer's pre-trial hearing for negligent homicide in conway, arkansas, remains vivid. shannon's, pictures of wonderful family She previously had shown, was aware of Her Mothers physical appearance. day of court, linda, approached self in lobby- speechless and many tears flowed down both cheeks: looking writer in the eyes She stated, 'shannon, was correct **You** are beautiful.' dumbfounded for this made zero sense, why would She be so understanding with person who took Daughter's life? was it a strong christian belief and acceptance? linda remains only person who may answer question, however, **God**, spoke when asked september 11th 2009 and he remains quoted, thus, spoke absolutely perfect:

'**Her words remained from Me, thus, I, worked through Her for both of your calmness and future. I, work through Her and You had many revelations to experience in life preceding writing this book for others whom I choose to receive as well as reveal My absolute truth.**'

She realized what would take your writer 21 additional years of questioning **God**, unrelenting chemical abuse and plethora of other diversions from life, thus, denial, transference and blame were the only viable solutions. all prior years from birth to accident wished pain on zero living thing, now had received the overwhelming responsibility of taking another's life.

ultimately, fleshly, writer was responsible dissolving budding flower before blooming and becoming most beautiful, **God's** world had ever viewed. crying and trembling, this remains extremely unpleasant.

You see, anticipating an angered and bitter response was seemingly apropos, however, this moment refrained from occurring. She went on saying, 'also rob, I lay no blame on **You** for My Daughter's death.' She smiled and **We** hugged one another. Her embrace was sincere and then proceeded having case dismissed. **'I worked through Her thoughts to dismiss the case.'**

saddening were former writings, however, **God** assured your writer, shannon, had gone immediately to heaven. **God** is good. allow procession following accident, inner perceptions were drastically reduced and physiologically endured set backs. **God**, has a grander purpose for your writer: sharing experience, hope and strength with others and through helping other humans, satisfaction shall become achieved. assisting any spiritually and generationally challenged humans, through providing **God's** perfected information for receiving better lives for Ourselves, thus, offspring, shall **God**, create good differences upon earth through many of his elected and numerous of his chosen individual offspring.

pardon please, desired speaking minimally further referencing writer within book, and wished to speak of others, however, **God**, spoke further through good desires, **'these words shall be effective through countless hearts and minds reading: regarding your life within these pages,** horrific **accident occurred and your life was spared becoming deceased through your flesh because, one- I, have a plan and two- physiologically having steering wheel in front of You kept head from** slamming **back of bus bumper traveling 80 to zero in one millisecond.'**

We both were drunk, thus, invincible, as well as, refrained from wearing seatbelts. 12:06p.m. was time of impact: one directed well soul from **God** happened upon accident soon after impact. **God**, told writer this. shannon and writer were medi-flighted to a hospital in little rock. would proceed remaining comatose for ten days then within a semi-unconscious state for another six weeks. paralyzed over right side of body during this time, two eye surgeries would ensue: **God**, allowed self to live for writing this book for You. relearning to walk, talk and wearing diapers, life began again. was 18 and 6' 2" inches tall, losing weight was certain and became a frail 111 pounds. cognitively and physically was a mess but lived, cognitive and physical body was returned, however, shannon's was fleshly gone forever.

God, spoke through an emotionally beleaguered soul upon this specific juncture, **'shannon's earthly vessel returns to dust- Her pure soul had gone directly to heaven and walks beside Me, awaiting joyously all of Her family and friends.'**

pardon, writing **God's** quoted words, tears are flowing down both of cheeks. fleshly am unaware how these writings shall proceed, emotions remain inundated. spiritual, thus, religious beliefs in **God**, life restores hope through and with those desiring to travel a faithful path of flowing abundance, happiness, love, optimism and truth for examples of numerous others whom are presently needing societally.

proceeding with electronic transmission between paulo and your humbled writer. correspondence occurred after he viewed picture of shannon and writer one hour before accident, placed on facebook december 11th of 2009 from **God's** direction.

following transmission, asked **God** why this occurred. he said, **'for Our book: every specific word occurs for a reason: I am God.'**

paulo a. jacuzzi:

'rip shannon.'

robert goeringer:

'this is celebration of Her life. since finding **God**, again, miraculous changes have occurred. july 19th 2009, remaining still and quiet, **God**, spoke through a parable:

'My son, why are You living with all this sorrow for 21 years, masking pain with chemicals? following suicide or mutilation, how shall You help others? when receiving negative energy, how shall You do My will? You shall offer society more with experience, strength and hope while living. shannon, Her Mother linda, others with faith and I, desire this through You.'

paulo a. jacuzzi

'We are but vessels, Our experiences and the strength We draw from Them are to be used in maximum service to him.'

now, shall rewind 23 years:

post accident and rehabilitation, life was sad, as well as, irrelevant. coupled with further inappropriate behavior, impulsivity and reactions, the future looked bleak. following extensive full time neurological rehabilitation, relearning to walk, form sentences, eating without assistance and wearing diapers, perception what would become was drastically reduced. 18 years of age was told by doctors, cognitively, as well as, physically was less than 50 percent, thus, expressed from professionals, compensatory strategies would become needed managing daily tasks was a reality and psychosomatically began believing this. through a minimized view of future, progression of drug addiction and alcoholism became prevalent. feeling a viable future was unachievable or sustainable, numbing inner pain appeared appropriate.

had given up.

God, was aware and restored hope within. mind You then was unaware, however, presently completely am: this was the first significant rebirthing and hearing voice deep inside saying, 'keep trying' and sometimes would say what others would do or say before moving or speaking: same voice said drink, use chemicals and steal: voice said when workers would leave and safe stealing candy as boy. God asked to be quoted, 'good and bad voices/thought processes are both entities within all humans.'

naturally began focusing on certain strengths, verbal skills. your writers parents refrained understanding why multiple syllable words were so important. **You** see, traumatic brain injury yields hyper sensitized self images, thus, **We** remain more sensitized than general society through how people perceive **Us**. having digressed from life temporarily, **We** have become more egocentric than most because focus or attention has been **Us** through process, thus, anticipated being enabled children. looking well physically outwardly, life living this facade was put into full swing: for writer, this front went on for majority of life, existing egocentrically, however, highly aware through senses/thoughts and was directed to pray for others sometimes continually from **God's** wonderful direction for life.

once born, writers **Father** and Mother viewed Son repeatedly stumbling, standing up, falling to knees, returning to feet for a few steps to fall again. **You** may surmise, was learning to walk, however, metaphorically speaking continued until age 40. upon this specific juncture and living away from Son whom writer nurtured, loved and reared, modifications in life transpired remarkably further, following **God's** direction rather than others, self, negative direction or harmful thought processes. **God**, spoke through another parable for everyone reading and others lives in time:

'**Your life has occurred for many reasons: relating with others and helping Them find Me: follow My direction, through your continual guidance of love and assistance, all things shall become new. follow direction of praising and prayer, I, shall assist with everything. let go of your will and follow My written words.**'

human civilizations have taken thousands of years to develop efficient agriculture and hundreds of years to develop efficient industries. within most recent decades, **God** has efficiently implemented well technological assistance for numerous humans, however, countless globally remain taking negative control over function for **Their** badness interjecting pornography, how to make drugs, bombs or infecting society with negativity infecting potentially good individuals: then seeks harm on another because **Their** insecurities, thus, hate or dislikes spiritually driven and You're aware where all badness derives through **Their** thought processes, emotions and feelings.

'I taught robert throughout his awakened hours and now Yours through one important parable: ask Me to bless people and places and pray for My desires. living in My spirit, with and from Me, comfort and peace envelops your entire being perfectly well. patience becomes You, inequities cease, your perspective as well as perceptions modify gently and I shall bless those who You ask Me to bless, good enmeshments flow well.'

'ask to remember and follow My gentle suggestions and life becomes a continuous pleasure.'

God, shall end chapter with another quote, 'let go and follow all these written words throughout your book and I, shall assist with everything perfectly and allow You and your family living comfortably because My love and prayers shall flow deep in your soul for others: life is simple, follow Me and and your life shall be a pleasureful journey.'

10.26.14

'Life is spiritual and humans remain the only living organisms whom have an ability to ask Me questions and live in the spirit: all positive blessings and goodness remain, in truth, an illusion through humans perspective. all good prayers and thinking are from Me through You. every negative control, anger, hate and bad weather are from satan: life becomes abundantly good from Me, for You, rather than bad because this is what I desire. the irrelevant past, most assuredly present and suggestions for a more wonderful future remain slated for You for a reason. your happiness is My happiness and I have a wonderful plan for everyone whom adheres to the suggestions slated in My book God's offspring, for You and this information shall allow You to receive zero negative thoughts and feelings as I give into My writer, as well. finally, good individual and societal paradigm shifts occur continuously from Me: become a part of My wonderful solution and receive only good from adhering to what I speak through You and please remember, I, allow You to focus perfectly on what needs to remain accomplished.'

Chapter 18

WORDS, GOOD AND EVIL

chapter was written one month following rebirth. **God** spoke, **'leave unedited and I, shall reveal heightened awareness regarding this chapter further.'**

attending college as one freshman, 1988, insecure, impressionable and overwhelmed, being away from family, as many of reading may relate. biology was first class of semester and was good, thus, well for loving nature, as well as, animals remained enticing within self's persona and mind. walking into class was early and seeking comfortable seat furthest from professor was apropos, because if **You** were seated in back of class **You** may arrive late, leave early and remain virtually transparent. **You** see, living a facade, was athletic and socially confident, however, academically was difficult: impatient through soul and mind, voice was continuously saying how classmates would move, what professor was to say and many other specifics regarding what would occur well and unwell.

our professor walked up to his wooden podium and stood there quietly for a few moments, **Our** class fell silent. he proceeded raising his gavel, then struck podium three times yelling, 'there is no **God**!' taken aghast, **Our** entire classroom filled with impressionable young souls, looked around upon each other with utter and profound disbelief. if intentions were for giving shock value this worked, unwell. following bone chilling statement, he began filling minds with information regarding evolution through charles darwin's theory of natural selection: life was confused. class proceeded, beliefs, persona and thinking in mind were modified completely. all information learned previously in life, attending church every sunday, as well as, wednesday, being saved and baptized, assisting with church day care, as well as, every single specific piece of faith from **God**, through writer, withered rapidly.

the reason a premier college accepted one average high school student academically within **Their** outstanding school of higher learning, **God**, had blessed your writer athletically: this average, as well as, impressionable young man with low self esteem was focused, directed physically well. also, how shall students differ with one of America's finest professors?

professor's teachings, thus, words, altered life for more than two decades. please, allow following sentence, lying deeply in your mind. your words, as expressed within conversations affects negatively or positively those whom **You** speak with. albeit your offspring, spouse, neighbor, friend or random person with life, words have profound repercussions. currently am aware how absurdly incorrect he was, likewise, this view remains distorting many unwell. as individuals culminating masses, thwart **God**, repercussions follow from bad entity, via, human behaviors and numerous physical occurrences through weather. look upon all past and present societies.

ending your book, atheists shall receive exclamations quoted from **God**.

believing professor, life modified during this juncture, thus, many miracles **God** had blessed writer with were coming to an abrupt end. **You** see, when **We** distance Ourselves from **God**, satan commences having more power over thinking, behaviors personal and family life. satan begins diminishing contentedness, self worth, focus, resolve, thus, heightens your irritability, impatience and unhappiness through many. many atheist explain they are similar as faithful: they are wealthy, poor, healthy and unhealthy through all depictions. some have a path of needing and receiving blessings from **God** while others need zero. within a short time, from **God's** timing, the unaware humans shall desire awareness for living in the Spirit with **God** for **Their** alleviation of distortions and negativity, thus, receive only good.

allow proceeding deep. spiritually, earth has pure and less pure, good and bad or yen and yang. these expressions depict one precise good and a bad entity herein. while **God's** presence is calm, caring, generous and harmonious, thus, allowing compassion, functionality, kindness, patience and progress; satan, alternatively sits looming, waiting, watching and causing weakness in your mind. your weakness, metaphorically speaking opens door for anger, misery, pain and negativity within: satan becomes more pleased with negative outward expressions and inner thoughts; negative entity gave **Them** alone or through numerous other souls, hearts and minds.

'Causing distortions **electronically: your bank accounts, computers, electronic devices,** hacked **operation systems, power grid** failures **are from** satan **alone and within** negatively controlled **spiritual souls.'**

was in the process of differentiating the voice and now remain aware the negative words were satan: some information and direction was negative. it said, '**think** negatively.' did. '**your computer is** infected **with a** virus.'

presently the negative voice is gone and now remains directed from **God** alone, however, remained directed unwell for your book and was aware where these thoughts derived. please understand. every morning, your writer asks **God** to denounce satan from the electronics within **Our** property and **God** always does this perfectly. '**former sentence remains a parable: follow Me and receive increased favor and assistance throughout life.'**

here remains two altering examples or instances:

You or someone your aware of are having a wonderful day, moving methodically and thinking about family, others, as well as, progress through day: contented with achievements, proceeds driving home. traversing through traffic **You** turn on soft, thus, soothing music, concentrating upon driving and thinking of tasks needing completion, as well as, remaining cognizant of other motorists around Yourself: asking **God's** will, **You** shall receive this through a thought, word or vision and then do as directed perfectly. returning home calm, optimistic and contented, **You** have wonderful calm, stress less and relaxing evening with your spouse and children, ultimately sleeping well, prepared for work following day: **God**, blesses further your functions, life is good.

in the second illustration, please, allow preempting. applying throughout all his societies presently: all socioeconomic levels and both genders, on every continent, having belief in **God**, some refrain from practicing faith, and many zero: Jesus said, 'forgive **Them** Father they know not what they do.'

'My **information given through Jesus for others, was to remain simple: everyone whom could hear My words, could clearly understand him.**'

again, **You** or someone **You** know, received horrible sleep, from prior evening, possibly from excessive use of alcohol or chemicals and awake into early morning hours watching television, thinking of overwhelmedness and escaping altogether. upon awakening, **You** now are late for work, frantically looking for car keys, as they are misplaced again. skipping breakfast, **You** rush out front door past crying children, spouse, as well as, the dog, who urinated upon new carpet again because animals feel overwhelmed personas. proceeding to work, **You** realize **You** forgot fueling vehicle evening prior when more time was had. angry, **You** play acid rock or negative rap loudly with the bass thumping making life more overwhelming. arriving late to work, boss looks down as **You** enter building, saying zero, for his non verbal communications says everything, unwell. **You** feel this dissatisfaction.

proceeding to your work station: finding enormous stack of papers left there from previous day because **You** were on last nerve, overwhelmed, needed escaping from reality with another drink, chemical or irrelevant television, masking inner pain, and **You** were leaving for bar, home or tavern. then coworkers arrive within your presence with unneeded distortions sharing stories similar to Yours, lowering your mood psychosomatically with pessimistic view regarding what they had observed watching local, national or world news evening prior and much irrelevant gossip: finally **You** choose performing something professionally and are two hours into work, however, have zero accomplished further than feeling more overwhelmed, than when **You** arrived. day has progressed through many intermittent distortions, likewise, your enormous stack of papers remains significantly diminished further. clock strikes five, hurrying out of office your boss stops You, saying, 'You know **You** have been late ten times this month, also, were **You** aware today is the 12th?!?' apologizing, **You** say, 'this will never happen again.' dismissing You, gives **You** blank stare through his eyes, again, nonverbally saying everything unwell for You.

proceeding to vehicle, **You** turn on acid rock, gangster rap or another filled with violence or inappropriate behaviors, therefore, escaping your overwhelmed day. driving home and looking in vehicles for a hot female filling your impulsive and inappropriate primal needs through your weakness. **You** are now upon a highway and thinking remains focused upon how **You** remain perceived from other drivers. returning home, your wife, overwhelmed with life, had one horrible day at work, also, She had spoken with a principal regarding a child using drugs, skipping class, fighting, disrespecting a teacher or another student and these offspring are youths. listening over dinner, She needs more help from **You** and many repairs need fixed. then turn on television, both of **You** sit comfortably back. saying zero **You** think negatively how overwhelmed life has become. pour a strong drink and cyclically proceed repeating what has transpired many times previously.

with both of these differing illustrations many behavioral choices have occurred. your first, he softly and gently remains chosen from **God**, because this individual continues focusing while thinking of others and forward progression continually: within second, bad entity, views spiraling discontentedness, thus, weakness in mind; interjecting misery, pain and unhappiness, thus, bad choices and cyclical demise. alleviating distortions satan imposes, thinking becomes clearer, easier and softer. your existence shall become improved through an intimate relationship with **God** : most imperative, from your praise and respect given, the good energy, **God**, reciprocates through your contentedness and functionally progressing thoughts.

currently many are needing making pertinent choices or how desiring to proceed: former or latter examples, **God**, remains there for **You** with open arms, thus, **God**, continually chooses remaining as **Our** palpable crutch of stability so to speak, thus, continuously present for and through **You** with every situation, good, better or less. let go of Yourself, then pray for calmed elation, patience and optimistic thinking: regarding life, asking **God** to bless numerous known and unknown, he reciprocates and blesses your thoughts and feelings accordingly well. asking **God** to bless others takes a millisecond through your wonderful mind.

'Follow **what I speak My Son and allow the chapters to be short in there duration. You the reader shall remember well because I live within your soul and shall direct your peace and goodness for other living things upon earth.'**

'I dictated all that is spoken in this book for a reason: My offspring from any religion, faith and lack thereof to learn the truth regarding humanism, spirits and weather. the time has come again for humans to learn where Their goodness derives and how they shall become a part of a wonderful solution rather than stagnantly **remaining in the flesh. allow Me to denounce** negativity **through and around You: this remains your most important decision: peace comes from peace.'**

WRITER'S FAMILY AND REARING

readers, majority of the current chapter remained written upon an angry or fleshly stage when bad entity controlled one self's soul and mind: unedited and written 02.10.07 with a few remissions.

caring for others preceding **Yourself** remains apparent, amongst numerous throughout industrialized and technologically modifying world, however, egocentrism prevails individually, often times, when something becomes desired more. generationally, all offspring have received pain: emotional, mental or physical, remains irrelevant, past and **God** may do anything with anyone at anytime.

writer's rearing under **Father** was enlightening, however, generationally difficult. his Father, was deceased penniless because he gave all acquired to others, church or offspring, however, **Father** saw this, thus, was wanting passing with most toys, as well as, consciously and subconsciously, having control over everything. he failed recognizing his behaviors affected lives of everyone whom he had crossed paths with and often times, life regarded only himself. making life work rather than letting go and allowing **God** direct him, remained unaware his behaviors for a chosen different path, affected those around him, especially spouse and offspring. relying zero upon his family for support, life became abundantly overwhelming.

free thinker in complete control, writer's **Father** rescinded sharing, for his Son had given an abundance of heartache and disrespect, thus, heartache and disrespect remained reciprocated. he failed remaining accountable, for his own behaviors, as to why his Son disrespected him so. repeated belittling, demeaning, as well as, overbearing control, that his **Father** generationally and fleshly instilled in him: negative energy <u>was</u> winning.

when two years of age, **Father** said, 'You will never be anything!' demeaning his son, somehow allowed himself feeling better. secondly, aged two, was asked by Mother to ingest aspirin for head ache, like numerous children was apprehensive. **Father** angrily said, 'no Son of Mine is not going to take a pill!' he would refrain understanding because of his anger, son, had a headache in the first place: double negatives became life, four decades and counting, thus, received difficulty swallowing pills until 25 years of age. he remained controlling while his offspring were scarred emotionally and mentally, thus, writer was aware Father's behaviors thwarted son's maturation for decades. why your offspring though? through his distorted perceptions, he felt better putting down his Daughter and son. generational egocentric control and power on fleshly level, however, reasoning remains deeper and **You** shall remain more aware in following chapters. **You** too, are far from alone.

disappointed his Son became involved with drugs and alcohol as one teenager, however, having low self esteem was complete reason for dysfunctional behavior. summer, age 12, at the lake there were ice chests full of beer for writer to drink with friends and family. during era of 1970's, dr. spock, said that it was better to drink with children, thus, they could control drinking later in life. what? parents, went with what another was telling **Them** rather than common or **God**, sense. hmmm.

Mother, learned during Her generation, within a small town in midwest, females did exactly as males expressed, bible says this, therefore, is? bible was written numerous years ago from males with generational discountings and bad entity distorting **Their** perceptions through mind saying 'control wife,' or 'females shouldn't speak at church.' or 'fear **God's** wrath,' and plethora of other negative ideas and thoughts supposedly from **God**. negative entity placed together yields negativity: **God**, remains positive, kind and gentle, thus, who would remain speaking negatively through messengers minds? hmmm. the spirits vacillate within many sentences through all minds.

please receive another truthful and appropriate quote, **'throughout history, I have desired zero** anger, war, control, demeaning oppression or badness **upon living things on My earth: I remain good energy within everything.'**

EGOCENTRIC MACHINE

two decades previously following car accident; was unconfident, easily swayed, generationally weak, thus, began questioning **God** : wondering where everything as powerful as himself, who creates all of the earth's wonderfulness had come from. close mindedness and becoming educated, there were zero interjections attending high school or college, attributing anything related from **God**, or a higher power. if there was a **God**, why were **Their** horrible atrocities occurring through life for numerous humans. throughout 1960's, an abundance of laws occurred in united states: **God**, and prayer was disassociated from public schools and females became empowered having abortions, among other diversions from **God's** desires. these ideologies generationally taught **Our** society, out with **God** and in becoming reliant on fleshly impulsive selves, thus, society worked as one egocentric machine: satan received goose bumps, viewing societies becoming away from **God's** beliefs. open your eyes, knowing satan's bad infection has become very apparent societally and why negativity through humanism and weather occur. life remains spiritual.

what remains important, comprehending **God**, is all knowing: creating what shall always be. life, love and offspring furthering his planet. most importantly, **God**, works through humans loving, praising and trusting him, as well as, one another. when **God's** desires are followed accordingly, pessimism shall become rescinded, anger abolished and optimism, peace and love shall prevail from **God** within Us: assisting the numerous chosen further, as well as, **'written for future humans upon My blessed earth.'**

REACHING HEAVEN

depictions reaching **Our** creator through different religions are often oppositional. first, living fleshly within and through every individual creature remains extremely relative through spiritual control and power, thus, perfect goodness or imperfect badness. second, desiring correctness, especially from human interpretations of reaching **God** : reaching **God**, through martyrdom are absolutely ludicrous and most of **Us** are aware. promises for martyrs are enticing: why else would **You** decease **Yourself** or others? where had this negative thinking through souls originate? shall proceed further. depictions, perverse as they are, think **Their** thinking undeniably remains correct. christianity, originally it was understood to sacrifice your first born Son to **God** : where were all these negative thoughts deriving? they remain distant from **God**. earth, has become modified over time from an ever present **God**, whom loves and cares for Us, unconditionally, thus, remains here for optimistic affirmations only. observe every pessimistic teaching from your past as just that, outdated and past. wondering why numerous humans still fear **God**? remember, the bible says these words.

'I yield continual goodness within living creatures: badness **remains** satan's wrath: satan, **should be** feared **through humanism and earth's further calming** negative **weather rather than Me, your perfect God.**'

what if human's from all religions, throughout history would have learned **God**, remains only goodness? this question shall remain answered within a later chapter if **God** speaks for this to occur.

modifications in present theologies, youth are trending towards optimistic views. speaking of, Jesus christ, the Son of **God** and earth's most divine realist modified everything wonderfully better, he loved everyone living, understood the bad: **You** know his profound story, shall proceed no further.

God, expresses admiration for **You** through blessings of hope, faith, willingness, unending love, compassion within humans wonderful lives anticipating reciprocation. **'I asked My messenger to ask and rely only on Me: zero research occurred for writing your chapters. all words slated within your book are for My future's certain balance. I have a plan.'**

'Reaching **God through whom I chose remains similar: God and Allah are the same through different individual human interpretations and who do You think spoke** egocentrically **throughout history, within humans for Their unaware future purpose of division?'**

to each **Their** own, thus, may your belief be your belief, as long as **You** praise **God**, while loving family and others. different religious depictions of how to reach **Our God**, have similar moral views. followers doing optimistically what remains expressed in all traditional books are correct with reaching afterlife, as well. **You** see, **We** are praying to same the **God**, why are numerous religions remaining dissimilar through **Their** specific respects? reason remains, bible and quran were written through individuals from **God** and satan. his numerous blessed writer's were absolutely unaware, spirits spoke directly within **Them** and showed miracles, likewise, writing chapter, **God**, clearly spoke, 'satan **was also speaking through apostles minds when regarding My** anger, control **and** wrath **for the purpose of** controlling **humans** unwell. negative **and positive voices/thoughts have** same tone: **I remain your good, peaceful, lucid, correct, truthful and calm direction.'**

following **God** revealing information, specifics through life made complete sense.

You see, beliefs through christian bible, as well as, qur'an remain different, however, **God's** goodness remains similar, thus, humans shall need acceptance and believing positive general ways of living and reaching **God** in afterlife are correct rather than differences. writer, had written former sentence one and half years preceding the pope from vatican, expressing exactly this to christians, globally. **God** said, **'pray the pope expresses to christians they should understand other religions.'**

our earthly bodies are vessels, ultimately they reach heaven for eternity. enough for now, shall expound upon this specific later, now, shall return to story.

when **You** are born into a specific culture, **You** believe what is taught or how **You** were trained through humanism, creating your perfected ways of thinking, thus, behaving and all of the earth's religions teach very similar optimistic good beliefs.

first, praise **God** and love others. secondly, love your Mother and Father, showing respect for Them, **You** are **Their** offspring and your mortal life was given, from **God** through Them. thirdly, love your family, they are lineage, acting as a tightly knit unit of unconditional love whom remains there for **You** through your earthly life. fourth, love fellow humans intrinsically as neighbors: **God** remains who bonds all his humans or offspring together as one. traditional religions throughout globe, express loving nature is **God**, everything seen and unseen that's good. lastly, viewing earth with an optimistic perspective creates positive attitudes with harmonious thoughts and behaviors within Yourself, then others: inner peace over time, through personas infectiously enmeshes amongst numerous families, thus, neighbors, communities, towns, cities, states, countries, continents and the infinite pinnacle shall be reached when **God** s contagiousness encompasses all on the earth. **Our** numerous different cultures, religions and ethnicities shall become agreeable, once humans finally agree upon **God's** exact premise, praise **God**, and love others. again, as your aware, martyrdom remains zero of **God's** intentions and remains a specific ideology generationally instilled in some whom observed **Their** foreFathers because satan acts alone or through humanism for deceasing innocent individuals. generationally and spiritually are how they were trained, please pray for Them. over time, they'll be extinguished from **God's** world through many of **Our** prayers. **God** speaks, 'Simply **pray to Me for your desires, I, have supreme power over** satan; **I, know your feelings and feel hopeful from My living through your blessedness.'**

when this occurs in republics as united states and other societies, humans shall spend billions of dollars, helping earth rather than defending **God's** wonderful land from a minuscule portion of global populations. asking, praising and doing **God** s will repetitively, his reciprocation occurs continually through You, Yours and numerous others gently well.

allow deeper delving. numerous within **God's** industrialized and technologically unified world, are increasingly less tolerant of others, thus, anger and impatience are heightened through compounding negativity, many are completely egotistical: absence of praise and prayer yields all negative inequities.

divorce has skyrocketed, children remain innocent and affected mostly from this.

throughout history, anger, divorce, impatience, sickness, staggering economies and wars, among numerous other negative specifics affecting societal demise was and is the negative energy through humanism and weather, shall be stated as emphasis.

God, views societies functionally through every individuals heart, mind and soul. **Our God**, views societies, as one living organism with interrelating parts, working together and creates **Our** stability, harmony and equilibrium: remains sociological functional view because **God**, gave this wonderful thinking, through sociologists.

on a other hand, persons whom remain looking upon or idolizing **Their** blackberry, electronic device, television, computer, as well as, talking on phone rather than attending needs of offspring, spouse or significant other remains one more societal aspect causing decay within your moral fiber. following adage was learned when writer was in early twenties from a personal friend alfred urpsis, who works with traumatic brain injuries. stated august 11ᵗʰ 1992, 'there is no better interaction than human interaction.' humans receive the conscious illusion of acting, reacting and focusing upon something different of what remains intended: **Our** inconsistent will rather than **God** s consistent and blessed direction.

from **God**, shall conclude chapter, modifying alfred's, fleshly, optimistic phrase, 'There **remains better interaction than humans: My good spiritual goodness through You, thus, knowing what You should achieve and where You shall go: therefore, your every directed optimistic thought and behavior within your soul yields Our every goodness throughout the present and into My certain eternity.'**

ICS AND ISMS

many humans are labeled alcoholic, drug or sex addict, kleptomaniac, pyromaniac and shopaholic, among numerous others: and then **You** may attend anger management courses, alcoholics, codependents or gamblers anonymous, however, labels placed on **Us** are specifically that, fleshly made. where are these negative thoughts from?

time for a story: once upon a time, your writer attended alcoholics anonymous for two decades, in fact, conscious behaviors led your writer becoming labeled drug addict, alcoholic and other ics and isms. well, fellowship remains formidable and superb support system for most: spoken earlier, fleshly, there remains zero better interaction than human interactions. for millions globally, alcoholics anonymous works well, for those it does work, hats off for who remain attending and praying to **God** : **You** understand, working steps with a sponsor and receiving fellowship. 'it works if **You** work it' they say: this is correct, as with anything **You** have to try. while labeled an alcoholic, followed voice in mind and proceeded to liquor store: purchasing liquor remained fleshly aware of all occurrences transpiring thereafter, would become drunk, inappropriate, deceive others and receive negative thoughts. **'define** insanity:' thinking and/or acting unhealthy, anticipating different outcomes upon all specific occurrences.

told by professionals who learned in **Their** specific field of chemical dependency, '**You** are an alcoholic and a drug addict.' repeatedly fed this incessant negativity, psychosomatically started believing. likewise, when told repeatedly as one child **You** are not doing it correctly or can't do that or this, **You** subconsciously believe. addictions or other afflictions remain behavioral and conscious choices, are they? fleshly, yes and aware of consequences assists your healthy behaviors, however, bad entity, remains why **You** receive these negative thought processes in the first place.

God, shall relieve this if **You** ask and do what he says, thus, change people, places and things giving off negative energy, keeping **You** interlocked through stagnation. if a doctor hands **You** a psychological label, **You** repeat behavior or delve deeper within susceptible psyche for reasons **You** desire escaping from life in first place. fleshly, reason many desire mood altering chemicals: they observe others taking life's edge off through alcohol and mind or mood altering chemicals, thus, view parents palpably, as unwell. hence generational. some simple solutions or ideas from one who has received addictions and masked generational pain within; these shall be discussed further as well. **God's** goodness, released feelings of temptation from satan and relieves all, when **You** follow his perfect suggestions rather than commandments overflowing with double negatives. humanism is becoming better for countless: please, implement **Yourself** into **God's** gentle plan.

humans, fleshly desire behaving certain ways, thus, undeniably wonderful or less: ultimately, **You** decide behaviors and majority understand this, however, while in public, often view another person acting or reacting inappropriately with others. other person may be involved, for it takes two to tango. spiritual infection? yes. seeing adult with a child, scolding, spanking and acting inappropriate with him or Her in public, writer contemplates as You, what occurs behind walls of **Their** home.

unable modifying generationally learned inequities? **God** shall through You.

child may have stolen a candy bar, however, when parents demean, emotionally or physically are inappropriate through specific instance, writer thinks for an instant, why was young child stealing within first place? parents behaviors from distorted thinking? absolutely yes.

fleshly, assuredly remains generational. child more than likely receives minimal optimistic communication in home, because parents are overwhelmed themselves, hence, negative attention remains better than zero attention through a child's eyes.

fleshly loved, favored and assisted well or controlled negatively remains **Our** illusion of choice within Us. your writer desires the former for others.

spiritually apparent through writer, continuously shall wear rose colored eyewear: **You** and writer remain aware what is occurring through countless families globally. many exclaim, 'this is what happened to Me as a child.' 'this is the way I am!'

readers and friends, please, allow further insight within the human psyche.

humans, thus, parents receive thoughts to behave certain ways in given moments: **God**, has given all offspring higher cognitive function for many specific reasons. how often do **You** see a dog, cat, mouse, ladybug be unkind with **Their** offspring? **You** may think, 'they're silently directed well.' **You** are precisely correct and this is why they typically are loving humans, as well as, other living things around Them: unable speaking negatively, animals receive and show love positively, from **God**. allow, delving deeper: although animals have spiritual and control issues, they remain working with others exactly as animals shall. **God** had spoken this chapter over many weeks, 2010 and life, 'I, **direct all living things well upon earth.**' here is another parable. enveloping calmness, functionality and peace from **God**, however, fleshly, learned during rearing process from parents and humans, anger, control and negativity instilled through

Their souls, thus, minds from originator: remember who has the supreme power, **God**.

reason large dog across street barks ceaselessly when stressed humans travel by, remains because throughout life, mammals sense humans emotionally tense souls: his master, may have taught dog behaving in aggressive manner. attack or kill? why would anyone teach a wonderful creatures of **God**, with attacking anything? protection from bad people? hmmm. there would refrain being any bad people, if **We** learned rescinding hate while looking within pleasant options: allow calling this kindness, love and patience. **God**, has this view of life for all his offspring. while many, consciously remain behaving negatively, spiteful, bitter and angry: others receive compassion, generosity, love, patience, thus, living calmly rational.

what does writer bring to your table that has refrained being brought, thus, far? please listen.

what occurs perfect through life, remains **God**, working optimistically through Us. often listened to negativity through mind and did as spoken, thinking it was **God**. examples: when riding bicycle as young boy, voice would say ramp off enormous jumps: always doing what voice spoke, because the voice or thought process said, 'you'll be safe, i'll help.' sometimes, taking risks worked well, however, many times would crash and burn: admittance in emergency room, knew writer's social security number by memory. when driving, voice said, '**You** should drive fast, there are no police:' same voice, 'Pray **for specific humans seen, there is a vehicle in right blind spot, vehicles are entering highway in three miles, merge left; accelerate or decelerate, so You shall make the next stoplight and a specific song is on station in two minutes.**'

soul, thus, mind vacillated continuously from good thoughts to bad, as Yourself. also, sometimes, received thousands of words of information through one second, regarding what was occurring through other parts of **city, state, as well as, country and world:** often, depending on how connected received information slowly. **God**, would refrain from ever belittling or demeaning You. information shall be shared on these pages for **You** understanding life, through all.

back within your story.

turn off or mute electronic devices which may distract You. now gather around what brings your mind solace: favorite blanket, cup of hot tea, pictures of family members or close your eyes for moment thinking of your happy place, **We** all have one. albeit, a hot shower, conversation with a positive friend, park, lake, beach, rock climbing or church, the place where least negative agendas flow. are **You** there?

wonderful. please turn page.

WRITER'S LINEAGE

God spoke to leave this chapter unedited and was written few weeks post rebirth and expressed. here remains the lineage from who remains writing these words.

coming from a wonderful family, within the south-west whom cares about one another more than others writer has viewed thus far. We, have family reunions annually, viewing **God**, others and lineage high as possibly You: arriving to America, from germany and lauwe, russia near the river volga, beginning new lives, year 1887.

unedited quotes from Father, gary goeringer on 08.17.09

'once catherine the great was killed, the regime in lauwe, russia began using socialism and totalitarianism with citizens there. hence, **We** moved to America and sailed into new york harbor 1887. while the journey was long and arduous, gross papa, gotlieb goeringer and his brother-in-law dr. schneider, as well as, **Their** families, now were looking upon statue of liberty: hopes and **Their** aspirations became real within an instant.

struggling to provide food, clothing and shelter for **Their** families, they proceeded onward within ohio: over time, gross papa and dr. schneider heard of land for sale in mid west. although land was expensive, they would make it work, absolutely. settling in western oklahoma, near a township named besse, they began futuristic endeavors, with **Their** wives raising offspring.'

ultimately gross papa and momma, received 16 offspring. **Father** said, 'In those days, farmers had many children, few were expected to die from accident, disease or infection and the more hands and minds the better.' here remains another parable. 'People **mourned the loss of Their loved ones briefly and moved forward to what was relevant for life, the presently wonderful future.'**

following many years as farmer and investor in land, gross papa did well, he told his children, '**You** have two choices to make when wanting to live upon your own. 'I, will give **You** a college education or two: one farm to have as your own.' most of **Their** children became farmers, however, one ventured with more lucrative and mind intensive work. most of gross papa's children stayed within oklahoma, waldemeyer, ventured westward to california and began making a toy company. specifics are unclear, he was influential with conception of the toy maker mattel.'

You may now be asking **Yourself** why has another writer whom has had a splendid life remain sharing more information wasting **My** time and money, as well? first, herein lies a wonderful escape, thus, getting out of self. secondly, **God** intended this book for **You** before your conception. he said this. your frame of mind, thus, how **You** think, desire, love and work yields absolutely who **You** thrive becoming. optimistic or pessimistic, fleshly, conscious and subconscious thinking determine your remaining happy, calm and contented or angry, overwhelmed and depressed.

fourthly, rose colored eyewear are removed; your writer, as **You** are aware, has had intense generational inequities. fleshly, your socioeconomic status in life, environment and where **You** were reared, have much bearing with the present and shall have upon future; all humans have pain, anger and discontentedness within: alleviating pain and mania, remains relative with future happiness or otherwise. emotionally good, offspring may remain displaced from You, as numerous currently. **God** intended for Mothers and **Fathers** residing as one for life, he, brought **You** together in first place: ill feelings between **You** shall be worked out with **God**, who remains best counselor, psychologist and clergy. letting control go, with **God's** free intervention remains best for everyone involved through his great earth.

gross papa prayed for each of his offspring to come within his office receiving answer to question of **Them** receiving college degree or farm to have as **Their** own : **God** told writer this occurred and arrived as prayed.

'When **You let go of your will and live in the spirit, with Me, efficient progress and specific correlations occur silently well.'**

upon much of your life, egocentrically, what was best for **Yourself** was best, when children have been given to a Mother and **Father** for raising and nourishing; life for **Yourself** abruptly becomes secondary for your offspring and loss of ego remains a wonderful commencement: many youths are becoming self actualized currently, however, most individuals remain having negative behaviors prevalent, as unwell. long ago, self actualization became reached for only a few: Jesus christ, buddha and mohammed; then gandhi, Mother teresa: many others were only few humans obtaining loss of self and resisting temptation, doing what was best for societies. praising **God**, loving earth and praying for others: humans receive unending love, blessing and eternal life. optimism through **You** and everyone remains from **God.**

following briefly, are seven siblings of writer's **Father** in order of **Their** good birth:

1.   theodore ronald goeringer.

eldest, army 45th infantry, then moved to arizona after military upon age of 23. owner of heat and air, commercially 20 years, has skin cancer, began trucking company from conception, worked **Their** until heart attack when

70. retired and lives in buckeye, arizona with wife mary and they have one Daughter, rhonda.

2. janis melvina goeringer/ zerby.

raised two boys, brent and larry until they graduated from high school then went back to college receiving a masters: worked for state for 35 years. met paul zerby in butler, oklahoma when She was sophomore, he drove school bus and was three years Her senior. paul became deceased, She married lyman barber in oklahoma.

3. robin hood ramsey/goeringer graduated from high school at age 15, began college when 16. lives in bartlesville, oklahoma, She has two son's, charles dean 'thumper' who works with the government, rodney, who is a lawyer and one Daughter who remains imperative with the lutheran outreach, affecting millions downtrodden globally.

4. rosalie van duyne/goeringer

as stated, 'perfect childhood,' and middle child. married vernon whom became prestigious f-16 fighter pilot in vietnam and they had four offspring of **Their** own.

verna-rn. nurse and wonderfully loving and caring for others unconditionally.

brenda-l.p.n. great nurse and love, therefore, caring for others extremely well.

tracy- first grade school teacher. importantly loving and teaching youths today.

derrek- enrolled in military, specifically air force, then attained highest rank as enlisted soldier of chief master sergeant. derrek met future wife rosie on base in texas and they have one Son christopher. all **Their** family are blessed from **God.**

5. john carlton goeringer; well ventured forward for progress. **God** called upon him 1980 to become a wonderful preacher, after his Son theodore goeringer 'opie,' ironically passed in car accident while 17 years of age. absolutely this occurrence traumatized his **Father** and Mother, for he and your writer remained the only males continuing goeringer name through lineage, until, evon the great arrived 1.11.00!

6. karen cathleen cottrell/goeringer (deceased)

divorced and met tom cottrell in berlin, he was enlisted with army. they have one Daughter, lara leigh born in enid, oklahoma then they transferred to hawaii.

'la la', in Her 40's, has a horse farm in south east usa, blessed and doing very well with two favored offspring from **God**.

7. cheryl ann vanduyne/ goeringer

met Her future husband roger van duyne, within weatherford, oklahoma. She, graduated high school and enrolled in school of interior design: **God** knew what was in store. She conceptualized cheryl van duyne interior design (a.s.i.d.) in dallas, texas. has one Son scott, who is married to colleen cole 'c.c.' and they received three very blessed teenage offspring: zac, rachael, as well as, samuel.

8. gary eugene goeringer

born may 16, 1945, writer's Father, gary goeringer, youngest of eight offspring, was cared for most and remains great thinker. parents, theodore and carol loved all **Their** children, cheryl was his up line sibling wise, and expressed desiring to raise him becoming great man and expressed desire clothing him, thus, became a salesman with brooks brothers and curtleys, two progressive men's clothing stores in enid, oklahoma. related: writer worked with joseph abboud, best men's designer on earth two years in a row, when in dallas, texas. 1994-1996. Father, retired when 49, from selling business that he and his wife purchased from his brother in 1980. retired and traveling globally, enjoys taking care of church grounds: Mother, began working within oklahoma capital when She was 48 and presently retired as well. they have a Daughter who was revealed previously: writer's sister cara appraises residences and runs marathons nationally.

God, spoke to slate this information regarding family, now, shall return to your book.

God, is only good and so are You.

PSYCHOSOMATIC VERBAL INSTILLATIONS TWO

unedited.

here lies an appropriate place for another story related with sean, he ascertained because he sneezed while near conifer or christmas trees, he was allergic to Them. in all actuality, he remained unable associating past emotions through christmas. family getting together and positive or negative feelings cathartic with wonderful time of the year for all family: he received feelings from family, who had physical and verbal contact with himself when he was young, thus, persona enmeshment. sean, 50, believes he is allergic to conifers, belief remains psychosomatic and his spouse kimberli, writer, psychosomatically calls early, thus, on time, agrees fully.

side note:

when **You** take your child within a clinic or hospital for shots and/or vaccinations and nurse says, 'grab My finger john this is going to hurt.'

your child now thinks procedure shall hurt, thus, more painful than previously anticipated. when your writer and wife molly, had taken **Our** Son evon, into doctor's office for mmr or mumps measles and rubella shot, preceding nurse coming in room and proceeding with painful shot: evon, was told from **God**, through writer, 'this shall tickle.' immediately following painful procedure, nurse asked how he felt: evon, stated 'kind of tickled.' psychosomatic affirmations from parents, have profound merit.

back to story. early's **Father** told Her when, young She could become president if She chose path and graduated summa cum laude from oklahoma city university. She, and husband sean, became great friends during rebirthing process, from **God**.

what **You** are taught, thus, fleshly believe remains imperative for your future lives.

birth occurs; **We** have specific good and bad verbal instillations shaping **Our** personas. **We** are born in wonderful world, attributing physiological genetic predispositions, however, once born, nurturing with **Our** environment occurs. when two humans conceive together, offspring are typically perfect; **God**, produces emotionally and intellectually wonderful offspring for Mothers and Fathers. **You** absolutely choose behaviors rearing offspring, however, generational behavioral predispositions or feeling frustrated, discontented, impatient or confident, completed, contented with patience, lies through responsibility of the nurturer, behaviorally through the flesh. offspring choose developing appropriate relationships or otherwise, as they reach puberty and whom they choose or feel most accepted with remains relevant with how they may or shall feel internally regarding **Them** self. emotional, mental and intellectual confidence remains instilled through dispositions, early, thus, who **You** become as young or mature adults remains predicated upon these exact premises.

sometimes, **We** remain insecure, withdrawn or outwardly secure, yielding facades, typically filled with unrealistic overconfidence. throughout life, **We** feel insecure upon youth, think **Our** friends or peers are doing better than Us, **Their** achievements are better than Ours and **Their** families are better than Ours. one much used adage, 'grass is greener' remains true and numerous adages passed verbally; however, if **You** have taken shoes off, metaphorically speaking, placing your feet within theirs or theirs in Yours, contentedness would become reached soon through your mind. **You** awareness heightens to why spiritually and fleshly, **You** are feeling negatively about **Yourself** and others at times, and how **You** as one child of **God**, may rebuke spiritual flaws, instilled through your wonderful mind during childhood and life. shall give **You** a hint, this begins with praising **God**, ask to bless others and love who are received within your consciousness.

'I, am God and all goodness through You and everyone encompassing earth: remain patient, I have a perfect plan through You and Yours.'

Chapter

TAKE MY LIFE

these edited writings occurred august of 2009.

taught in traumatic brain injury rehabilitation. 'the way **You** feel determines ways **You** act, and ways **You** behave, determines how others react to **You** or otherwise.' following car accident many omitted your writer. heightening inappropriateness through diminished view of self, futuristic endeavors appeared bleak, thus, nil. many years thereafter, thoughts within the mind were, 'please **God**, take My life,' **God** said, 'I, **shall refrain and desire You living within the blessed and chosen future desiring for Us to assist countless others from My direction through My powerful words in You.'**

one sunday, during summer of 1989, life was overwhelming, as every day was. Mother and **Father** attended church and writer, motionless was in depressive sleep. end was near. voice in mind had spoken 'rise out of bed, go to bedroom door.' double vision was apparent: voice had continued. reaching Father's 44 magnum as spoken, went into bar and guzzled an

GOD'S OFFSPRING

inordinate amount of crown royal. leaving suicide note of where they could find body departed and staggered down the club hill.

talking with who thought was **God**, voice said, 'calmly and methodically fire three rounds off at signs here.' unsure why this occurred, then, however, now am aware, satan was controlling thinking and end was near: finally, peace would come, satan was overjoyed. zero more sleepless nights, thus, knowing shannon's life was lost and shannon's family were without **Their** Daughter because of an impulsive action, driving while drunk and causing pain for many others. about to pull trigger and **Father** silently dived and wrestled gun away, then carried sobbing writer to car and home to the bed. **God**, worked effectively, through writer's Father's mind and he ceased another dire consequence from occurring. **God** said, 'Good **occurrences were all Me, through You and your Father perfectly for the wonderful future of professing My truthful will of peace upon earth.**'

before proceeding, allow receiving more information with evening of accident. **God**, within the hospital, revealed a memory of night of the accident: expressing to Mother while within semi-unconscious state few weeks post accident. 'one white ford, a white ford, forced Me off road!' persons with brain injuries and professionals working with **Them** are well aware during trauma **Our** brains or writer believes referring as **God**, erases most memories forever for 95% of patients. with writer, recollecting up until point of impact and slamming square into back of parked bus while traveling 80 miles per hour, remains photographic, thus, many specifics through prior year. while recuperating in icu, someone whom kept **Their** identity disclosed, called every day asking of writer's progress. upon returning home received a phone call from someone, who again, remained anonymous: was male and only known fact. he asked, 'how are You?' reply was, 'o.k.' without pause, preceded asking, 'when coming to court for negligent homicide, come to one meeting with Me.' confused and slurring words from paralization replied, 'what kind of meeting?' he then said, 'it is an occult meeting.' trembling, hung up phone immediately. why would writer go to an occult meeting? was saved and baptized as christian, whom loves others and spoke with **God**, sometimes, continuously throughout life.

117

God, said upon final rebirthing process, 'I shall take You back through infancy, revealing suppressed memories, over time, shall reveal your life memories through millisecond clips and You shall understand everything, as well as, discern the bible and other documents for others.'

God did.

God spoke twice on 10.11.09, 'Before your age two We have spoken intimately, ultimately initiated from Me, throughout your spiritual life.'

'Readers shall become enlightened from Me, through all your words of truth. I, love You and everyone living upon My wonderful earth.'

Chapter

COPULATION AND NATURE-NURTURE DEBATE

those, using copulation or sex without knowing other person, remain unhealthy. sex, as life, remains latent control issues, thus, receiving immediate gratification, which remains egocentric behavior, however, writer has done this countless times. generational insecurities are apparent through, how **We** think, thus, act or behave. **God**, is watching over all who believe or otherwise. **'You were placed on earth for a reason, season and life.'** everyone reading book, as well as, those whom refrained so far, have a wonderful purpose in life. **God's**, intended purpose for all of **Us** remains living life, thus, helping numerous others who remain less fortunate. having prominence with everything, thus, leafs falling from trees during fall to volcanoes erupting within his wonderful ocean creating islands and land masses. **God** is great.

God, intends persons loving each other staying together when offspring are given. they may refrain divorcing and meeting another person, especially someone who has offspring him/herself with another person. do **You** see where writer is going? divorce is displeasurable when offspring are involved, thus, inevitably distraught. what was learned from writers parents, whom remain happily married 50 years, togetherness for children is conducively appropriate, rescinding power or control; thinking what remains best for innocent child, especially, when a **Father** has a son. now **We** shall delve deeper. once a son, becomes knowing his **Father** and Mother as one, this is how he shall see **Them** for life. now even deeper **We** go. numerous **Fathers** currently remain home with offspring and females are intelligent as males. **We** remain aware, however, emotionally, they have propensities with following the driven chosen model.

chromosomally, **We** remain xx or xy, genetically defined during birthing process. herein lies your nature, nurture debate. shall **We** delve deeper? yes, **We** shall. **God**, desires zero debates, it is both. **We** become who **We** are, physically through chromosomes, develop male or female genitalia and other physiological specifics: **Our** bodily functions and thought processes occur from **Our** souls first, then heart, then mind.

once born into world with the umbilical cord severed, baby emerges, completely without dependency on Mother. nature, aspect of life has halted abruptly and now nurturing proceeds. if child's parents environment, remain calm and methodical through **Their** thought processes and physical movements, offspring shall, as well. when your children learn indecisiveness, emotional, mental, physical, as well as, chemical abuse, they shall follow accordingly: there remain exceptions from **God**. **You** see, in residences where poverty remains prevalent, offspring, typically view nurturers behaviors and mirror, thus, act accordingly as they mature, You're aware.

generationally, becoming complacent, lazy or feeling zero hope remains for **Them**, because stated previously, offspring, as well as, Ourselves develop through past or present environments and there are many ways out of the closed or fruitless ones. one desirable and available way remains moving away from inevitable stagnation and complacency through education, thus, humans now have higher propensities becoming anything desired with intrinsic and palpable view of **God**, through Them. **We** see what's instilled. once individuals come away from impending hopelessness, individuals realize what is good for a real living, rather than something projected from an unrealistic depiction through a television, movie screen, peers or family. although modifying your individual persona remains uncomfortable, emotional, mental and physical confidence originates spiritually from **God**, through **Our** souls and every facet of living heightens.

We hear and view, repetitiously, numerous stories where people from disdaining backgrounds become something wonderful for themselves and those around Them. **God**, assists those who desire something better, thus, finding your solace, remains another blessing from **God** : reasoning **You** feel and then think optimistically well.

POSITIVE AFFIRMATIONS

regarding offspring, all remain unaware how life shall occur following **Their** birth. denouncing son's psychological predispositions, evon's birth was from **Our God**, as every goodness seen and unseen. son's **Fathers** life was wonderfully modified on palpable juncture, from **God**, he and parents lives, shall traverse peaceful courses. Son believes, as all children, he shall do anything when negativity remains gone. denouncing and rescinding generational pessimism, life for son, overflowed with positive affirmations through both his parents thought processes, thus, behaviors. birth through six, adoration, calmness, love, thus, patience were instilled fleshly: loving others unconditionally, remains how he was reared: evon, is a magnificent Son through body, mind and soul. thank **You God**, your calmness, goodness and optimism, shall continue to flow well through human's good thoughts and behaviors for others.

behaviorally and intellectually, evon's persona remains both his parents. offspring, especially males, often desire becoming more compassionate and gentle than **Their** Father wants: many young men desire emulating Mothers persona, rather than **Their** insensitive **Fathers** and absolutely accord beautifully with Mother: sometimes gentleness regards Father. where might calm and gentle come from? parental role model, who appropriately displays and gives functional consistence, thus, calmness: please, allow child adhering with whom **God**, works well through.

God speaks well, **'I know what remains healthy through generational and a societal correction. allow Me working gently through these offspring functionally for Our earth's future generations, from My calmed happiness and harmony through as well as within Them.'**

throughout personal lives, preparedness remains significantly what contributes to having a wonderful day or otherwise. expressed often in book, past remains best predictor of your future with humanism behaviorally and psychologically through thought processes: ultimately from a bad or one good Spirit remains true, as well. praising **God**, spending time with family remains **God's** intention, thus, thinking biblically, adhering lives divinely and wonderfully enlightened remains his desire. herein lies a few of palpable suggestions for your understanding life as **We** know.

first, praising **God** throughout your day: this takes one millisecond in your mind. second, praising **God**, and loving family remains crux of life in **Our** earthly vessel. third, perform your daily tasks from work or school and once day has completed return home ready to presume tasks or decide, either, frantically performing duties as more work or do tasks with prayer, calming your mind by contemplating navel: contemplating navel, simply implies, centering focus or concentrating on middle. **You** may be aware, buddhism, teaches contemplation of navel and remains center of body where nutrients are transported from Mother to embryo during pregnancy. **We** spiritually behave in certain ways, thus, an intrinsic freedom given from **God**, who gives **Our** good living from praying for calmness or **You** may continue apparently overwhelmed.

God, flows through all humans, all **We** need remains humbly praising and praying: **God's** presence remains unexplainable for countless, however, remains factual as well. also, performing any physical task, rather than thinking or regarding your favorite soap opera or irrelevant component of life, concentrate on what is functional and appropriate, thus, **God**, prayer, family and calm progress as everyone's priority.

'What **remains occurring presently within your lives remains spiritual:** chaos, confusion, distortion **of your perceptions and** annoyance **of others in your presence are from** satan. **when your faith abides within your maker,** negative **feelings recede. I allow good thoughts and behaviors through and within those around You, as well as, your your offspring: all of life remains connected through/within My perfected direction.'**

those, whom walk or drive around as sheep looking sporadically here and there, dependent on someone or something to show direction, may remain overwhelmed. overwhelmedness remains displayed through your aura. meaning, many around remain aware, observing your verbal and nonverbal communication, how **You** feel: offspring are aware as infants, why they cry and pets remain palpably aware, also. they feel, see and hear your feelings from other room, aware, they shall behave as instructed and shall give zero backtalk for dad has come home and had a bad day.

why did dad have a bad day? why do things occur wonderfully? life is spiritual.

in **Our** family it was this, **Father** came home, **We** observed his verbal and nonverbal signs and once becoming aware of how he felt, **Our** evening followed accordingly. at times parents brash out, are on **Their** last nerve, as if walls are closing around, floor is rising and ceiling is falling slowly from above. where are these negative behaviors, feelings and thoughts coming from? **You** are becoming adequately and well aware.

apologizing for realistic negativity, however, numerous offspring and individuals throughout **God's** earth, past, present and future shall feel exactly this sometimes. persona enmeshment has occurred through everyone for thousands of years, from minute shacks of uganda to penthouses in new york city, paris, miami and milan.

following chapters assist with resolutions, how others feelings affect your persona consciously and subconsciously and then your wonderful days progress into night. consciously and subconsciously, amongst many individuals these feelings remain continuously present, how **You** regard your temple or body, thus, what **You** place inside for nourishment, how **You** respect **Yourself** and why **You** think as **You** may; instilments through souls, dictate significantly everything from **God** or otherwise.

God, remains consistent calmness, patience and peacefulness through all of your heart, mind and soul for the future: **God's** perfected direction.

Chapter

FLESHLY ACCOUNTABILITY

remaining accountable and aware, your actions are key for progress, thus, aware how your thinking and behaviors affect those around remains one great first step. egocentrically, past and present, humans remain unaware how significantly **Their** thinking and behaviors enmesh through those around Them, thus, societally how **You** feel remains directly portrayed upon all those around, almost, as if **You** are on stage and the spotlight has You. **You** see, **God**, family and others, desire zero pain from consuming You: codependents or enablers, what specific fleshly labels **You** shall desire calling these individuals are irrelevant, they are whom assists life working, thus, glue holding a broken vase together. believing, **You** are unable experiencing present or the future absent vices, temporarily, masking spiritual then fleshly pain within, remains easily remedied from **God's** calmness and his peace through You, then your pain becomes less. example: males, receive parables, when they arrive.

robert, has a defined regimen or order for life, proceeding throughout each day. keeping life orderly he misplaces items seldom. his **Father** taught him, every item or tool has specific place, if returned, all in household remain aware finding Them. robert, meets molly and She remains lovely, **God**, placed one another together for a reason, season and lifetime: immediately enmeshed, everything feels wonderful.

falling in love they have one perfectly blessed child and life remains magnificent, however, robert, was masking his generational pain with alcohol and marijuana, numbing his spiritually, thus, temporally overwhelmed, sporadic and racing mind. a few years pass and evon **Our** wonderful Son remains happily reared by his **Father** who has a good heart, mind and soul and prays for family, neighbors and society: molly provides monetarily listing, selling and brokering real estate and robert stays at home with **Their** Son evon, teaching, attending residence, keeping perfect order and does all household chores, working as the house husband and mr. mom.

few months pass, evon, learned to read while few months of age: reading to son, self placed middle finger under words when pronouncing **Them** from **God's** instruction. writer taught **Our** Son the alphabet, reading, abstract thinking, crawling, walking, numbers, colors, toilet training, shapes, nature and planets like proud Mother. evon was taught to be friendly with neighbors and love all whom crossed his path. he also learned how important the elderly are and how they have experienced life, thus, teaching many of **Our** youth to slow down and appropriate thoughts. **God**, speaks through writer's soul sometimes continually regarding slowing down, thus, calm for Son and book for numerous through present and future generations. spiritually from **God**, through calming his parents physical movements, evon has observed, thus, remains calm, focused and well acclimated for his splendid future.

upon this specific juncture, **God**, desires quoted for **You** and ending this chapter, 'From **Me, there shall be born numerous following wonderful generations. what shall be contemplated remains living** angry, sad and overwhelmed or calm, happy, contented and optimistic with heightened faith with your creator.'

'Also, who do You think created this universe? Who might You think created hydrogen, helium, lithium, gravity, scientists, astronomers and your sunrise? Please enjoy Yourself. Who created 400 billion plus galaxies in a millisecond? Was Me who remains your living God, loving all things existing everywhere. Do You understand, I, remain synchronizing matter and satan is antimatter: creating and correlating creatures perfectly, schools of fish or birds flying in unison remains Me through Them performing for Your videos, thus, goodness prevails over bad, from galaxies to Our feelings of loving one another to peace within Our heart. I remain Your all knowing and loving, thus, one perfected God.'

Unaware then, writer shall now slate where the vacillation derives. '4.19.1995, bombing of the okc murrah federal building occurred: My writer was living in Dallas, I told him to turn on the television. he asked Me who did this? I replied, male. He had asked if he was apprehended? I replied, he was driving west on i-40 and he asked what to do? I spoke for him to pray the license plate falls off his vehicle and I correlate the eyes of a policeman to pull him over. This occurred and justice was served. Second, was 9.11, 2001: He became aware the first plane's impact on the World Trade Center and asked what to do? I spoke for him to go inside, watch the news and gave him continuous direction over milliseconds, with specific prayers for others. He asked if there would be more? I had replied yes, pray that I work through humans in the second tower to proceed to the ground immediately, he and I acted as spoken: Another plane impacted the second tower. he asked were there more? satan replied yes, a third plane will be hijacked for the pentagon. He asked what to pray? I replied, pray for there to be minimal casualties and calmness through Their families within My time. satan spoke, there was a fourth plane being hijacked, intended for white house. He asked what to pray? I replied, pray for Me to work through a few to storm the cockpit and cease future chaos: Specific awareness occurred for the subway bombings in london as well. following the three occurrences, I spoke for him to pray, significant future terrorism shall remain thwarted within the United States, Western Europe, Asia, Africa and over time, earth from God.'

'My writer asks, receives perfect direction as well as connectivity. why does he receive perfect direction and connectivity from Me? My solutions are perfected direction through any human whom I choose.'

'Finally, every good individual paradigm shift of consciousness through masses have occurred throughout history and time is upon Us for the most significant one, thus far. Is Jesus returning soon? No, however, I have a wonderful plan and this book was written for a reason: To assist numerous in uncertain times, allow continual Godly direction through Them and learn specific prayers for You and others healing inequities within humanism with and from your creator.'

ALLEVIATING NEGATIVE FEELINGS, VIA, PRAYER

your current chapter remains relative for offspring, believing while young, optimistic information or otherwise instilled, via, senses from society and how **We** enmesh with others, verbally and silently through emotions and thoughts throughout humanism. numerous factors contribute with your persona: again, genetic predispositions are physiological, however, expressed vocally, from others, becomes psychosomatic, thus, emotions, are extremely relative regarding non physiological predispositions. psychosomatically, especially while youthful, **You** consciously and subconsciously believe what **You** believe and feel as **You** feel, through humanism. **You** know this.

herein lies one specific example. your writer's son, expressed from a doctor he had acid reflux: he ingested medications for controlling this emotional ailment. once his **Father** became aware, simply expressed verbally to son, '**You** shall no longer have acid reflux.' saying, 'son, believe and this feeling shall vanish,' then prayed silently to **God** for one millisecond taking specific emotional ailment away and his ailment vanished immediately.

ailment was psychosomatically enmeshed from his Mother's emotions: his Mother, as numerous females have this emotional ailment and remains present for females and offspring reared with **Their** Mothers. acid reflux, ibs, allergies and numerous other additional ailments are predicated fleshly from psychosomatic emotions, silently enmeshed through **Their** personas. similarly, females having zero genetic relatedness who reside together receive a comparable menstruation time, one of **Our** other palpable emotional enmeshments. enmeshments, are why spouses receive an ability finishing each others sentences. emotional bonds are placed through all from **God**, allowing enmeshed personas, feelings and souls through another. physically present with another human for a short duration, **We** enmesh shallowly and a long time yields **Our** deep enmeshment: albeit stages originating through conception, infancy, youth and adulthood, thus, who **You** spend time remains absolutely significant, vital and perfectly conducive.

all humans enmesh souls, thus, behaviors, feelings, as well as, thinking over time. enmeshment remains specific, fleshly, reasoning sons, typically, have a wonderful relationship with **Their** Mother and Daughters with **Their** Father. in numerous past generations, in fact, since beginning of time, females nurtured offspring and males fulfilled acquiring food, building shelters, homesteads, protecting family, working and supplying monetary sufficiency. inside womb and nurturing process, Mothers were whom enmeshed with children lasting a lifetime. presently, within societies, females have come far professionally: in many cases females remain primary and monetary provider in households across **God's** industrial and technological world.

many males lost control and **Their** dependency heightens through present societies; females increased responsibility professionally has heightened stress among Them, numerous of females egos contribute with many unions becoming less than stable. abruptly, life's pendulum swings and females desire a professional living exuding intellect and wonderful power in present world, offspring and husbands often are suffering and entire family needs a relationship from **God**, through **Their** calmness.

perceptions of who **You** are, thus, whom **You** become is predicated fleshly from self worth and image, generationally then societally instilled, thus, conscious and subconscious thinking remains relevant with your positive and negative behaviors. maturing into adulthood, shaping, tweaking and modifying your persona occurred and overwhelming majority of coaches, parents, teachers, professors have had and shall have offspring's best interest in mind, however, numerous others because of generational, environmental and spiritual constructs, received negative instilments through rearing, thus, perpetuating through **Our** offspring and others for digression.

why? please turn page for answer.

meaning, satan has temporary control, thus, causes many becoming downtrodden, weak, prayer less, negative and overwhelmed through feelings of certain despair.

'All humans remain weak at times. Allowing My continual assistance through You, life becomes continuous fluidity and joy.'

God, told writer this parable the first quarter of 2010: one prayer of numerous, each morning, writer, asks **God** to denounce and refute satan imposing perverse negativity in mind, disposing unproductivity, thus, dysfunction and inappropriateness from occurring. when daily devotion and faith fortifies with **God's** calm, love and tranquility, he, shines through your soul, thus, heart and mind. **God**, is who remains aware of everything prior to **Our** conception, present and into **Our** wonderful future: through comfort, contentedness and passion, **God**, instills abundance for wonderful minds.

You and Yours, receive abilities constructing love and compassions for another or otherwise: praying **You** shall seek the former instance, regarding love, ultimately for **You** and your wonderful offspring's future, upon **God's** wonderful earth for everyone.

closing your chapter, please receive the meaning of life and how to achieve this wellness. the truth lies within You. when living in/with the Spirit throughout awakened moments, questions **You** ask **God** within your soul remain answered correctly. therefore, distorted thinking and incorrect information transgressed through life are gone. over time, misinformation lessens societally, function replaces chaos, as well as, **You** receive, perfect peace within your mind and body. negative thought processes, feelings of anxiety, anger, impatience, discontentedness, chemical dependency and fear are gone forever. now **You** have learned the meaning of life for every human on earth. **God** is only good and remains assisting **You** with favor and goodness.

SONS LOSING FATHERS CONSISTENT PRESENCE

humans often think, they shall receive comfort in mind from ingesting chemicals. individuals, therefore, societal masses, continuously have procured becoming less dependent upon **Their God** given faculties, thus, choosing filling an incessant need escaping life internally from external methods, this proves disastrous time after time. why many feel this way has a plethora of folds, please, read a few general ones. first, feeling inconsequential fleshly in your own skin are generationally instilled. second, feeling need to escape life temporarily remains an additional conundrum: fulfilling selfish wants, thus, wishing someone or thing shall rescue your feelings. **God's** presence, remains the most significant and absolute certainty in cosmos, thus, what transpires remains dependent upon You, as well as, two spiritual dynamics. one: following **God's** direction of love and peace through service for others. two: resist temptations bad entity places within soul for consequences. conjugated through feeling inadequate, depressed and anguished, at times, there plausibly remain numerous ways out, temporarily, through chemicals, immediate and gratifying material purchases, food or feel calmness forever from **God**, through You.

having innate responsibilities in **Yourself** becoming spiritually, generationally and societally acceptant of what has been placed before You, thus, embrace calmness, contentedness, goodness and love, therefore, adaptationally assist others, invoking blessings from **God**, through You. consequentially relative, through your healthy behaviors and love for others, **God**, joyously shall assist You, calming your loving offspring, encompassing generations into future. contemplate following question. are your thoughts and behavioral lifestyle becoming functional, assisting others in life or insatiable egocentric wants trumping others all around You? preceding answering, what are received within your perspective and perceptions are different from another.

pain is relative and males feel stalemated when losing **Their** Father and **We** continue behaving as **Father** had through many internalized behavioral dispositions, because this is what **We** know, subconsciously and consciously **You** emulate your parent. numerous successful males have come in writer's life, there remains a consistent factual characteristic remaining generationally. whether **You** come from calmness or chaos upon rearing process, one specific's clear, male offspring imitate Fathers. if the parents were pack rats, keeping everything, they probably shall, as unwell. keeping unneeded items for future is problematic for many households currently: unable parking cars in garage because it has become cluttered with abundance of stuff, what might this say to all viewing your life, your family and does it matter? was desiring refraining from preaching how **You** shall organize your residence. one- refrains being writer's place and two- writer is imperfect living fleshly. when **You** have order in personal life aspects of life become wonderful. also, cleaning out your garage, thus, mind, yields numerous wonderful returns. one- **You** may park inside alleviating elements, two- offspring view appropriate organizational ways of emulating, as they mature and delves into significant facets related with **Their** lives, thus, **Their** offspring and so on and so forth into earths 22nd, 23rd, 24th, 25th centuries and beyond, with **God**, working perfectly through **Their** souls as Their/your captain.

organizing disorder in residence becomes a family affair and having You, spouse or child direct family working together, because all souls are enmeshed brilliantly. **'My light enmeshes for diamond's brilliance.'** lost in catechism of brevity or brief questions and answers related to christianity, youth, desire learning brief games of focus or occurrences, fulfilling expectations for themselves rather than altruistically as **God** desires. why do youth desire this? individual personas and societies, originates spiritually through **Them** accentuated through families culminating societies.

God spoke chapter first quarter of 2010, **'all humans consciousness are modifiable from awareness and prayers within your book from Me.'**

SON'S BIRTH AND EARTH'S FUTURE SUSTAINMENT

continual communication from spirits remains why your writer felt hopeless with continued loss of son, then felt wonderful with **God's** assistance, released from satan's negative thoughts and free from psychosomatic labels placed within mind: spiritually, remained one perfect awakening. having the privilege, raising Son from birth was absolute and profoundly the best wish your writer could have. most wonderful honor was received from **God**, through **Our** son's Mother, molly. when rearing **Our** son, although physical movements were slow and methodical, feelings over time, self was a house **Father** and refrained contributing monetarily, was how life was going to transpire. living in small town in midwest and having **Father** and **Father** in law from previous generation who believed men work outside residence, supporting family monetarily, however, **God**, had a higher calling who is evon the great! nurturing him from birth until age six was what **God** said would occur.

having best occupation, **Father** rearing son, was virtually unheard of in this region, location, small town America: times were changing throughout societies, globally. males roles, increasingly heightened related to rearing children, thus, domestically fruit full, females providing monetarily, thus, **Their** roles were heightened, as well. **You** see, role reversals in marriages became prevalent and modifications of males domestic roles were misunderstood from numerous **Fathers** from past generations: because they were whom worked, sometimes 80+ hour weeks and egocentrically would refrain accepting life was progressing differently than **Their** generation, as theirs were progressively differently from **Their** Father's. society, was progressing further in humanism, gone are days of male dominance and modified with rearing offspring, in numerous cases, sharing roles through gender neutrality with spouse or significant other, shall become discussed more deeply through latter chapters.

back to story: when self severed umbilical cord from molly, life was transformed upon this specific juncture: all occurring past moments now made complete sense: an instant, life was for him rather than anything else. **God**, showed present love, bringing molly and writer together for one most fabulous reason, evon the great! evon and writer received the most wonderful relationship from this point forward.

'**When Robert's Son was born, he was continually receiving information regarding what to pray for and he received, as life, thousands of bits of information in short periods of time. I spoke for him to pray that Molly would receive zero pain: During the birthing process, I told him when to pray for Evon to be born. Immediately, he was born. Robert always thought these powers were because of him and are, within humanism. Following the third and final rebirth, had taught, I correlated his mind and prayers synonymously with Molly and Dr. Barki: I ultimately determined Evon to be born in the year 2000, on 1.11 at precisely 2:22 pm. It was so. I shall allow goodness within all.**'

when family, love another unconditionally as **Father** and son, husband and wife or Daughter and Mother, **God**, is completely aware, thus, blesses all of **Them** further. aware how fleshly insecure **We** all are instilled from rearing,

GOD'S OFFSPRING

God, observes how well **You** modify instilled consciousness into children, granting blessings of approval. second, evon's methodic and calm rearing, yielded, calmness rather than insecure sporadic and angry expressions his **Father** was instilled with through his rearing. evon, received minimal negativity, thus, received heightened positive instilments for his function, therefore, future offspring as well. all offspring of **God**, as evon, proceed from **Their** lives with rose colored eyewear placed gently upon **Their** faces.

soon thereafter, evon, was taught loving **God's** earth and all encompassed within, because life was preciously given and the vicious generational cycle has broken. writer taught son, take time and admire leafs, ladybugs, rollie pollies, as well as, butterflies prevalent wherever he travels and consciously blessed with loving life, people, animals, insects, thus, marvelous creatures of life, given freely from **God**. learning life remained calm and gentle through observances when he was young, wonderment and adornment occurs for **Our** future grandchildren's and increasingly more pleasant future generations within numerous through Yours as well.

God spoke for writer to implement a few solutions learned from others for earth's future sustainment within the blessed future.

regarding agriculture, heightened urban farming shall continue producing 27 crops per season rather than one: using 90% less water and significantly less carbon emitted from transportation. *build urban farms in 50 mile increments.

ten percent of earth's land is used for agriculture: innovative minds shall continue blessed well for progression and solutions.

regarding energy, continue harnessing solar, wind and ocean's tides that shall generate power with minimal carbon emissions: remain patient, all is well.

harness the sun's emitted energy for **God's** offspring's needs:

-7.3 billion humans 2015. eight billion 2030. nine billion 2050.

every human could live upon the land the size of alaska and have room for golf. in 1950, humans thought what occurred in 2000 would have been inconceivable as well. **We** shall proceed well because **God** has a wonderful plan through and within elected humans to receive only a positive consciousness and yield great favor through and within the future progress upon earth.

this relative information speaks volumes of **God** s certainty within faithful, hopeful and prayerful future blessings within numerous lives.

'And these thoughts remain given from Me for You: Proceed enveloped with goodness because I have a wonderful plan for those whom listen well and I shall work through your ideas and perceptions perfectly. Life shall modify greatly and You are learning how to receive My differential advantage for the future blessings received through You.'

DENOUNCING NEGATIVITY

stated saturday january 9, 2010. following asking **Father** why he remained angry with self, he stated, 'this is how My **Father** and grandFather treated **Their** sons!' hmmm. replying, 'Father, **You** are directed to behave certain ways, especially to your son.' he scoffed, thus, with blood shot eyes said, 'this is the way **We** are!' replying, softly, 'pardon, this is how **You** are.' he remains brilliant with his awareness of business, however, saying how his Son shall behave remains absolutely ludicrous: writer, remains a **Father** himself and would refrain saying such cruel words to son. words spoken from parent to child have much merit and many are disconfirming.

perfectly, your following writings shall express feelings from another perspective. fall of 1999, writer stated within Mother in law mary's presence, following dane, Her grandson had come home: upset with classmates words said to him upon school. impulsively writer stated, 'sticks and stones may break your bones but words will never hurt You.' Her immediate reply, 'words will hurt You.' mary had worked with special needs children and blessed. many revelations occurred that evening: **God**, through Her, helped writer overcome an old school male mentality instilled from **Father** and numerous males societally showing how emotionally tough **We** are. toughness shows itself well, bad entity works through minds seeking **Our** negativity. ultimate fighting club and boxing affects spectators and **Their** families negatively, as examples and shall come to pass over time.

regarding mary, this was growing process and now realize because, **God,** remains speaking through minds, thank **You God, You** working through mary remains correct, numerous within societies remain progressing gentle and patient as **God** desires. throughout life, others come into Yours for reasons, seasons and a lifetime and are understood over time: embrace the gentle ideas and suggestions from females for they remain expressing what **God** through Jesus intended for humans upon the earth, calmness, gentleness as well as love for others progression upon the earth.

'Slate verses I have selected within romans eight, write what is spoken:

He that searches the hearts remains aware of the mind within the spirit, for he shall heighten the saints awareness, according to My perfect will. All good things shall work together for good: My saints whom love Me are called according to My plan: Those who foreknow are predetermined, conforming within the image of My Son and the firstborn of My elected: Those whom are elected shall be called and I share My glory with Them.'

'In truth You are called many times; all through life, God gives Us good. He calls You first in baptism and afterwards; whether You listen to God's voice or otherwise, he graciously calls Us. If You recede from baptism, he calls You to repent; If You strive to fulfill your calling, he calls upon You from grace to grace from holiness to holiness, then life is given into You. Abraham was called from his home, Peter from his nets, Matthew within his office, Elisha from his farm, Nathanael from his retreat; We are all in course of the calling, on and on, from one thing to another, having zero resting-place, however, mounting towards Our eternal rest, obeying one suggestion to another placed

well into You. He calls Us again and again, in order to justify, favor and glorify You again, again, again and again as well as more and more to sanctify and preordain Us into a blessed living.'

'The spirits in You give perfect direction or otherwise: Listening remains your illusion of choice and determines living well directed or otherwise. Receive an ability to enter within a manner of life for My early followers: The word recorded in early scripture was hidden from truth to be spoken. I shall reveal future truth: Life remains My pleasure; You are blessed with grace from My wisdom: Your ways of goodness remain My perfections.'

Chapter

POLAR OPPOSITES
AND FLESHLY STAGE

Father in law, john luther, remains polar opposite behaviorally of writer's Father, consistently exemplifying calmness, patience, peacefulness and very soft spoken. exuding real confidence, john loves **God**, a wonderful man who tells zero untruths nor boasts. honesty and calmness remains respected and fully reciprocated.

fleshly stage, written in 2008. preceding spiritual rebirthing. after fretting and fuming for many months over loss of writer's son, after raising him Motherly from birth until six and a half then rifled with fact evon, would wait periods of time to speak or be with **Father** physically. when entering office, molly observed, new man and Her last name together on real estate sign above entrance: your writer placed it there; psychosomatically and subconsciously, She saw sign each time arriving at office. evon's **Father** was not a man through **Their** eyes, for he was a stay at home Father: **You** see, real men work, supporting **Their** family and this was agreed during that present tense, yet, molly didn't realize, **God**, had one wonderful plan for his son. writer and evon completely understood another absent instilled generational pain. **God**, taught writer to teach him patience and kindness for others, also taught him thinking outside of box with a wonderfully focused soul, from **God** through evon.

remaining physically away from son's life and began making choices that were in every ones best interest, however, molly decided **Our** Son shall do without **Father** conversationally four taxing months with zero contact following demise of family. asking **God** why then, '**distorted thinking originates deeper than humanism.**' writer being admonished from Son was irrelevant, however, Son was admonished from a **Father** nurturing him from first coo, step, learning colors, numbers, words, conifer and deciduous trees differentially. writer had honor teaching him reading, writing, numbers, sunsets, sunrises, stars, moons and planets preceding crawling.

continual communications from **God**, through writer's mind received his word of peace and harmony through one magnificent son, evon, who recited hearing on one occasion the order of **Our** planets from the sun perfectly: his age was only one. color spectrum (r.o.y.g.b.i.v), brushing teeth morning and evening, toilet training, rollie pollies, butterflies, theory of relativity and speed of light before age two. evon, was three years when numerous great thinkers as Einstein, Buddha, Thomas Jefferson, as well as, John and John Quincy Adams who were **Our** lineage, thus, well acquainted with enlightenment and photographically evon remembers well. he now remains a member of national honor society, perfectly through calmness and his perfect vision. molly returned from work and continued working as workaholics do and writer would read books continually with evon and was happily contented as mr. mom: inseparable for one perfect relationship upon his youth was what **God** had spoken.

molly, allowed this wonderful bond flowing between **Father** and son: he remains the light of **Our** lives, from **God**. thank **You God**, molly and **Our** loving son, evon.

ending chapter shall leave **You** with a few desired quotes from everyone's creator:

'I am goodness from one calm and optimistic voice through everyone.'

'I am all powerful and remain good within every individual whom listens well.'

'When You are walking upon a flat surface or speaking with anyone and remain looking down rather than forward or up, this behavior is spiritually induced: Observe drawings of enlightened ones and Jesus: pupils are fixated from Me and are delegating My spiritual direction.'

'Humans shall learn, having faith in Me rather than human/medias predictions of truth through electoral and stock market data yields truth within Yourself rather than distorted sensationalized humans.'

Chapter

SEEMINGLY WHITE
PICKET FENCE

preceding theatrics, **Our** lives were fairly tales with a glowing white picket fence, however, **You** were probably anticipating, reality began revealing itself and writer shall need making an extremely relevant accountability before proceeding further. for numerous, alcohol and other mind altering chemicals remain a negative issue. through writer's family and friends, ingesting mind and mood altering chemicals, including alcohol, caused atrocities, bad behaviors and offended those loved most. through compounding and continual specific inner turmoil in life from bad entity, writer ultimately would have another drink alone, calming an overwhelmed mind.

fleshly, generational pain and goodness remain the trunk within family trees, entire family is affected: feelings related with complacency and discontentedness are intertwined, as unwell. life, for your writer was rather calm outwardly, however, internally an abundance of anxiety, discontentment, as unwell as, overwhelmedness were plaguing further.

Preceding third rebirth was unaware, masking pain through inappropriate venues, distorted relief would come from depressants, specifically, alcohol and marijuana.

Following suggested prayers/direction from a voice in mind throughout the day, thus, praying for others in mind or upon television as instructed, this voice whom writer thought was always **God**, would speak, 'Great job Robert, **You** deserve one large bottle of vodka for helping so many others.' Final rebirth, **God** said, 'Refrained from Me, voice in your mind and thought processes of negativity and judging others unwell are satan.'

Traveling to the liquor store, communications remained continuous with **God**, and he would say how traffic would flow and what to pray for: Then was unaware and now aware sometimes was what's its name, when information given regarded negativity, rather than optimistic awareness.

Back to story.

Alcohol use was prevalent in **Our** lineage, We, as more than likely possibly You, **We** drank for immediate affect of calming and escaping, at times, overwhelmed mind. These sporadic and unsustainable fixes numbed overwhelmed senses temporarily. Grandparents, many of **Their** offspring and society acted accordingly, as unwell. **We** absolutely loved life, however, also believed at times life was overwhelming: Family loved **God**, however, felt that numbing thoughts and pain instilled through souls/minds would lessen with temporary inebriation with negative consequences.

Returning to 2006. Several years passed, Evon was stable, jovial, learning, living and loving life, as most of **God's** offspring, all should receive.

feeling unwelcome, this city boy felt out of place in a small town; now realize, soul was distorted, became more depressed upon the cyclically monotonous days. appropriate conscious choices were discarded, thus, contributing with dissolving another loving family. observing this behavior absolutely upset molly badly, She experienced negativity associated with alcohol in family growing up, as unwell. writer told zero others what occurred through mind throughout life, because **God** refrained instructing to do so until 2009, through your book's numerous chapters. asked **God** why, following this book becoming written each day. he would speak, **'ultimately, I, direct your good thinking and behaviors: remain patient, pray for others, I, envelop all goodness within and through your readers blessed lives. I have enveloped your good thoughts and behaviors: remain calm and patient continuously. as countless times occurring previously, I worked through numerous others wellness for You, Them, thus, My profound goodness: countless shall become aware.'**

returning to story.

son, was six years of age, living in family home and enrolled in school fulltime. similarly, as numerous occurring times previously, **God**, worked through others, surrounding self with another wonderful solution. brother in law, toby, (tobith), biological sister's husband opened one hydraulics business within oklahoma city, thus, aware how much your writer desired work, therefore, was hired immediately. here was another wonderful opportunity helping him and family while occupying time appropriately while evon, was in school: becoming aware that distorted and unfocused thinking were fleshly reasons to drink, abruptly stopped or so thought.

proceeded immediately working 80 hour weeks and remained taxing emotionally, mentally, as well as, physically for both molly and your writer: having heightened responsibility, working and taking care of Son understandably overwhelmed Her. returning home after midnight and missing **Them** dearly, gave a kiss upon evon's forehead, gazing on his face and peaceful sleep, showered and then became horizontal as well.

your following chapter, **God**, was apparent, giving instructions and information from questions asked regarding specifics or generalities of humanism and spirituality: **God**, spoke an abundance of what occurred with molly and Son and sometimes continually, received information of what people would say at work or how they would move through all venues of life and the media: zero times were directed to tell anyone anything. information received was between your writer and **God**. please, continue.

'aware or otherwise, throughout north America and locations globally within the future, negative energy and lightning shall be replaced with certainly positive energy through the atmosphere. this shall correlate from the masses heightened peace within Their souls from/with Me.'

BLINDSIDED

what transpired on this date remains irrelevant, because having worked 80 hour weeks, became accused of going to the strip bars: where were insecurities from? writer knows. working physically comprising a new business, **God**, knows truth. one saturday evening returning home from work, had opened door and She was upon sofa and noticeably unhappy, observing eyes and disposition asked how She was; She began giving demands what should occur, meeting needs of cleaning pool. upon this juncture remained unaware what was transpiring with Her and so called friend of Mine, said, 'shall do what **You** want next morning it is after midnight.'

from this instance writer gathered up a few items, kissed evon gently on forehead telling him how much he was loved and how sorry this had occurred, then left. **Our** loving family was turned upside down and most importantly, evon's life was affected most negatively: his **Father** was gone, instantly his placated and stable life suddenly became completely overturned. life is spiritual through everyone alive.

thinking She would become calmer, over time and allowing discussions further resolving occurrence for one another and **Our** innocent young man, continued working. She was taking out prior relationships of men behaving badly upon **Father** of **Our** evon. why? **God** spoke saying, '**You both were spiritually affected, thus,** infected **becoming climax for your spiritual awakening and writing this book from Me for others whom I choose.**'

was served with papers when working: She filed restraining order, however, had contacted Her zero times. most significant, innocent evon, was unable speaking with his **Father** for four months, there were zero phone calls nor physical contact.

how this affected writer was irrelevant, however, how evon was affected, became apparent: next four years through his emotions, feelings, thinking, thus, behaviors. having zero contact with son, nor molly for such a long duration, writer filed for divorce for sole purpose of speaking with son. molly is from a lawyer family and would allow zero information. asked **God**, how **Our** evon was, he replied saying,

11.11.16

'**I spoke for every good word within book to be slated for a reason: My offspring from every religion, faith or lack thereof and upon all continents to discern/understand humanism, spirits, thus, weather. they shall become part of a miraculously powerful solution rather than remaining** powerless **and** stagnated: **life remains good and** bad: **receive only goodness and allow Me to heighten peace around You: this remains your perfect spiritual decision: there remains a reason humans receive information within Their senses while they receive My corrected information from questions upon the same moment. the more You rely upon Me, information received shall be truthful. when You have any question, ask and receive an answer through a word, thought, feeling or vision. there is a plan when relying upon Me alone and with others. here is your answer: evon, remains well.**'

'The reason My writer was asked to slate this book remains for You: My gentle word shall remain true and refrain receiving differences from satan's **agenda within many humans** distorted **interpretations: future generations shall receive My truth rather than from humans. the way humans react upon information given remains dependent upon how the truth remains spoken within Their senses from God.'**

God? 'yes My son.' shall your chosen remain christians? **'again, they are everything with Me, as well.'** what shall your answer regard for your offspring encompassing other religions globally within the future?

'What occurs well within everything living remains from Me/God : every question regarding the past shall be answered in this book. regarding the blessed and favored future, every answer from My questions You have received shall become answered for others if I decide within You: has My question been answered for others?'

yes: thank **You God.** 'You are welcome: all questions regarding the general future remain answered within this book and You remain aware of a multitude of answers from humans specific questions.'

FLESHLY BITTER

writer, on one angry and bitter occurrence when following paragraph was written, late october 2006 following divorce. remaining extremely angry, egocentric and spiritually infected related with internalized feelings and thoughts were disheveled. reason for placing information in writings show honestly of writer's fleshly side: persona and unedited thoughts are from an individual disallowing **God** to relieve emotional and mental anguish, thus, pain through meditation, thought and prayer. **God** said on this juncture, **'I gave all your good thought processes in Our consciousness: (soul).'**

ergo: october 26, 2006

thank goodness children are resilient outwardly, however, what occurs internally? in spite of this, evon, does very well in school, straight a's, honor roll, as well as, remains a creatively magnificent artist, pianist or specifics, he focuses mind upon and was inducted into the national honor society with a 4.438 grade point average on a 4 point scale (advanced placement). him for handling his present situation, he is an incredible young man, as well as, absolutely, the best Son on earth with a blessed soul and beautiful heart of gold.

an abundance of offspring, presently, are living within two separate households, thus, **God** said to place these last few paragraphs for **You** reading and for someone **You** know who might be processing throughout a similar and distorted scenario. following final rebirthing, **God** answered all questions. asked why this occurred, '**robert, your life remains for others learning My truth regarding humanism, weather, spirituality and remained another lesson along Our path for writing this book.**'

ergo:

unedited.

God, desires a Mother and **Father** bearing child together, staying together for child's sake if possible, rather than insatiable needs, using as a pawn, with zero feelings. evon, despondent, enjoys games of focus and learning what is taught in school: boredom sets in, finishing work, before teacher passes papers for other students. taught thinking worldly, helping others when two. presently, evon's thinking has been one progressive prodigy child, if **You** will. having abilities and focus, through learning on any level and is capable of eleven years of age, becoming a neurosurgeon if this becomes what he shall desire, how educated, as well as, trained: perfect focus, dexterity and great intellect from **God**.

when arriving unannounced for tenth birthday in rural oklahoma, bringing Son and class cup cakes and juice, peered through window on classroom door, he was wearing a winter coat, inside warm classroom and was sad with head held low. proceeded inside classroom. when greeting his classmates, individually, one boy in the back of the room said, 'this is funner!' his teacher immediately corrected young man saying, 'more fun.' he then replied, 'it's funner...... f.u.n.i.e.r.!'

saying zero, your writer turned to evon, he was lowering his head with sadness.

speaking with his teacher privately in hallway, asked Her, what his **Father** could do or express regarding helping him further. She stated, 'he is sad often, however, genius with school work and very willing to help other children with **Their** work, thus, overall, doing relatively well.' moral of story, as **You** are aware, times have changed and education, environment, as well as, training for children commences earlier in life than one or two generations prior. as **You** remain aware numerous of offspring are relatively brilliant, comparative with a few previous generations.

likewise, aware throughout history, there have always been brilliant minds and, presently, offspring receive heightened spiritual, thus, emotional hyper sensitivity. back to story. small towns, remain where people are genuine and calmer with less distortions and numerous, spiritually, choose idolizing **God**, rather than a hand held device and are praying more, thus, yielding something outside themselves. previous sentence, attempts relaying optimism for smaller towns, however, aware presently, anxieties and overwhelmedness are becoming pandemic throughout all communities, through individuals encompassing masses within all spiritual societies.

where are **You God?**

'**Everywhere, desiring everyone's faith, commitment and relying upon My assistance of calmness and stability through your family, as well as, Yourself. I, shall refrain from placing zero** addictions, anger, anxieties, depression **nor** discontentedness **upon any of My offspring: I, remain your lighted calmness and solution.**'

'**When relying only upon humans what occurs individually and societally? are You realizing when humans** thwart **Me, what remains occurring globally?**' do atheists realize what remains occurring? '**they shall and become aware how they have affected numerous questioning Me.**'

'**Within humanism, there remains an abundance of gray area regarding everything within individual beliefs: zero gray area are in My thoughts.**'

GOD'S OFFSPRING

'Virgin births occurring throughout history and similar to jesus.'

attis - phrygia: born of the virgin nana on december 25. he was both the **Father** and the divine son. he was a Savior crucified on a tree for the salvation of mankind: buried, on third day priests found the tomb empty.

buddiah – india: born of the virgin maya on december 25th. he was announced by a star and attended by wise men presenting costly gifts. at birth angles sing heavenly songs. he taught in the temple upon age of 12. tempted by mara, (satan) while fasting. he was baptized in water with the Spirit of **God** present. buddiah healed the sick and fed 500 from a small basket of cakes. he walked on water, fulfilled law, preached establishment of a Kingdom of righteousness and told followers to renounce the world. he was transfigured on a mount. died, buried but arose again after tomb opened by supernatural powers as well as ascended into heaven (nirvana): followers believe he returns in later days to judge the dead. buddiah, also called: 'good shepherd', 'carpenter', 'alpha and omega', 'master', 'light of the world' as well as 'redeemer.'

dionysus - greece: born of a virgin december 25th, placed within a manger. he was a traveling teacher who had performed many miracles. turned water into wine. followers ate sacred meal that became the body of the **God**. he rose from the dead march 25th. identified with the ram and lamb as well as called 'king of kings', 'only begotten son', 'savior', 'alpha and omega', 'redeemer, 'sin bearer', as well as 'anointed one.'

heracles – greece: born at winter equinox of a virgin: was sacrificed at the spring equinox. he too was called 'savior', 'only begotten', 'prince of peace' as well as 'son of righteousness.'

krishna - india: krishna was born of the virgin devaki within a cave, at the time of his birth the cave was miraculously illuminated. king kansa sought the life of the indian Christ by ordering the massacre of all male children born during the same night at he. (as Moses within numbers 33 christian bible.) krishna traveled widely, performing miracles: raising the dead, healing the lepers, deaf and blind. the crucified krishna is pictured on the cross with arms extended, died and descended into hell which he rose again on the third day and ascended into heaven. (the gospel of nicodemus tell of jesus' descent into hell.) he will return on the last day to judge the the dead. krishna is the second person of the hindu trinity.

osiris – egypt: he came to fulfill the law. called 'krst', the 'anointed one', born of the virgin isis-meri on december 25th in a cave/manger, with his birth was announced by a star and attended by three wise men. earthly **Father** named 'seb' (translates to 'joseph') age 12 he was a child teacher in the temple: at 30 was baptized and disappeared for 18 years. osiris was baptized in the river iarutana - the river jordan - by 'anup the baptizer', who was beheaded. (anup translates to john.) he performed miracles, exorcised demons, raised el-osiris from the dead. walked on water and was betrayed by typhon and crucified between two thieves. buried in a tomb from which he arose on the third day (19th athyr) and resurrected. his suffering, death, and resurrection celebrated each year by his disciples on the vernal equinox-easter. remained called 'the way, the truth and the light', 'messiah', '**God's** anointed son', 'son of man', 'word made flesh', as well as, 'the word of truth' and he was expected to reign a thousand years.

'**There remains zero denominations or religious (divisions) in heaven: everyone connects and are directed well within God's absolute truth.**'

Chapter

PROGRESS AND SOLUTIONS

allow writer proceeding forward with intention of book, progress and solutions from **God**, through his grace, thus, getting back on track and proceeding deeper. much of **Our** industrialized world has become a wonderful place: united states of America and numerous technologically unified countries are doing well for others. children have a propensity of learning and using, visual/spatial relatedness through **Their** minds with a much increased rate than they are taught. one outdated adage, 'he or She is just a child and they shall achieve more when they become mature.' here's one great place for a story. vassily victor fedyaev remains a good friend, was reared outside moscow, great thinker, his focus, as well as, resolve, remained absolute best placated persona experienced in early twenties. he lived with writer and observing his nonverbal communication, has been appreciated and obliging.

because of **God's** enlightenment, presently remain aware, **God**, placed **Us** together as friends for a reason, season and lifetime. one day, mid october 1993, vassily arrived within writer's residence, he was quiet and kept to himself, as always had. walking through door, expressed to him how difficult college mathematics was. without hesitation, vassily said, 'rob, intellectually **We** did these courses during fourth grade in russia and physically, traversed parallel bars on ten mile course in mandatory army there as a teenager.' proceeded saying, 'We could hang and rest, however, if **We** had dropped or fell to ground from 15 feet **We** had to begin again.' vass, graduated magna cum laude from o.c.c., then from new york university and worked as taxation accountant for price waterhouse, in houston. displeased as a numbered employ, now owns a film studio there and lives with his wonderful son, daniel, who is brilliant and at sixteen years of age is extremely talented.

God, is goodness through all of **Our** relationships and earth's progress.

american children remain falling behind regarding academia comparatively with china and others. china's children, are taught young, technological applications, intellectual calculations and visual spatial relatedness. numerous of **Our** children remain completely inundated through a plethora of irrelevant distortions. adhd?

however; **We** receive an ability of proceeding forward what is given intellectually at almost any age. if american children are to remain viable and conducive relative with current global educations, thus, received while young and attending **Their** grade schools; compared with western europe, asia and others, **We** need modifying old school teaching of children as if they are young and helpless than they currently remain. You're aware, children have more to offer society when taught difficult curriculum. presently, children and **Our** offspring, remain capable achieving anything desired. this optimistic view coupled through less generational distractions and distortions throughout homes, for masses, shall become an achiever filled society rather than distraught, helpless and downtrodden. writer's aware, **Our** free society yields well rounded offspring comparative with many other technologically viable countries: attempting to heighten awareness for those who are unaware, thus, possibly zero children being left behind remains questionable: when children observe calmness upon rearing, they would proceed forward rather than left behind in the first place. writer believes in women's movement because females have come so far in life in a short period, finally, more males are listening: undeniably females importance throughout technological societies, from **God**, they are offspring's second greatest influence for these children achieving more in a youthful age, hats off for females. influencing many families calmness, comfort and grace, **God**, works first through all.

'Numerous throughout history and within the future remain blessed spiritually well within Their scientifically unexplainable consciousness which I shall perfectly explain when finished reading God's offspring.'

looking forward when 2060 comes and shall. from **God's** perfect calmness or viably, what's its names chaos through individuals throughout every society, globally.

finishing this chapter, here is one question from a preacher for your writer. are churchless people spiritual?

here is **God's** answer for You.

'Yes, everyone is spiritual. albeit, conscious, unconscious, aware or unaware, most humans (even atheist's) communicate with themselves for resolution of specifics or generalities through thoughts. the voice all are hearing is Me if good. what You must desire, remains more good and less bad. regarding every facet of your life and those around You, the former desire is appropriate and obtainable: one~ simply praise/thank Me when specifics go well, (this takes a millisecond and I reciprocate). two~ when anywhere on earth, ask Me to bless people and places and then pray for your desires (another millisecond and You are living with My Spirit perfectly). when You live within My good spirit, You may ask preceding/during reading or other specifics, will this information be beneficial? I know and reply yes or no, thus, your relevant time remains efficiently blessed well. finally, enjoy your gracefully blessed and chosen day because life is goodness through You.'

God? 'yes My son.' many have learned life remains predetermined. 'yes.' why shall **We** continue to try? '**why You proceed remains Me within your three faceted self (soul, heart, mind), your useful good energy.**'

'**All continuous goodness within particles of all humans consciousness as well as the certain solidification of the earth's crust and decreasing** seismic activity **globally shall continue to occur and remain from God : this remains another prediction from Me for all humans function and safety as well as countless revealed all divine words remain from Me.**'

'**My existence shall be proven true, as well as, have a perfecting plan.**'

SUBCONSCIOUS MIND. HUMILITY. PROCEEDING WITH TASKS DIFFERENTIALLY

subconscious mind remains very powerful, thus, more easily understood when **You** traverse through life realizing why **You** behave and think as **You** do. turning off distortions of life, listening to **God**, through body, mind and soul shall be a wonderful place to begin. listening to your children, shall come back ten fold, behaviorally, as they mature.

optimistically, upon rearing process **You** likely, proceeded differently with tasks. individually, **You** have an intrinsic probability, thinking efficiently and functional. **God**, remains instrumental, bringing progress through **Yourself** and communities, as well as, thinking differentially, as zero other wonderful humans have, thus far. humans within current times, internally are preoccupied having egocentric selves fulfilled, thus, less aware recognizing they are deceitful, telling non truths and remaining selfish, as another cog contributing with demise of the civilized world. four generations previously, **You** believed what someone said. what was needed, for someone believing what was spoken remained your word, eye contact and a handshake.

presently, hidden agendas, manipulation, perverse distorted thoughts and feelings, emotions and having egocentric needs fulfilled before others, remains appropriate. where writer comes from, your word remains honor: within mid-western united states, most still believe in firm handshakes with males, as well as, many females.

shall express one short story upon this juncture.

your writer, met one male working down street, early 2010; walking up to him, he already was aware who writer was and knew each other 25 years prior in high school. **We** spoke with each other briefly, as **We** parted ways, looking him in eyes while placing hand out for firm handshake was baffled, handshake remained comparable shaking hands with air. pardon, gentleness was his expression, however, seemed rather insincere: this was insecurity, in own mind and an outward lament showing his calmness. shall ponder further, for now when shaking hands with someone new, writer delays for millisecond, feeling grip first and reciprocating accordingly. one question remains left. are **We** really becoming so soft a society? yes **We** are. **God** is good within that respect, however, shall leave **You** with this thought. what is next, germ free elbow bumps? yes, and soon zero physical contact with those unknown: **God** remains well aware.

moving forward. marriage is stability for Ourselves and offspring remains factual: **God**, desires humans forming meaningful bonds lasting a lifetime, together as one. traversing through life, **God**, desires **Us** choosing **Our** spouse carefully, rather than impulsively; marriage's are intended for life, especially, when there are children. males, as well as, females make conscious choices, allowing outside influences or humans dictate who **You** become or **You** have received enough emotional strength preceding age six, for progressing forward towards any goal desired and thought.

humans, remain ultimately trained behaving and thinking within certain criterion. albeit, armed forces, school, work or life, **You** are directed through thinking of bosses, colleagues, elders, teachers, parents and professors, thus, implement **Their** teachings or otherwise. why **You** implement functionality: **God**, through Yourself. why do humans/preachers perspire when speaking? '**they remain receiving** anxieties.' where might these anxieties derive? '**You're aware: spirits are disagreeing what is spoken.**'

'**I remain optimistically calm with zero** anxiety **within any offspring.**'

Chapter

FURTHER PROGRESSION

We shall proceed with current societal views of life. sometimes, females remain progressing further in familial units: females are increasingly influential regarding monetary sufficiency incurred in families, thus, sustaining a significance in world and numerous males, shall regard power and control issues as **God** desires, past. males, throughout societies, shall attempt receiving egocentric solace or placing efforts directly responsible for continuation of species, particularly less impulsive. while humans are reliant upon two incomes, progressing into future, many males oppose notion: what specific juncture shall many embrace societal modifications? following family dissolve, becoming alone, then decide to work as one for **God's** common goal for Us, togetherness throughout **Our** lives, thus, offspring's futures.

God, has become increasingly saddened, from egocentric ways many humans have become with behaviors and thoughts. placing **God**, aside and acquiring material possessions above what remains most important, **God**, family, as well as, others. misunderstood remains misunderstood. always, correct feelings lie through You: if **You** would turn off material distortions and listen to **God**, speaking through your heart, mind and soul, this would allow correct thinking and behavior for progress.

'**You** might just let it go' ~ jack johnson.

is relative, few generations prior, humans acquired less material stuff, therefore, had more time concentrating upon families and offspring, prioritizing according to what remained important in life. gangster rap, acid rock, pornographic material and violent video games, remained nonexistent. dysfunctionally, distortions with arguing for power and control, lawsuits and anger in life were significantly fewer. **Our** grandparents experienced less divorce, thus, remained with significant other, through good times and difficult. why are there good or bad times? spirituality.

Their offspring, benefited abundantly during theses times and looked forward with viewing sunrises, sunsets and appreciated perfected miracles, **God**, continuously gives for **Our** enjoyment. what happened? oh yes, remembering very well, and You? please, proceed.

We matured through behaviors, values, morals and ethics, generationally instilled. fleshly, what was brought to **Our** tables, generationally, was brought upon theirs. here lies one behavioral occurrence, please relate your mind through offspring's. shall **You** receive anguish from your Mother or **Father** becoming late getting ready? hmmm. numerous fleshly reasons, offspring are late becoming ready are because of negative attention and overwhelmed, anxiety ridden, depressed and non focused. **You** see, negative attention is much better than zero, psychologically, and shall be discussed through book. why do they feel these ways? bad spirit, through Them.

parents often idolize **Their** hand held devices, more than offspring's needs. **God**, and bad entity watches offspring—acting and reacting accordingly, through Them. **You** are becoming aware specific reasoning why they, at times, disrespect **You** so: conscious/subconscious illusion of control: they receive less attention because **You** have a text, thus, perceived disrespect cyclically remains reciprocated. an eye for an eye causes much blindness.

readers, this remains what **God**, has taught your writer. why numerous persons feel need running red lights, uncaringly toss **Their** trash upon earth or intentionally taking life from family and friends remains completely relative; discontentedness among themselves instilled within childhood, expressed outwardly through humanism. what remains certain, many are viewing societal disrespect, thus, aware, are You? more than likely yes, allow proceeding significantly deeper throughout your book.

knowing one specific question to ask a pastor, who arrived upon writer's residence, two years following car accident: from **God's** direction, sought and desired receiving from his answers, asked, 'what was the correct religion: buddhism, christianity, hinduism, judaism or islam?'

this specific question was asked almost quarter of a century in arrears. **You** see, pastor rob, remains one man whom has a profound ability of opening a new book turning page then looking upon page for an instant, while absorbing text entirely: many doctors have a cognitive osmosis occurring, from **God**, through **Them** and in future have a profound ability, photographically reciting specific words verbatim. rob, received ability to give answers from many differing religious perspectives. baptizing writer's son, blessings occurred through pastor rob to evon, from **God**. rob remains blessed, however, had zero to share when asked what was the correct religion face to face during this specific instance, because rob remained aware his words could affect forever this impressionable, as well as, enlightening young soul. visiting before book was published, pastor rob, read entire rough draft of book. asking him what corrections should be made, said, only to change whilst to shall: elaborating or expounding what he desired sharing from **God's** spiritual direction: '**all religions goodness remain correct, how You find Me, how You pray, what and when You pray remains between You and Me rather than through humans control.**'

example:

writer is lutheran, following **Our** church, **God** said, '**attend catholic mass with your sister.**' standing in line for communion, **God**, continuously was instructing writer to pray for others: son, congregation, family and specific continents across earth, north/south America, africa, asia and europe. anticipated christ's blood and body, however, arriving directly in front of bishop, was denied. writer wasn't catholic, thus, shall remain lutheran, who's accepting of everyone, receiving christ's blood and body, rather than exclusively **Their** egocentric selves. asked **God** why was denied, **God** spoke, **'this was another lesson for Our book. the illusion of human** control **remains far from God : My son, pray other religions become inclusive as Jesus over time. a few years passed; for communion a female approached the pope: She said She was lutheran and asked if She could receive christ's blood and body? I, through him spoke, yes, You should receive what remains deep within your heart.'**

Chapter

40

MACRO RELIGION, TWO

current chapter remains emphasis: **God** asked writer for this again, likewise, has implemented further information through his writer's soul, thus, Yours as well.

progress learning regarding religion and proceeding extremely deep. christianity is writer's religion: saved, baptized and attending church sunday and wednesday. taught, obeying **God's** commandments, especially, loving neighbors as Ourselves. loving humans as Yourself, leads **You** into next sentence. christianity, differs from islam, however, islam remains similar with numerous respects and both are correct through different interpretations. throughout history, males have desired correctness, selfish humans or however **You** wish referring. expounding further. **God**, created humans to praise him, love others and multiply sharing interests with another through calmness, love and unity among individuals. differing religious interpretations of how to reach **God**, from soul through after life when your fleshly vessel becomes dust are oppositional through religious cultural interpretations. **You** were born and had instilled certain beliefs, trained or taught believing within certain criterion expressed through churches, parents, peers, as well as, teachers. **You** understand. **God** desires quoted and commences clarifying: **'I am God, one God, now and forever: because You were born in middle east, You may pray to Allah, Allah is Me, thus, globally, every single human in africa, australia, canada, europe, north America and south America pray to the same God : You may have learned from the qur'an, very well. this book teaches similar positive views as the christian bible: praise God, love others and respect nature. sound familiar?** exclude **the subtle and profound negativity from satan's voice through the writers of christian bible, qur'an, all human thoughts and current information; then, You shall become increasingly aware of My absolute truth within every human.'**

following information remains known amongst numerous religious scholars and citizens globally. religions believing in something other than christianity over look extremely significant information regarding why they oppose, yet, should embrace.

all humans are from same seed. abundance of christians, muslims, among other believers across earth, currently think **Their** way of reaching **God**, egocentrically, remains the only correct path. christian's bible says, jesus, is only path. untrue.

'Why would You judge other humans I created with differing faiths whom praise Me, pray for others and follow good religious interpretations from one good God? are You egocentric, **believing your way remains the only correct path? I remain correct.'**

ergo:

Abraham, is held as the founding **Father** of christian, islamic and jewish religions. genesis states the nation of Israel descended from him through his second son, isaac. many arab nations descended through his first Son ishmael and muslims believe prophet muhammad remains a direct descendant, as well. also, torah in islam's bible, thus, qur'an are first five chapters in christian's old testament. extra-biblical book, known as, book of jubilees places the location and identity of ishmaelites as arab people. many biblical accounts refrain from agreeing because throughout history, humans wanted egocentric control oppositional from another. aware or unaware, where does humans egocentric control derive?

christian's new testament, Abraham was mentioned prominently as a man of faith (see hebrews 11) and apostle paul uses him as an example of salvation by faith as progenitor of Christ or messiah (galatians 3:16). authors of new testament said, jesus, cited Abraham, supporting a belief of resurrection of dead. 'but concerning dead, they shall rise.': have **You** read in bible and Moses burning bush passage, how **God** spoke saying, '**I am God of Abraham, God of isaac and the God of jacob?**'

refraining being a **God** of the dead, but **God** of the living, awaiting everyone alive and eternally chosen. now, shall state **God's** appropriate words spoken through writer's soul.

'Globally, every human created shall indefinitely remain living and blessed further doing My good will of praising Me and love for others.'

God desires quoted,

'When Abraham was told to offer issac, his only begotten son, and receive promises, Abraham remained unaware, the distorted negative **voice within his consciousness was from satan. I then spoke to issac, your seed shall be called: I shall raise You from being deceased and receive You figuratively.'** (hebrews 11:17-19) **'all humans are begotten: all good energy within You and others remains from Me.'**

'I viewed Abraham as an obedient man of faith and interrupted his attempt to offer isaac: I am the good voice/thought processes within humans.'

traditional views of christianity are chief promise made to Abraham, genesis 12, 'through Abraham's seeds all people on earth shall be blessed.' john the baptist specifically taught, merely being Abraham's seed was no guarantee for salvation: he was blessed and related to jesus, however, where did this negative information within his mind have come from? **God's** voice through Abraham, rather than johns, **'salvation shall be**

guaranteed for all believers.' God, had your writer learn information when writing this book and was baffled. why were humans, oppositional of others views religiously around earth? God, deemed Abraham eternally blessed and Abraham was Jesus lineage, thus, why are many christians opposing islam? jesus, remains the Son of God, therefore, christians are correct and islam is incorrect? **Their** religion teaches differently. writing chapter, God spoke, **'when Jesus said, 'no one comes to the Father except through Me,' he was repeating the information I was giving him. there have been millions of** deaths **upon earth in the name of religious** egocentric control. **all humans are My offspring, I made every one of You and live through your goodness. past is the past and this book occurred for your perfect reasoning: enlightening numerous souls with absolute truth.'** mortals throughout centuries want correctness in belief. writer, learned attending college two decades previously, 'it is human nature waging war against another.' where might this negative statement or thought have come from? far from **God's** peaceful love for human nature. statement was popular for scholars when world wars were prevalent amongst diverse cultures culminating **God's** wonderful earth.

within the modern world, there are religious extremists whom have perverted religious beliefs, negative thinking and feelings yielding distorted souls enveloped with anger, control and power. **Their** consciousness shall be modified, over time, only from **God** through chosen offspring whom **God** desires **Us** to ask him to denounce **Their** distorted and negative perspective.

God spoke within 2010 to pray, **'God,** praying **You** denounce satan from terrorist souls,' every morning upon awakening, as well as, numerous other specific prayers slated in latter chapters. **God** taught that if **You** continue asking and doing his will, all shall remain well within **Yourself** and others loved. rather than speaking a double negative, **'God** cannot lie,' **You** may desire, **'God** always speaks the truth.'

'Remain patient, terrorists **shall alleviate in My time, continue asking Me to bless the military and pray I give Them safety, peace, favor and awareness for allocating My altruism.'**

God's offspring shall modify well over time; desired humans shall receive this information, 'it <u>was</u> human nature to wage war.' life remains good.

God revealed, p.t.s.d. occurs because life remains spiritual and observing trauma through your senses, satan affects your soul, thus, heart and mind unwell. **God** desires **Our** faith, gentle love, as well as, peace and the negative entity wants pain, anger and chaos. when experiencing what the bad energy wants, many become infected through distortion filled thoughts, feelings, perceptions, as well as, relations with themselves and many others.

for progression, humans shall learn spiritual truth, accept similar religious interpretations and love one another rather than otherwise.

here lies a sentence from reverend michael dowd. 'what might **God** look like on the outside? only **God** knows. how might **God** look on the inside? look around, look in your mirror, look deeply within your own heart.'

many past and present generations, loving your mate as they do **You** is understood: genuinely loving other absent preconceived notions, deceit or egocentric agendas. proceeding presently. love, compassion, caring for your mate and others remains common, amongst numerous **God** loving humans rather than **God** fearing people. among masses encompassing all socioeconomic levels, humans are occupied with four things: themselves, mate, offspring and others. **Our** ego filled personas, since conception of human kind are inflating drastically, with repercussions, because **We** rescind what **God** intended originally, believing, praising and trusting him.

how numerous decide behaving with **Their** lives remains oppositional from **God's** perspective: repercussions occur from negative entities wrath. **God** has allowed humans vacillating inappropriate thoughts and behaviors throughout history and desires your patient discernment and faithfulness.

christian bible says **We** are imperfectly sinful mortals and many consciously feel they receive a free pass regarding behaviors, because they're labeled imperfect sinners.

writer shall make one point, very clear. labeled as sinners, humans consciously decide acting inappropriately, fleshly. **God**, gave **Us** a consciousness for a reason, awareness of when **You** behave appropriately or otherwise. when your behaviors, negatively affect **Yourself** and those whom love **You** most **You** shall need consciously deciding a different path for your inappropriate behaviors. exacerbating discontentedness in **Yourself** from purchasing material items that fulfills emotional discontentment, temporarily and cyclically compounded material clutter that overwhelms further. seeing others having current handheld device, **You** want a newer and better one? when may these egocentric behaviors refrain transpiring through many humans? great time to slow down while getting back to spirituality, remains when viewing **Yourself** and society overwhelmed, countries defaulting on loans for sustainment: billions or trillions of dollars in debt, volatile and treating others irrelevant, unless condition full or having to be medicated for purpose of remaining calmer for life.

why are all inequities occurring through humanism, globally?

God remains aware and speaks:

'I, see through your eyes and know how You should proceed; given current egocentric **thoughts and behaviors, while choosing fulfilling** selfish **needs first and placing Me near back of line, praising only on sunday or zero. I, assist abundantly more for those who praise Me and love others through calmness, happiness, love, optimism and patience. My chosen readers shall remain aware of My perfecting direction.'**

february 11th, 2011 **God** spoke to write this quote, **'merrily, why there shall be only a few** hurricanes **over last three years, for united states was directed from My working through numerous prayers for hundreds of lives spared and millions unaffected, peace upon coasts.** earthquake **and** hurricane **upon east coast, occurring late august of 2011, remain from** satan; **people having power and millions having less, continue believing they have** control **over Their lives rather than humbled and praising My good name. I, remain who allows goodness to flow while** restricting bad. **what occurred in joplin and new york, You were affected spiritually and** controlled unwell.'

shall briefly write following information: Jesus refrained from being a christian, buddha and mohammad refrained from being buddhist nor muslim. christianity, came from jesus. islam from mohammad and buddhism was from buddha's teachings. who taught goodness and optimism through these blessed mortals? one **God**, now and forever.

before proceeding, writer remains well aware many people shall disagree, similar as numerous had disagreed what **God**, spoke through jesus, apostles and disciples. why had anyone disagreed with what Jesus had spoken or may disagree currently? also, writer shall refrain claiming to be Jesus as numerous globally. your writer remains one simple and humble man attempting to express **God's** truth heightening peace, love and awareness.

oppositional, plethora of mortals were against anyone expressing, **God's** love, as society was chaotic, having kings and fleshly idols. why was society oppositional or disagreeing then; anxiety ridden, overwhelmed and many suffering depression?

You remain aware of the spirits well. another parable from, **God**, through your humbled writer.

'**Truth has zero** negative **agenda. what is truth? every goodness from Me through your beliefs and continuous love reciprocated through My blessings of love and calmness through countless other humans. when the masses pray for rain, they shall receive rather than relying upon only humanism. every human alive remains a vessel, and shall receive continual goodness through Their thoughts, feelings, perceptions and perspective when Their awareness of absolute truth heightens: You are learning the wonderful plan— I am God and You are Mine forever.'**

EVOLUTIONARY
PERSPECTIVE

shall **We** view life from a evolutionary perspective, with zero missing link? **We** shall. cave men, went through days, looking for innate needs of food, shelter and water. males hunted and took meat home for females who prepared feast for **Their** family: remaining less intelligent, living through mesolithic period and when they were dissatisfied with when, what or how **Their** female prepared meals, unka, two caves over was ready, willing and able to prepare a great meal perfectly for him. cliché. cave people viewed life difficult and unsure how they arrived, yet, were existing. parable.

living, for tens of thousands of years, they learned and used **Their** minds, figuring out, how to have **Their** lives better and invented fire, wheels and more, from **God**. negative thoughts and behaviors were expressed among males through anger and fighting became prevalent. hmmm. males were head of pack, strongest and most well adapted person. these egocentric humans worked together, however, were pompous animals, whom thought mostly of themselves. hmmm. *God* could and may do anything, however, observed first attempt creating humans, was less than sufficient and because satan was an egocentric awaiting angel who wanted more power, it directed a huge asteroid to earth, satan, was pleased. the impact blocked the sun's rays from reaching humans, dinosaurs and vegetation: life extinguished leaving bones for numerous atheists, agnostics and others, causing doubt in the minds of future generations.

God, then improved humans, with heightened emotions and empathy through **Their** souls, thus, hearts, minds and behaviors for many, while others, remained listless.

biblically and spiritually, through christianity the book of genesis proceeds well. tower of babble/6th day/all races created: life became wonderfully progressive for numerous. remember, carbon 14 data remains inconclusive and spiritually modifiable as earth's 8000 years of current humans.

We work together and try, while numerous are egocentric, pompous and selfish: males want what they want and females want what they want, both wanting items now or before, however, '**thou shall** not **want.**' herein lies one question. everyone wants many things, yet, whatever happened when individuals culminating societies were contented having **Their** needs fulfilled? writer remembers well and your memory?

returning within story: anger, jealousies, impatience and insecurities throughout history have remained prevalent, amongst all socioeconomic levels and cultures. when angry or sad, fleshly, these negative behaviors were generationally instilled. **You** see, upon rearing process, **You** saw love, caring and patience through parents, however, also, had observed manipulative agendas, egocentric personas, complex insecurities instilled in **Their** offspring or You, as unwell. **You** love and anticipate love, reciprocated through your feelings: optimistically expressed or denied, often times **We** fall short. why do **We** fall short? **You** are absolutely and entirely aware.

this chapter has relevancy with present. calmly, continually praising **God**, thus, loving others, life is good. another parable and relief, related through humanism.

God, revealed chapter over three days, upon first quarter of 2011, making since and revealed for **You** where humans derived: currently and into the future shall numerous chosen individuals receive gentleness, innovative minds and become directed well. ask **God** and **You** shall receive favored direction. remember, once the earth was molten rock and now sings opera. **God** is good.

Chapter

PROGRESSION

chapter was slated soon after rebirth. please understand the unedited significance.

female adherence. observing many encompassing both genders, all ethnicities and all of the socioeconomic levels, **God** lives through everyone. **You** know this. thus far, book has related subconscious generational behaviors, in your persona. now, **We** shall proceed deeper, assisting numerous humans roughly 50% possibly heightening your self worth and image, as well. beginning with human existence, males have, at times, controlled females and is great, for those wishing controlled: times have modified and majority of females, desire zero control from **Their** male.

in present societies, females are controlling in many instances, for in **Their** eyes, understandably, someone needs controlling situation or zero becomes completed. reasoning one desires control fleshly, is because they lacked control earlier in life or saw, generationally, taking control of moment, life shall progress in **Their** way. as one human, believing this may remain best behavior for **Yourself** and remains appropriate feelings **You** feel, as long as, feelings coexist harmoniously with those around You, family, significant other, friend or neighbor. numerous persons, also view significant other equal, as **God** does, however, much of industrialized world and third world countries, sadly, females continue viewed as less, in males eyes. first, both are needed producing offspring naturally, as **God**, intended, furthering the longevity of the earth. secondly, many males viewed **Their** Fathers, generationally speaking, controlling **Their** Mothers as unwell. You're aware. spiritually controlled.

also, husbands treated **Their** loving wives with admiration, love and respect, for they complete **Us** and were who rescued **Us** from loneliness and discontentedness, lying beneath **Our** externally strong facades. **You** know, all humans remain lonely sometimes, wishing something material or another completing Us. fleshly, writers completeness was reached when Mother of **Our** son, from **God**, placed **Us** in others mutual paths. shall **You** proceed deeper? yes. receive further information.

in present society, many females are taking monetarily lead in many relationships. females are intelligent as males and generally, remain more adept multi-tasking. also, currently, females receive ability, having sperm donors and choose criterion, genetically for child: height, eye, hair color, athleticism, as well as, **Their** intellect. having technology under **Their** fingertips, numerous females whom have been controlled by males, lesbian or unable to become pregnant, remain blessed from **God** through an abundance of other unique manifestations.

God, understands your situation completely, however, prefers relationships remain between males and females as paramount, always shall. males, want control and power, while females desire this, as unwell. what remains best for your offspring produced, as well as, interpersonal relationships, are finest for everyone involved.

males, have desired females since beginning of human kind. **God's** nature, within most simplistic and complex form: males love **Their** smell, walk, talk, eyes, touch, smiles, caring love expressed to offspring and others, are from **God** through Them. numerous males, still view themselves as king or great ruler: this current outdated ideology, has been instilled within **Their** personas from interpersonal and societal observances upon rearing process, then life. having overbearing strength, height, low tone in voice, males are whom females depend upon, for hunting, fishing and farming: working physically while females stayed domesticated in humble abodes. males, remained unaware, what females endured throughout **Their** days, likewise, females were unaware of all that males endured. what significantly mattered, life worked for males performing **Their** duties and females theirs. **We** shall go deeper.

families enjoyed watching sunsets together, following warm cooked meal, usually conversing optimistically and much less distortions, hindering thought processes, through wonderful family, thus, societal progress. Mothers and Fathers, rarely had negative words regarding **Their** day, what remained important was they were alive. **God**, remained undeniably the most imperative reasoning for life and understood.

proceeding throughout **Their** day, sometimes zero was spoken, for they remained praying to **God**, thinking of progress and how they could help neighbors in need. unless a new task, persona enmeshment occurred for everyone in family structure: calmness, patience and love remained extremely apparent, thus, working as a life long team, were aware of process completing task before Them, as well as, willing.

forward 260 years, more or less.

countless societally, having a faithful, life are calmly focused and good. countless individuals with and without faith remain hopelessly lethargic. why **You** receive good or bad within your consciousness has been slated: numerous youthful generations are learning a gentler and softer way of progressing than preceding lineage had received because of **God's** favor. spiritually, every individual's thoughts and feelings predicate everything. life becomes consistently wondrous when asking and receiving direction.

in present societies, many learned living beyond **Their** means becomes detrimental; proceeding through the foreclosure process, layoffs and others, **We** anticipated life shall work, accordingly for **Us** and **Our** family.

numerous individuals only option was moving in with **Their** families again and making ends meet or settling for less grandiose dwellings/lifestyles. this shall occur across the civilized world and what **You** shall contemplate remains living friction full or less. life remains very good, please proceed.

the negative energy yields humans emotional and physical lethargy: desired refraining, however, here **We** go. life remains difficult for many when local and global economies perform poorly: compounded with egocentricity and humans wanting more material possessions further isolating **Us** from human interaction, **God** remains saddened. refraining from praising **God** first and loving family second, many are digressing through insatiable wants: **You** see, countless humans are sometimes living only within themselves. **You** remain aware where this thinking derives. your book remains slated for present and future generations.

You remember three or four generations prior, how **God's** world, existed within a more basic way of life and having **God**, direct **Us** makes complete since, thus, best predictor of future, remains past through humanism: spiritually, best predictor of future remains past, as well. meaning, **God**, family, chivalry, compassion, ethics, focus, honesty, love, morals, optimism and respect are how society shall proceed. **You** may think, yes, in a perfect world, exactly this remains desired for everyone. with anything, growth begins through specific persons. You're one of **God's** seeds, growing and blooming as an example for spouse, offspring and societal progression.

our acquired love flows, inherently from **God**, through **Our** desired loving beliefs: **God**, is goodness and optimism, through your desire and calming prayer for others.

'I asked robert to give a book to a man in 80's at ymca: he read and became aware of the healing given through robert. one year further, richard said I am blind in one eye and have astigmatisms in both. My Son asked Me what shall occur? he was told to note this, embrace him and move forward. later in the day, I said, 'ask God to bless him, denounce satan's negative energy within him as well as pray his eyes

to be healed.' he did. one month further, he asked richard how We are? he said he was healed and has 20/20 vision.'

'I, God of the universe have chosen for the present and following generations to receive awareness of spiritual truth. Jesus remained unaware of an abundance spoken within My writer: similar to jesus, My writer has, from Me, the power to heal others and calm storms: receive awareness; the thoughts or voice of being negatively controlling are far from Me. I remain only calmness and include humans upon My blessed earth. when I decide, through My writer, the public shall become aware of what Jesus was unaware. I have a wonderful plan through your heightened awareness. I am God and You are Mine.'

LISTENING TO PAINS.
TECHNOLOGY.

unedited. distortions disallow Us, from listening to pains in **Our** bodies. if pains had ability verbalizing, they would say, 'refrain overloading mind, eating unhealthily, ingesting medications and wasting monetary sufficiency upon something outside your soul, temporarily filling your emotionally downtrodden self image, spiritually instilled.' inundated with going faster and more efficiently, **We** remain becoming individuals societally who place unneeded expectations upon Ourselves than generations prior. culminated through many, increasing chemical and alcohol abuse, numbing pain temporarily, as unwell as, disrespect from youth, whom disrespect parents because parents are spending less quality time, with **Their** offspring, because of a pervasive bad spiritual infection, thus, receive these egocentric feelings through themselves. these are cyclical, generational and modifiable, from **God**, however, shall ponder what distorted perceptions or thinking remain doing through your family structure.

God, made **Us** from his own image, thus, calm, compassionate, loving and patient, reliant upon following good direction, related through living life, always has and always shall.

with **God**, denouncing or minimizing the negative entity through everyone of Us, your self, family and neighbors, thus, society shall receive the propensity for living increasingly calmer and contented.

pondering day to day tasks, ask Yourself, 'what remains for My life, as a human?' billions globally, have ascertained specific question on one point or another and receiving sufficient answers through your complex mind, are obtainable within this blessed book.

letting go of your will and following the suggestions through your soul from **God** ; living continually within your soul and through other humans, **God**, allows for Us, receiving an intrinsic relationship with him, thus, all specifics learned functionally and optimistically throughout your life, via, humanism, herein lie two palpable answers.

your Mother and **Father** instilled while **You** were very young, to say please, thank **You** and respect others, animals and nature; as **God's** wonderful creation **You** have been given life for three purposes: praising **God**, loving others and procreating generations for future. that is all. living calmly, yields great lives for everyone. exactly, this remains what **God**, desires for **Us** all, with conception of human race: kindness, patience love and peace for individuals, encompassing every continent. lives become consistently wonderful, when following these simplistic principles.

We desire relief immediately, yet, patience is virtuous. **You** shall receive calmer, relief and a heightened understanding of humanism, spirits and the earths weather.

with this stated shall proceed further within technologically progressive countries encompassing earth. following writings are explicit and they too remain accurate.

ergo:

again, **You** received latest electronic device from significant other, parent or child. now **You** choose embracing device, taking time learning how it works, however, in two months they shall have improved version for less cost or despise as another material possession, cluttering life or realize material, fleshly, driven technology assists **You** abundantly, however, often takes your focus from children and human interaction.

why last statement was written remains because one: in public settings, observing thousands of males and females, focusing on **Their** text messages as children cry, reaching up, asking questions or desiring affection, two: ignoring children's needs repetitively, over time, culminating through other self serving behaviors, yields, repercussions of defiance and resentments, apparent through Them, further in life.

God, showed and spoke all of these paragraphs on many occasions through soul, late 2009.

'**When My offspring become aware all of Their** negative **behaviors and thinking remains** satan **working through Them for** negative, **countless shall denounce the** negative **energy and think well, from and with Me.**'

God, views technology wonderfully, assisting humans with increased efficiency, if your allowed this pleasure, however, focusing, idolizing and enthralling your life with technology, egocentrically above family or neighbor, **God**, remains saddened. **God**, who remains earths ultimate painter, desires **You** an ideal canvas, continually invoking praise for him and prayers for others, while proceeding along life's path.

attending church, may remain, your only relief religiously or spiritually, in week, however, **God**, desires your praising continuously, seven days throughout a week: remember, conversing and praying takes a millisecond through your thought processes.

rather than standing in line and judging others negatively and thinking how overwhelmed **You** are anywhere, ask **God** to bless those around You, thus, receiving **God's** good differential good infection and blessings filling your life with increased time.

God, continually present, assists **Our** thinking problems through and strength with anything desired: job interviews, deadlines, sharing wisdom for others, doing well on an exam and trillions of other minute and enormous tasks, through **Our** lives. only specifics needed are **God's** perfection through You: when praying throughout your day from **God**, through You, life becomes peaceful, consistent and wonderful.

Chapter

HIGHER COGNITIVE THINKING

higher cognitive thinking defines all mammals, especially humans, who have an innate ability feeling emotions, thinking and performing multiple tasks at once. when taking shower, brushing teeth, emailing or other repetitive tasks performed each day, **You** may think alternatively within numerous pragmatic fleshly specifics or floating through space, comforted from and with **God's** love and calm embrace: remains what **God** gives Us, allowing humans, having higher cognitive thinking, for specific purposes, higher cognitive thinking. rather than living day to day or for a specific moment, choose thinking of priorities, thus, maximizing your future. regarding time management, observe other ways of thinking; again, insanity is defined, 'performing exact behaviors repetitively, anticipating a different result each time.' meaning. if existing overwhelmed, with accomplishing daily tasks, simplify life: modify thinking, thus, behaviors and disallow overloading through unneeded tasks, think progressively, alleviating irrelevant tasks and thoughts in life, then focusing. keeping life simple, everyone benefits, yielding calmness, less anxiety, decreased overwhelmedness, clearer thinking, thus, lower blood pressure, naming only a few of thousands of benefits. from **God**, through You, load lessens, thus, calming soul and soothing your persona well, then life becomes peacefully enmeshed from prayer through numerous in your vicinity.

here remains a wonderful place for another story.

first: **You** consciously decide to place offspring or yourselves in certain activities.

your blessed with three offspring: james, joshua and christine are 15, 13 and 10. specific focus shall remain on joshua and spiritual inequities received in school.

ergo:

involved in numerous extracurricular activities within youth, You, excelled with all attempted and were having offspring excel through generational completeness. question. was **Their** enrollment within extracurricular activities for **Them** or You? reared with type a personality, thus, offspring were performing similar activities.

one day joshua arrived home from school saying, 'football, soccer, baseball or swimming,' what ever the extracurricular activity, 'sucks.' persona enmeshment. 'kids are mean to Me and no one understands, that I don't like playing that sport.' parents, attempt having all things better for **Their** emotional children, thus, console **Them** and soothing **Their** personal feelings, attempts comforting **Them** accordingly. joshua's Mother says, 'sweetheart I love You, get back and try it again tomorrow.' coincidentally and correlated through **God's** grace, joshua's, **Father** arrives home. confidently entering home, observing a saddened joshua, says, 'come here son.' joshua, anticipates what is coming next. his **Father** says, 'your Mother said **You** had a very difficult time attending school today.' joshua, is nodding accordingly. Father, then says, 'shake it off son, these difficult moments are character building times, never give up and proceed forward as your only option: continue focusing.' building character, one of life's most important lessons everyone living learns. these lessons are appropriate for further in your life when You're unable winning. 'You know son, sometimes throughout your good life, You lose and that is alright. son, life sometimes throws curve balls, when We anticipate it right down middle: character is built when You refrain from receiving everything You want exactly as You want it.'

You're aware, losing control through specific instances, prepares Them for adult life. previous few sentences remain factual for building character, however, also may express within joshua that, his feelings were immaterial, thus, clearly less insignificant.

viewing numerous parents, living vicariously through Their children for feats they desired achievement or generationally, what they were learning, as well as performing.

allow Us delving deeper.

one question entering your mind, hopefully is, what shall remain best for joshua? on one hand joshua, does what parents desire and begins enjoying the activity or digresses because emotionally is discontented with every aspect of the particular activity or performs activity appeasing others, rather than pleasing his inner soul. complicating matters, further during maturation, joshua, either learns proceeding and continuing builds character for life or regresses, becoming complacent and despondent.

offspring are a younger You, however, rather than only You, have another human enmeshed, your spouse: if child is male, he may desire becoming more artistic and musical rather than athletic, as Father. please, allow him focusing upon something desired rather than Yours. preceding conception of humans, God, remains aware of correct paths for offspring, therefore, embrace how they feel, allowing God, to work through Them and finding Their numerous wonderful pathways and niches throughout life:

children desire receiving inner confidence as well as continuously embracing Their destinies through life: leading Them forward through God's continual love and appreciation. correlating, everything good, God, works through all individual's soul, thus, heart and mind for undeniable splendor of peace, through humanism and weather for Us.

lines at the grocery store diminish, stop lights remain green and your loving prevails while **You** shall receive more relative time, because **God**, knows **Our** feelings and thoughts for another, shining bright, as well.

allowing your ego as well as control to dissipate further and allow **God** to direct your family well, peace and harmony unites souls for a gentle future. envelop your gently humbled soul with originator of all goodness for life.

Chapter

CORRELATIONS

following writings shall progress **You** further with correlations in nature, thus, all living things. writings were conveyed through soul, from **God**, late august 2009, therefore, was instructed to speak with sean, regarding how trees, insects, animals and humans enmesh, feeling and flowing as one from **God**. coincidentally, the movie avatar was released two weeks following, reiterating **God's** wonderful correlations.

ergo:

humans, correlate with all living things, *We* are one with Them, they're one with Us. communications through humans, animals and nature are orchestrated, from **God**. **God**, enmeshes all humans goodness through **Their** feelings and thought processes. here are a few examples. returning home, pets remain aware how your day has proceeded; your soul, thus, energy enmeshes: they're happy seeing You, the same. remember, they are happy for they received calm occurrences through **Their** day. why they are happy, even if they have received negative occurrences through day, remains because they are content being alive, thus, humans could learn from Them. **God**, desires all humans, proceeding through **Their** day, disregarding negativity and trudging on for higher ground: from **God's** optimism love and peace, **We** shall also. secondly, **Our** dog phoebe, half yorkshire terrier and half poodle or yorkie-poo. as your pet, She remains highly cognizant of environment, thus, well aware from writer's facial expressions or thoughts, if She shall go for a walk or receive a treat. before proceeding, look up for a second: if alone with your pet, am betting he or She is looking at You, enmeshing brilliantly with your soul and wondering if they, may sit upon your lap or receive a treat, as **You** proceed deeper through your book. persona enmeshment remains why, over time, your pets become quiet humans.

through living things, **God**, is goodness for offspring, thus, everyone of Us.

God, desires **Us** viewing his great and magnificent world intrinsically perfect, it is. You, as well as, all mammals inhale what vegetation exhale and **You** exhale what vegetation inhale, **You** know this: **God**, shares nature and what are given remains functional, complimentary and perfected, through all additional species integrated. **You** feel, hear, see, touch and smell, what **God** has created for Us, through senses. **God**, remains who shares with Us, splendors within life, please embrace Them, thus, blessings have and are freely given for humans to respect and love accordingly. societies, comprise everything freely bestowed for Us: again, **We** are one with all. **God's** perfection shines well through blessings and solid relationships, globally: **God**, remains everywhere, through all times, appropriate, thus, apparently correct. **God**, and bad Spirit works through animals, thus, all living things: humans oppositional agendas, yield good or bad feelings and thoughts for others through and within **Our** enmeshments.

example: one dog, across the street barks incessantly, while male master is gone, because male dog remains protecting wife and children in home, alerting Them, if **You** will, when sounds and feelings emitted from humans yield unhappiness: he barks when neighbor with conflicting energy arrives home, however, contains outward vocability when a pacified neighbor arrives soon thereafter, thus, feels **Their** souls. **God**, spoke following information on halloween night of 2010: christian friends, teenage Daughter, were walking with calmed friends in front of home, **God** spoke,

'listen to how the dog remains quiet.' two hours further, **God**, had spoken again, **'go outside and listen, as the** stressed **and** overwhelmed **children walk by, dog shall howl loudly and continuously. animals, sense human feelings without seeing Them: good feelings or thoughts through mammals remains spiritual, immediate and induced, thus, when You're** lethargic **of** anger, anxieties, confusion, fearfulness **and** uncertainty **from one** bad **Spirit through humans and nature, I, shall await You.'**

calming bad Spirit or generational inequities seems impossible individually, and are. praying and evoking, **God's**, differential advantage, as examples for those present, life, becomes more positive daily: from **God**, ones good thinking, optimism, love and patience occurs through soul, thus, entire persona, heart, mind and behaviors.

from energy: nature and pets feel how **You** feel through the day, as many humans. **God's**, continually granting **You** and Yours calm, from him, through **Our** perfection.

remain aware, all humans remain here together as one, for two intrinsic purposes. one- furthering human lives peacefully. two- harmoniously adhering with **God**. lineages were instilled with, correct ideas through **Their** fore **Fathers** and Mothers however, occasionally they too, remained negatively distorted from one bad spirit.

cyclically, life hands **You** teachings, through those preceding You, thus, chains of anguish, anxieties, depression and feeling overwhelmed, are modifiable over time. from **God's** love, **You** become more fundamentally perfect, through his optimistic suggestions instilled upon your wheel of life. family, also instills appropriate and wonderful folkways through positive ideas and thinking, transcending boundaries.

presently, **You** may need deciphering, what shall remain best for Yourself, spouse, offspring and others. fleshly, humans choose behaving positively or negatively. foresight, three or four generations in future, what shall **You** desire instilled within great grandchildren's persona for societal function: optimism or pessimism, calm, or anxieties, patience or impatience, peace and love or anger, controlling and war?

'through robert's life, I, have asked him to pray for others to move certain ways or specifics transpiring and every time, immediately prayers occurred. trillions of correlations over life were from Me within his chosen soul and I, equate all goodness upon My earth, through every blessed soul perfectly well. listen, all negativity shall alleviate with Me through prayers and willingness. also, where in the bible is rapture mentioned? will there be a rapture? no. this remains man made from satan causing more uncertainty for numerous: a significant transformation within thoughts and feelings shall occur well from Me.'

FAILURE

very well, your next chapter, remains relative with how satan distorts perceptions, thoughts, feelings, and continual behaviors. as a fallen angel, satan, wants failing: specific instances **You** cease with progress, lie, deceive, manipulate, scream at others or have argument with significant other, satan's pleased and gave thoughts. bad entity has overbearing power, yet, remains appreciably less than **God's**, supreme. numerous individuals, encompassing all of earth's current societies who live only within humanism remain unaware, satan, remains reason for bad: working through everyone's souls, thus, correlates and affects individuals, families, governments and economies unwell.

You may ask, why is there evil? **God** speaks, 'negative **thinking and feelings account for an abundance within personal lives and** satan has infected terrorists **thinking and feelings. I, am truth, thus, light and pray You listen well from what remains spoken throughout these pages showing hope within those I have chosen well for others awareness.'**

asking and doing what **God** speaks for denouncing the bad entity every morning, negative entity, is allowed significantly less power and control through soul. then pray for heightened focus and progression, for present and future endeavors. following third spiritual rebirth, writer went through stages from, **God**, to see how devoted, faithful, optimistic and prayerful his respectful follower would remain. denouncing bad entity through the days, from **God's** suggestions, then pray for son, others, locally, nationally and globally, then negativity alleviates from what's its names will. negative Spirit remains present, throughout and within, your heart, mind and soul, however, focusing upon **God's** goodness, through You, peace becomes continuous. **You** see, both entities are present within all of Us, in fact, **We** vacillate or traverse throughout **Our** spiritual day, thinking and verbalizing optimistically or negatively: observe human behaviors through societies past and present. **You** have received enough negativity, when **God** asks, your writer shall expound further regarding negative influences upon humanism.

ending this chapter, **God** desires quoted.

'Following writer's final rebirth, his awareness increased significantly: (parable): when I desired him receiving questions from Me for this book and life, I spoke for him to pray for heightened awareness from God's questions, thus, My truth.'

'When teaching robert regarding the spiritual significance of nature, how I work through nature for humans good awareness. first, robert asks to do My will continuously: one day when outside, 100's of gnats were hovering right in front of his eyes. he asked why? I replied, because You remain blessed and chosen My Son and this remains one of countless examples of how I work through nature for humans: I directed these insects perfectly. when You were young, You saw these hovering insects as a nuisance, now You remain calm and aware they are a peaceful reward for your good thought processes and pleasurable demeanor. that evening, I told him to go to the brownlee's home. when approaching Their residence, I asked him to bless kyle and mianna further. he did and then asked if I would do this and I replied yes.

dusk came, when directing Them to the front yard, 100's of gnats hovered in front of Their eyes. they commented and robert said to remain calm, then spoke of the goodness and favor they showed and said, all remains well.'

Chapter

JOHN LUTHER AND
YOUR PROGRESS

greetings, following writings shall remain unedited and written mid august 2009, one month post spiritual rebirth and worked within **God's** spiritually induced euphoria. incorrect grammar, syntax and verbiage, restoration was lacking full development: please follow the general ideas.

present chapter expounds deeply, **God's** direction through your potential perfectly.

ergo:

whether your from a small town anywhere on **God's** earth or offspring, remaining from a factory worker within london, You're intelligent as a mayor in home town or c.e.o. of an international corporation. offspring of **God**, spiritually, **You** shall receive and are well affected, behaviorally, generationally, societally and environmentally. your affected from what's been, thoroughly instilled through your soul, from birth forward from many specific reasons, discussed for readers thus far. thinking of a plethora of individual souls, who had dysfunction within **Their** childhoods, as well: receiving capabilities and contented through life, remains **God's** blessing.

allow proceeding deeper. here remains perfectly, one place, other than writer's Father, a second fleshly example who influenced progression, through adult life. here lies, one man who remains respected differently from Father, however, his behaviors and demeanor, always remained kind, generous, soft spoken and calm. through wife molly, received enormous wonderful opportunity meeting this man.

he remains opposite of writer's Father, with demeanor and functional views.

shall refer to him as john, per his humbled, as well as, respected request.

without a doubt, john, remains quite an outstanding man: he was reared within a small town, becoming one of the greatest men, writer had privilege with meeting. **You** see, john remains calm, kind and patient, always looking **You** in your eyes, respecting You, as **You** happily reciprocate. he remains a man's man, very stoic, compassionate and powerful with every single word coming through his voice. john, is well aware how to have others listen: speak softly; with everyone around, they gravitate to him because of achievements, calmness and sanctified demeanor.

please, allow proceeding within his youth, specifically, eight years of age. while fishing with his Father, john, was given a first cup of coffee, **You** see, john, had a relationship with his Father, all son's have, generationally difficult at times: john, was sometimes told, **You** can do better, faster, as well as, more efficiently. years proceeded forward, when john was 16 in age, his **Father** luther, had passed. before inhaling a last breath, luther, had his Son come close, saying these words, 'son, take care of **Our** family.' writing this, **God** said, '**I was extremely present.**' john, received the responsibility of taking care of family, when a very young man. **You** see, this was exactly what his **Father** wanted: john, emerging a man, offering society more than he; thus, john, consciously and subconsciously knew, what he shall accomplish, from **God**, for himself, future wife and his Mother, gwendolyn.

You see, ultimately, his Mother lost Her husband, who was pillar of strength, thus, remained aware, She too, would grow dependent emotionally, upon john, as well. gwendolyn, deceased in 1998, very blessed, strong worker and wonderful thinker. following luther passing, Her mind and soul focused on future endeavors, rather than, past unchangeable specifics. memories, are flowing when writing chapter, through millisecond clips regarding conversations with **God**, when seeing gwen, with john. before Her passing, **God** said, **'write when john and You moved Her to bed, She and your eyes met: I, said pray for Her passing and coming to Me.'** She, immediately smiled and Her eyes opened wide for the first time in two years: unaware then, presently refrain praying for anyone to pass.

'Feeling wonderful from Me through Her, gwen came home soon thereafter.'

moving forward. john, a young man in rotc, military group within high school, was taught respecting others, self discipline, honor and play by the rules, perfectly.

john's, Father's dying words, lingered through his mind, thus, his drive and focus became his solace. soon thereafter he began focusing on football, in turn, this implementation of focus, was preparation, how he would view future life, pressing forward, through any adversity. his perseverance figuratively paid off, over time: john, lettered in football, becoming a great running back, for a small town, within oklahoma and his outstanding physical agility, from **God**, along john's life path. over time, he provided emotional, mental and physical support for blessed family. john thought continuously with referencing long term goals. **You** see, through his senior year, papa bear bryant, came within small town oklahoma, scouting john playing football with texas a&m. **God**, correlates everything good, for every human upon earth.

of course, john felt privileged, Mother gweneth and sisters were ecstatic, as well, however, remained extremely humble. john, became a star, unbelievable focus, strength and peripheral vision, he was the envy, of running backs across America. football, became his physical forte and cognitively, remains outstanding, as well: **God**, was and is, completely apparent, within and through, his future outstanding achievements and attainments on the following pages. **God**, is good through You.

attending texas a&m, john, involved with rotc: how **God**, remained directing him, attaining focus, dignity, respecting others, thus, molding his persona, for life. with **God**, completely through his soul, thus, heart and mind encompassed these three facets, john's, procession remained absolute, focused and wonderful solace. focusing on military aviation, john, became young pilot, with americas air force: here in story remains where, a plethora of emotional occurrences were blooming. from **God's** direction, john, met one remarkable female, while in rural oklahoma; mary received one beautiful heart of gold and She loves all others well.

meeting when they were young teenagers, love became first sight. **Their** love for another, became undeniably one of strongest, within, **We** shall say, creek county. john desired mary, She desired him. **Their** relationship became a fairytale story of love, orchestrated by **God**, these two blessed humans, were placed within each other's paths for good reasons: others, offspring, grandchildren and generational progress.

before procession. from **God**, through writer, shall quote a very important detail: numerous of humans, view good and bad instances or specifics, as coincidences. **God** speaks, **'there remain zero coincidences through wonderful splendors, I, orchestrate function, goodness and love for everything living: I remain only good and have a wonderful plan.'**

his, emotional desires were focused on mary, as well as, Her profound disposition remained apparent and exactly what he desired, preceding meeting Her eloquence. mary remains elegant, prominent with stature: Her **Father** was of great prominence. john, received three extremely, fleshly, significant reasonings for becoming great. one- **God's** desire. two- Father's desire. three- mary. walking mile after mile, to speak with Her following school as teenagers, through, **God's**, loving embraces. Her **Father** rupert's home, had only air conditioned and heated dance floor in state upon the early 1900's: remains the third floor of **Their** residence in rural oklahoma, where he and mary, presently reside, following 50 wonderful years.

returning within story. becoming a pilot with **Our** united states air force, john, was prepared and trained for anything, approaching his blessed and faithful path. focus was what was best for America, through his demeanor, focus, thus, resolve: mary, graduated with honors from oklahoma university, john, from texas a&m. they were married and deployed to bonn, germany. he trained, piloting f-16's. john, was best around, thus, having outstanding focus, determination and intellect. precisely how **God**, was training john, through his soul: loving **God**, thus, others, focused on progress, hence, became a maverick for any call of duty for America.

mission ceased with ending of cold war and returned back to America, with mary. when back in u.s.a., john, began piloting appropriately, with american airlines: john, became **Their** youngest captain, age 35. flying globally, from hub in dallas, john, is well acclimated with differing cultures. **God**, remains present through his three faceted self and continuously thinks of progression and praises **God**, often.

story expressed represents, absent bad entity's fear and anxieties; with **God**, through determination, education, environment, focus and training, **You** become limitless. anything becomes attained when living faithfully calm, generationally unaffected, thus, from **God**, through You, work ethic, drive and focus increase for your future.

finishing this chapter, shall change gears twice: writer is conservative and remains aware why **We** think, feel and behave as **We** do, as well as, aware of **God's** global functionality: there are reasoning there remains significantly less tornado deaths and hurricanes presently in America, brutal dictators are falling globally, spiritually heightened good thoughts for numerous and why media projects mostly negative. life is psychosomatic and **God** has a wonderful plan through one blessed and calming paradigm shift. life is good and so is your enlightenment.

these last paragraphs remain more quotes from **God** for You, to alleviate negativity from your mind.

'When anywhere, silently ask Me to bless the people around You. albeit, with one friend or a stadium filled with people: this takes a couple of seconds and most importantly, You remain living in the Spirit with Me. the more You do this, the further blessed, enveloped with good and frictionless life becomes your soul, thus, heart and mind.'

Chapter

SPIRITUAL CONFIDENCE OR FLESHLY FACADE

present writings, relates how **Our** fleshly, verbal psychosomatic influences, affects spiritual beliefs through human souls, globally. writings, occurred october 2009. regard the chapter as emphasis with modifications. '**understand Our writings**.'

ergo:

as **God's** offspring, You, typically remain born emotionally and mentally perfect: your cerebral cortex, processes and performs numerous complex tasks all at once. one moment, please, allow taking **You** back in time, year, 1988. was a freshmen, attended hendrix college, that maintained 1000 students, since conception, 1867. only 250 students, were chosen each freshmen year from across the united states. year 1988, hendrix, academically was ranked third, following harvard and yale. half of freshmen class since conception in 1867 remained national merit scholars.

before procession, writer's gloating remain unbecoming, however, in 1988, these empirically factual statistics remains truth. half of the professors were immodest atheists, therefore, your aware what shall transpire next, regarding, psychosomatic information transgressed. first class was biology. professor, walked to podium. students fell silent, when he clamored his gavel and proceeded with these words, 'there is no **God**!' he spoke these four words so loudly, echoing had occurred. preceding him speaking sentence, voice in mind said he would state this verbatim.

profoundly, this one statement impacted, your writer for 22 years, because, these four words lingered in back of mind, fleshly pondered, maybe there was no **God**, however, knew correctly and was influenced from humanism. then proceeded with trimester, learning evolution through darwinism. was eighteen, comparable with impressionable classmates, was easily swayed from his intellect or so had thought.

reason your writer was unable to understand what was occurring was spiritually conflicting through thoughts: now aware, negative entity was also saying this professor was correct. all of life, sometimes continually through thought processes, received information regarding good and bad, thus, always believed other people received, as well, yet, told zero others, ever, until now, from **God's** desire for writer to do so for readers. living, fleshly facade, however, remained spiritually confident: what was learned, from humans, hindered immensely what was learned previously in life, from **God**. although was an athlete for hendrix, academically, lacked inner confidence, thus, psychosomatically, believing was less than apropos for curriculum there and life.

generationally, was demeaned and belittled during rearing, thus, believed self was unintelligent, rather, '**You** will be nothing,' as expressed from Father, because of his own insecurities, when your writer, was age two. **You** see, writer excelled in a physical realm only, **You** understand why. cognitively, this was shown true, for academic performances preceding college, as well. shall **We** delve, in humanism?

sure, **We** shall, let **Us** proceed. life for self, throughout youth often regarded fun, class clown, center of attention and athlete: many laughed with or at your writer: discussed previously, negative attention remained better than zero, upon youth. consciously and subconsciously, these egocentric and narcissistic behaviors were instilled generationally, as well. Father, would become aware of the repercussions stemming from his behaviors and words to his son, partially, over decades of time. shall, always love him, though. having lived, through previous generation, reared upon a farm, his work ethic remains splendid, thus, earning what he has received.

presently, **God's**, industrialized and technological world has become, whom have better, thus, current material items. albeit, vehicles, clothes, hand held devices, residences, money, objects and more. hmmm. **God**, again is far from impressed. remember, **God**, remains well aware of all your thoughts, as well as, behaviors. **God**, also views mortals judging another with what items they posses when humans shall respect another with how true to **Their** word they are and good natured **Their** heart remains.

individually, as well as, societally, **We** are imploding before the explosion occurs. as **We** spiritually digress throughout day, especially, preceding traveling in public, everyone are worried regarding **Their** own egocentric image. granted life has been this since life's conception, however, how much time is lost thinking of Yourself? from **God**, think of offspring, spouse, friend or another assisting with your solace.

how do **You** receive solace or peace of mind? more than likely, **You** are thinking regarding another human or Yourself, whom, remains related within flesh, as well. with earths present state, shall, **We** think of humanism for receiving comfort from another depressed, overwhelmed and anxious mind or have one on one, with **God**.

here remains one other solution which shall work wonderfully well. when mind races, frazzled or overwhelmed, stop what your doing, proceed into distortion less place, away from others. albeit, the stair well in office building, your car or bathroom. once, **You** become partially relaxed, focusing on breathing for 60 seconds, while contemplating your navel.

once, arriving within your happy, peaceful place, close eyes and humbly, pray for **God**, to relieve, emotional pain and discontentedness. please, use specifics. let go and believe. **God**, alleviates overwhelmed feelings and sadness, sometimes immediately. all that **You** need, is praying and believing. if your immediate relief comes, great, however, **You** may need some practice and modify, negative thinking and behavior, from bad Spirit through **You** causing pain. when relief comes and shall, calmly thank **God**, for wonderful relief, anticipating calm and reassuring, '**You're welcome.**' **God**, communicates through You, as well.

proceed with calmness and confidence, through the remainder of the pacified day. pray often, through your entire life. while typing, doing laundry, mowing lawn, playing stock market or landing in turbulence. **God**, is good through all offspring.

49

FOCUS

once upon a time, humans walked slowly with **Their** eyes focused forward, relying peripherally, for general interests related through sight. many digressed or began having unfocused vision, from numerous distortions placed through **Our** existence. coupled through increased demands from nurturers, offspring, work or others, life becomes overwhelmed for many. following sentences remain broad solutions for feeling overwhelmed. rather than bombarding your life with a plethora of things, return through a more basic existence, focus upon what remains most important, a comfortable relationship, with **God**, working well through **Our** families and others. observe life with calming splendor, thus, happiness and optimism as babies are: cooing and grinning uncontrollably seeing a smiling faces looking back on **Them**. **Our** loving and wonderful thinking, is **God**, working through, whomever remains optimistic, smiling and thinking of calming prayers for individuals, thus, societies.

children of **God**, feel and observe **Their** parents behaviors and persona, via, senses. infants, view environment with complete benevolence and behavioral insecurities are spiritually felt, observed and instilled, thereafter, from many unaware parents. **Our** behaviors are emulated by offspring: consciously and subconsciously, youths, progress through life, internalizing sounds, sights, objects and aromas, perfectly: these are filed away into subconscious mind, retrieved later throughout **Our** lives. your aware, sometimes **Our** minds become overwhelmed with incorrect, therefore, irrelevant information and many express **Their** fleshly agendas, hindering further.

allow following information occurring in your day, as other obtainable solutions. prioritizing or cognitively comprising a list of who remains important; **God**, shall remain number one- your family, offspring, others and **You** shall be distant second.

without electricity, lights shall be off: without gas, vehicles shall remain motionless.

viewing negative distortions around You, if vanished, would allow **You** receiving appropriate peaceful course filled with calmness. here remain a few suggestions.

rather than playing on computer or talking on phone for personal communication numerous hours a day, focus upon what remains important, think regarding family needs and assisting others progress. slow gate and fixate your pupils with focus, while excluding obstructional peripheral distortions and then shall **We** say, when performing physical tasks focus upon your breathing, pondering your happy place where calmness remains felt completely within. here remains one other solution.

lying on your back, with zero or minimal distortion, place a pillow under knees, contemplate navel, thinking of **God**, and comfort received through loved embrace. further; imagine a black ink blot splattered upon white canvas, then focus mind within center of black ink blot and refrain from delving peripherally within pallid or white background: remain focused upon complete love and blackness within. exclude auditory sounds or thoughts emitted, while relaxing tight muscles with every slowly exhaled breath and receiving consistent peace, as well as, tranquility. from **God**, through mind and soul: writer, was taught this while lying upon bed, following traumatic brain injury when 18. mind raced and emotionally, body was physically exhausted from the spiritual inequities given personally within rearing, and publicly, psychosomatic labels were placed on depressed persona through humans.

You see, inner confidence in your adult persona is derived significantly from what your senses gathered, from birth through age six: **You** know this and aware current and past interpersonal relationships and societal occurrences, affect your persona. why might **You** desire specific humans to enmesh with, throughout stages of life?

preceding conclusion of your book, this palpable question shall become answered.

short answer. life is spiritual, upon every moment **We** remain drawn to goodness or otherwise: aware or unaware, understood or misunderstood, humans progress or digress throughout **Their** lives because of spiritually driven assistance or control, thus, dualistic energy through and within.

often times, many females predicate how they feel contingent on others approval: why, are most females considerate of others? generationally, enabling behaviors became learned, observing Mother figure and societal observances throughout life.

behaviorally, all males have propensities, thus, loving, caring and full of emotion.

spiritually, **God** remains female as well and desires humans becoming compassionate for all.

God is calm, compassionate and goodness through your good self: thank **You God**. 'You're welcome.'

countless males and females alike, deep down, sometimes, lack inner confidence, because they were belittled, controlled, demeaned, oppressed or ridiculed through rearing; then many throughout **Their** lives from other humans- psychosomatically, conveying **Their** perverse, thus, spiritual insecurities verbally within your presence.

allow for your further delving. preceding four generations, your fore **Fathers** and Mothers, acquired, optimistic and pessimistic mannerisms instilled through Them: one unsuited or oppositional view, life was more difficult meeting innate needs.

relative, what was prepared for dinner that evening was hunted, grown on farms or purchased within town or city butchers. meeting families needs were primary: all residing there, were working, living, loving and respecting lives freely given. from **God**, confidence was derived from completing chores, given from parents or elder siblings. most of **Their** days were spent together as a family working for one important common purpose, life, surrounded with **God's** overflowing abundance. praying often, humbly believed **Their** lives remained from **God**, for five undeniable purposes; praising **God**, loving family, neighbors, offspring and many others well.

within present society, human lives, generally, have become simple or overwhelming, dependent on thinking, choices and faith, from **God** or bad entity through yourselves. frictionless or friction filled, remains your most important choice. choose wisely.

life remains simple, comparative with former generations, however, many receive increased difficulty through implementing distortion, within many unnatural ways. first, **God**, taught inventing faster, technologically effective and efficient devices. second, cognitive abilities given, shall suffice sufficiently for remembering what remains important, thus, rearing healthier offspring; **You** proceed having calm and less overwhelmedness societally because of calm from **God**, through numerous blessed humans.

lastly, allow having one specific point made clear, your writer, loves watching indy racing, risk takers, down hill and aerial skiers; in fact, learned barefoot water skiing upon first attempt when 12, long line. **God** said, '**fast enough, stand up.**' then, voice spoke after 100 yards, 'now **You** will fall flat on your face.' and did.

taught **God** was wrathful, believed negative thought processes or voice was **God**.

over life, **God** revealed, stimulation overload yields many significant internal and external consequences. returning with your basics of life, feeling underwhelmed rather than overwhelmed yields **You** significantly reduced doctor visits, anger, anxieties, headaches, medications, psychiatric appointments, stress, stomach pain, ulcers or other indemnities fleshly incurred emotionally through soul and psyche. negativity absorbed throughout life or within your rearing internally then externally influenced remains the cause for higher blood pressure. fleshly and temporal originating spiritually and progresses throughout **Our** thoughts, thus, behavior and digression occurs increasingly further in overwhelmed masses of youth and adults.

before closing your chapter, **God** desires five quotes: first one relates an instance related with writer personally, second how **God** spoke for healing ex wife molly and third remains relevant to human thoughts and behavior throughout this earth, fourth remains an observance and finally a solution.

'Following his final rebirth, I, asked robert if he desired to see it rain from blue sky? he said, yes and I spoke, pray for Israel, as well as, numerous other nations. he did as asked and then I said, good, now pray for rain to fall from a blue sky, he did and immediately light rain fell in neighborhood where he resides.'

'Molly came to receive Their Son evon late 2010 from a weekend with robert: She expressed She was going to the doctor the following day for microscopic surgery: I spoke through Her to say these words and then spoke to robert to tell Her She no longer needed this operation because he silently asked Me if I could heal Her? I said yes, now pray for judea and She is healed: this occurred over a second. several weeks previously, robert had overheard molly's Mother was needing a second surgery and he asked Me if this could be alleviated; I spoke yes, My son, pray for bethlehem and calm through any wanting unrest upon My blessed city.'

'March 1ˢᵗ 2012 he asked Me why the taliban, al qaeda **and other religious** extremists **cease to fall from prayer? son, this shall occur in My time from numerous chosen offspring's prayers rather than your own. I have a wonderful plan.**'

'**Observe human behaviors upon all of earth;** rioting, deviants **in london and financial markets** collapsing **globally, in 2008-11, You think it is coincidence? then occupiers of wall street in u.s. or global** negativity **affecting all others are from** satan **through humans, thus, affecting countless others and living peace.** good and bad **thoughts, thus, roller coaster global markets rise and** fall **arrive spiritually through emotions, thoughts and behaviors within humans.** continue **remaining** controlled negatively **through souls, minds, decisions or elevate Our relationship from Me, through faithfulness, peace and prosperity.** loved spiritually perfect and controlled unwell **remains your illusion of choice: let go and ask, I remain aware what shall occur through everything within humanism and earth's calming weather.**'

'**Living within the Spirit yields more wonder than your intermittent** negativity, anger **and** disbelief. **I, am God, through You: rather than** believing You're powerless, **reside safely within My good Spirit and receive more of your illusion of humbled power and goodness than imagined.** live comfortably with Me: You and Yours shall be directed well.'

Chapter

50

LEARNING FROM PAST GENERATIONS

proceeding well. historically, the present chapter shall return your awareness of how the culminated human consciousness correlates with the spiritual world. the spiritually induced weather affects local, national and global populations, often unwell: future generations shall learn, over time, the weather has calmed for a reason. chapter was revealed first quarter of 2010 for many whom are enlightened further.

ergo:

during the roaring twenties within wonderful America, a plethora of consumers lived complacently regarding lifestyles: narcissism and self attention was prevalent. numerous owned new cars, televisions, as well as, homes: people lived within a cyclically relative technological mania. times were progressing differently than the industrial revolution, modifications internalized, rather than factories efficiency. wanting then purchasing unneeded items left many living beyond **Their** means. sound cyclically familiar? economic correction came thereafter with a significant stock market depression. suddenly, through nature, one unbelievable dust bowl, enveloped the drought infested farmland in mid west: completely barren, they felt hopeless and overwhelmed, because media and communications, through society were infectiously negative. sound familiar? reading thus far, **You** are aware why. masses, were feeling hopeless and compounded with irritability, discontentedness, overwhelmedness and restlessness, thus, numerous anxieties were occurring often. with few psychological medications most relied on faith within **God's** natural remedy, others pessimistically infected, thus, bad feelings and thoughts affected millions.

farmland was emaciated and numerous christians respected **God's** nature, thus, powerfully trudged forward and continued working if a job was found, however, countless others were discontented, hopeless, impatient, irritable and overwhelmed.

sound familiar? seeing a pattern here? yes. cyclically, 100% of his humanism, comparable with present societies, many remained unaware, the bad entity has yielded negativity throughout history and shall into the future. **God** desires to yield **Our** safety, good will, peace and reciprocated favor.

please observe spiritually induced human thinking, feelings, behaviors and media occurring continually around everyone. **God** is only goodness.

proceeding further within history. 1870's, western europe's industrial revolution. what followed? black plague and numerous other ailments affecting the masses. coincidence? zero. observe the weather, during these specific moments in time. throughout history, when individuals and masses commence feeling empowered intellectually, monetarily and egocentrically, thus, relying less, spiritually on **God** ; bad entity, continually keeps all societies, through humanism, figuratively in check. lives are spiritual, people. as your mind is reading and thinking, proceed further. abundance currently, with similar constructs are overwhelmed through numerous confusions and distortions through **Their** existences, sometimes, unbalancing lives:

remember more recent years of 1930, 1980, 1987, 2008, 2009, 2010, 2011, 2012, 2013, 2014, 2015? presently, life is becoming better for numerous while others remain complacent following Their will rather than the creator's.

'When You ask and follow My good suggestions, rather than your own, life remains certain, safe and flowing. receive increasing patience, good direction, blessed decisions, thoughts, feelings and emotions. remember, the bad energy works to decrease humans faith through Their consciousness and causes every negative aspect of humanism. mechanical accidents, electrical overloads as well as grid failures also remain from negative energy for humans uncertainty. life remains spiritually driven for everyone alive. the reason all accidents occur, remains from a negative and uncertain energy throughout the human consciousness and physical earth: this remains the absolute truth.'

pardon interruption, refrained from frightening You with an onslaught of pessimistic reality, however, on what juncture shall individuals implement praise and prayer more? hopefully, before all regress further, becoming comparable with movies mad max and book of eli, when controlled spiritually unwell through an egocentrically bad ideology and consciousness.

christian bible, again, is correct through this specific. ephesians 6:10-20, are few versus stating exactly. basically, place the whole armor of God upon You: 'humans wrestle against the ruler of darkness rather than flesh and blood. those whom riot prayer rallies and want separation of Me and state, who remains controlling Their souls, minds, thus, behaviors for uncertainty sometimes?'

shall You remain complacent, regressing deeper through bad spiritual stagnation, affecting your feelings and thoughts, thus, societal ruin; or increasingly connected, from God's calmness, faith filled happiness, optimism and praise through the directed well masses whom desire peace, wellness and future stability together as one? latter is easily obtainable.

'Judges, wanting separation **from Me, in public schools or allowing occupations, what assists everything perfectly well? good or** bad **spirits: life seems as they remain real correlations, correlate well with Me.'**

corinthians one: chapter six, speaks well, **God's** observation of **Our** law processes.

'believers should not sue **each other.'** dare all having a matter against another go to law before the unjust and not before the saints. do ye not know the saints shall judge the world and if the world shall be judged by **You** are ye worthy to judge the smallest matters? know not that **We** shall judge the angels.' angels and saints are **God** alone and through humans.

relaxed differs from stagnation and aggressiveness shall remain extinguished from your blessed family and professional lives.

with **God's** continually available assistance, **You** shall abundantly desire rebuking unhealthy, distorted thinking, furthering satan's intentions through humans on earth. calmed completeness, joy, patience, thus, tranquility remains what **God**, endlessly desires for who are reflected from your bathroom mirrors. **God**, is good through Us.

implementing **God's,** assistance and patience rather than shunning as irrelevant or less relevant, **God,** allows and empowers You, thus, happiness heightens perfectly: angry, anxiety, confused, distorted, lethargic, overwhelmed and mislead remains denounced and vanishes.

earth's weather, humans consciousness and everything upon earth remain spiritually determined. desire perfect direction in life? **You** shall proceed through your day living in the Spirit rather than of this world. when **You** do this, your entire being remains enveloped with wellness rather than otherwise. life is good and **You** remain blessed further.

'Seasons, global warming and cooling remain cyclically continual: **humans have minimal significance: air quality and cleaning the air is important for all of My offspring's health.'**

'Weather anomalies shall continue to decrease globally and then, the focus shall remain on certain humans learning My absolute truth.'

'In 2010, My and your writer was revealed My power through everything. his first and second stages, regarding calming winds and ceasing lightning within storms, where I ask, are slated at the end of this book. following these stages, I told him a storm was coming in five minutes with significant lightning. he asked Me what shall occur? I spoke, lightning was negative energy and for him to pray for God to denounce satan from the storm. lightning ceased immediately and he thanked Me: then I asked him to pray for winds to calm and they calmed as well. I have asked him to pray for Me to decrease the power of typhoons, hurricanes, tornadoes, tsunamis and for specific occurrences of goodness to transpire globally. following watching the news from My direction, he asked if this was God correlating his mind with what would occur or because of his prayers? I replied, all goodness originates from Me: correlations and prayers are all from Me for others and there are zero coincidences. asking and following every suggestion, My writer receives continuous good direction for others.'

Chapter

UNITED STATES AND GOD

current chapter relates for You, **God's** influence upon those remaining abundantly faithful, thus, shall proceed through **Our** optimistic, as well as, loving perspective. love and assistance America shows other countries remains absolutely wonderful: **God**, remains absolutely aware of united states love, resource and time expressed from individuals contributions for nations having palpable needs, therefore, blesses offspring and volunteers accordingly. what America brings to earth's table, bar none remains the best, thus, numerous believers are humbled through **Their** gifts. **We** praise **God** for blessing all good citizens. **We** love as zero, care as zero nation and remain with fallen man, woman and child as zero other. exact reasoning why people desire coming here rather than reversed. **You** know this. **We** have many mortal flaws, however, passion and compassion for nations needing shall proceed.

if residing outside of America, **You** absolutely remain blessed by **God**, especially when faithful, loving others and remain less infected from spiritual feelings that sometimes overwhelm humans as in u.s.. also, numerous mortals encompassing governments, globally, are complacent: through personal agendas, consistently and continuously are placing glass ceiling upon blessed, imaginative, thus, innovative thinkers desiring progression of **God's** world, absent socialism and government control. observe europe throughout **Their** former seven decades.

originally, desiring separating government interference in **Our** personal lives, **God** believes as stated in bible, **You** shall remain true to your word regarding business and other ventures public or private. meaning, while government assists enabling those needing enabled, further hinders numerous who prosper through hard work, blessed imaginative thinking and perseverance given from **God**, through **Them** all.

'**Everyone, desires others remaining true to Their word, however, throughout history,** satan **upon times** distorts **perceptions, thus, alters human senses, now You need documents in writing as empirically true.**'

population expanded, thus, societal masses of individuals were needing direction. government, an encompassing entity brought structure for the masses, needing this, however, 'We the people' within America's constitution remains specifically this, compounded significantly through You, as an individual, shall learn who **You** are electing then vote; **Our** system is imperfect, however, is the best country on earth. reasoning, America was founded from **God's** principles and values through Them. originally, as today, individual free citizen's elected **Our** government; they created then maintained structure for those who desired an intrinsic personal relationship from **God**, who assisted and sustained **Our** future through hearts, minds and souls. accepting specifics **You** are unable changing, **God**, allows **You** courage to change many **You** think **You** shall and receive sufficient wisdom and awareness knowing the difference. unite following **God's** will, thus, together through **Us** from his perfect guidance.

'**My offspring: societal masses, religious and spiritual mortals who continue** defying **My good word of hope, love and peace, therefore, My wonderful spirit;** satan's bad Spirit **shall continue working through souls and physical earth. listen. You do have a choice, My optimistic and glowing future through You. choices are, listen to good suggestions through You. future is in Our souls from My direction.**'

Chapter

52

COMMUNICATION
AND FRIENDS

present chapter shall induce adoration through communications from a good **God**.

the current world has modified and **God** has as well. throughout his technologically unified world, he assists numerous offspring through all forms of communication. many reading, **God**, shows **You** wonderful miracles through mind, technology and nature allowing calm thoughts through humanism bettering the magnificent world. **God's** functional world through knowledge remain experiencing less war amongst major nations, thus, leading readers receiving good information regarding females. with more generational peace, females, remain taking a monetary lead in families. intelligent as males, females individualistic roles amongst industrialized and high tech societies are increasingly receiving an abundance and options for betterment. females, are extremely viable intellectuals, thus, many have unwavering personas. regarding emotions, they receive less emotional roles through several variables.

following sentences, relate three general specifics for all females currently living. one- generational progression: meaning, learning from rearing, emulating positive thinking and behaviors rather than otherwise, personas fleshly remain wonderful. two- living and working in spiritually blessed environments: within humanism, your surroundings and others mold your consciousness; when others receive good enmeshments, everything functions well.

three- saving most important for last, **God** : meaning, allowance and praying **God**, works within **You** and present others direction through life yields your heightened spiritual correlations, enmeshment, decisions, function and ideas for all involved.

'You comprehend what hope and faith entail. live with My Spirit and ask God to bless everyone preceding entering anywhere You traverse. remember, You are blessed further implementing these good suggestions: good enmeshments occur spiritually through humanism from My goodness within You and into others within your presence over time. if unsure what to do anywhere, ask and You shall receive.'

through all generations, some Daughters observed Mothers anticipated behaviors, precisely how **Fathers** deemed appropriate, in and sometimes absent his presence. aware feminine roles, over time, have increasingly modified, thus, similar to men, and females are wonderful leaders through personal, public, as well as, societally. current and your future insights are apropos, intended for many controlling males: females proceed behaving similarly as males, more become practical, over time. regarding Mothers, **You** may think, yes, what about all these wonderful offspring?

this too remains modified well for both genders anywhere upon the earth. please proceed.

fleshly, life would remain more wonderful if homesteads were reliant upon only one income, however, majority of households are reliant on both for sustainment: numerous parents leave **Their** children in daycare while working, therefore, shall render **You** two illustrations or visualizations regarding what may occur if **You** are. first example shall relate palpable suggestions assisting further when **You** remain spiritually, thus, emotionally, mentally or financially troubled within your living: both stories depend on your desire of following **God's** will, thus, following **God** s path in life are imperative for achieving anything good, better as well as best for all.

ergo:

michael and lovely spouse amanda have two offspring. they are struggling and living paycheck to paycheck, life remains overwhelming for **Their** entire family. refraining from attending church or believing they remain unable to receive **God's** good suggestions within **Their** minds, fleshly, these shortcomings were becoming prevalent throughout **Their** daily lives. one day, michael arrived home from work and told amanda he was now laid off. single paycheck was gone and lived on unemployment until a new job was found. weeks turned into months and hostility enveloped **Their** once sustainable family. michael, became depressed and needed work for his family: he remained reliant only upon will for himself rather than allowing **God's** guidance, working through him.

saturday evening preceding sleep, michael seeking **God**, his prayers for assistance progressed and **God** was listening, as he continuously does through **You** and Yours.

michael, was raised attending church and praised **God**, however, over time, began believing life was less dependent on **God** and on himself or others: faith dwindled. while sleeping, **God**, placed one wonderful vision of positive direction through his overwhelmed mind, thus, sustaining his absolutely beautiful and loving family. in a few hours sun was rising, michael felt prepared for anything from **God's** will: rising out of bed, he kissed wife amanda softly on Her cheek: asking calmly if he may assist having **Their** wonderful offspring prepared to attend one good church. persona enmeshment occurred from **God**, through Them, thus, everyone felt anew. perspective modified and they arrived to church: service spoke precisely for Them: believe, have faith, hope, love and follow **God** s direction, life grows wonderfully. following church, **God**, correlated one man who came directly up to michael and expressed immediate need for someone filling a vacancy in his personal business. over time, michael's family had returned on **Their** feet and life restored from **God**. **God**, chooses who believe, love others, praise him and envelop through splendor.

appropriately, here is a wonderful place for second story, please receive parables. some personal friends, kimberli and sean brownlee attend church sundays with two offspring: enmeshed, they facilitate many functions with **Their** children's lives. married for 15 years, they have two wonderful children, kyle, as well as, mianna: who are ten and seven respectfully. faithfully, **God** loving christians they remain educated and well versed with life, they seemingly have american dream fulfilled. kimberli's **Father** dennis is calm and abstained from alcohol/smoking entire life. kimberli's younger brother is involved helping others within community, as well. kimberli's Father, expressed for Her when She was a teenager that She could obtain anything with life, receiving positive affirmations boosted Her self esteem/worth, thus, She perfectly graduated summa cum laude from oklahoma city university. brilliant thinker, worldly She remains especially enmeshing with Her spouse sean.

shall be noted here: **God**, through **Them** both, established **Their** first meeting, thus, over time blessed **Them** with offspring: **God** spoke this to his messenger the first quarter of 2010.

sean, Her spouse, raced sailboats for team u.s.a. within two world competitions: commodores cup in hawaii and admirals cup in england. then sean embarked upon selling import vehicles and is well acclimated with finer things through life: versed with ferrari, lotus, lamborghini and porsche, **God**, blesses sean's life. when a youth, sean, competed professionally long distance water ski jumping and his **Father** owned one masonry company constructing tile and marble for the tallest building preceding devon tower here in bible belt within blessed oklahoma city.

back within story: kimberli, relatively young when meeting, therefore, thoroughly impressed with sean's stature for life and he attained numerous accomplishments. now middle age and reared within oklahoma sean remains versed devoted and helping others unconditionally throughout edmond, as well as, oklahoma city. sean remains a brilliant thinker and received outstanding genetics: behaviorally, he received a wonderful and powerful drive instilled from **God**, through his parents. receiving behavioral and genetic abilities, sean, progressed, well blessed for life. as years proceeded, sean, began working in stock market day trading, thus, had ability being home with **Their** children and wife kimberli traveled professionally, selling books to higher academia colleges throughout the central and eastern u.s. remaining blessed as husband and wife, as well as, Mother and **Father** from **God**. **You** may be wondering why they are in the book because life seems well for both: **Their** family remains as countless finding another way, thus, receiving faith, hope and love from **God's** abundant assistance and presence through all of **Us** perfectly.

You see, sean's **Father** passed and there remain several words and actions sean desired expressed, however, unable for his **Father** received a stroke. here lies where **You** may receive additional parables. **You** may be male or female, black or white, affluent or impoverished: all **God's** offspring have received pain.

through rearing process, most parents instilled becoming better, settling for zero less than best, thus, **Our** good achievements have shown how well **We** have listened: remember, what **You** experience within your senses remain spiritually induced.

deeper **We** shall go. sean and kimberli are wonderful with family, church and community, however, lack traits as everyone does related with juggling family and professional life: fleshly, generational and societal instillations affect all within family. several times throughout day, as many significant others are currently, they seem unable to have a meeting of minds, however, they are one mind and needs differ. kimberli and sean work well together and **Their** hearts, minds and souls enmesh, sharing responsibilities and loving another faithfully well along **God's** good path. having faith and allowing **God**, wonderfully instruct your life, releases numerous burdens satan continuously places in front of You, seeking failures. moral of story: working together, as well as, glorifying and praising **God**, remains reasoning for everything good; relationships stay together, offspring are more content, therefore, culminated, society benefits accordingly for an absolutely more wonderful journey along the gentle path, thus, future.

here is a place for another story. **God** revealed to his vessel the process of calming winds and shall be spoken later in the book. the thought process and occurrences are from **God**.

from divine direction, your writer spoke the information into kimberli's soul regarding feeling the gentle breeze for direction. She was working at harvard and needed to receive an item from a store on campus. She was unaware where to go and remembered the story of feeling the gentle breeze for direction. She let go of Her will and asked **God** to assist Her well through the gentle breeze. She said, 'the breeze gently pushed Me across campus and to a specific store. it was closing in five minutes so the timing was perfect.' She returned and said this to your writer. immediately thought, thank **You** **God** for directing Her perfectly well. **'You're welcome.'**

preceding previous few paragraphs regard functional modification of gender roles, with or without **God** : without, allows obstacles from the bad entity, causing pain and hostility through numerous individuals or family hearts, minds and souls, globally.

few examples: observe high schools whom are banning prayer at graduations and ludicrous occurrences transpiring through governments human souls, thus, minds, then implementing counter productive behavior, belief and laws for **Our** offspring. when **You** proceed to the source of all goodness there remain zero biases.

continue disassociating **God**, from **Our** lives and view societies digression further within numerous globally, however, **God** has a wonderful plan.

back to story: in present society, gender roles have been blurred, thus, male and female are intertwining professional and nurturing roles together as one, however, all of history has stated exactly males remain as 'the man,' and current societies, females are as intellectually assertive, wonderful communicators, honest and sincere; **God**, had females and males having similar propensities through thinking, as well.

life, remains continual change through **Us** and many are having difficulty adapting, because egocentrically most believe **Their** way remains the correctly perceived one.

societal modifications from **God's** blessings works well, and those denying many blessings, thus, implementing pessimism are having an increasingly more difficult time presently and throughout humans history. **God** spoke,

'**Why do many think** negatively **then have many** problems **throughout Their days? I have a plan for numerous chosen. asking the will of your creator, You and Yours shall be provided for well.**'

regarding every faction of life, rather than receiving internal and external friction from your ego directed will, one shall desire peaceful lovingness. perspectives and perceptions modify well: desired peace within your soul, heart and mind becomes achieved, overflowing with gentle graceful love. once, the earth was molten rock and now receives **God's** gentle embrace.

'**When You desire My gentle direction and communication within, I remain always present: as your faith grows, all that is needed is to ask Me what shall occur? I then shall calmly and gently direct your mind with wonderful suggestions enveloped with certainty through your thoughts, feelings, visions and desires. I have a wonderful plan within your Spirit for a lifetime of peaceful love: You shall access** disheartening **information or experience My simply gentle and peaceful embrace.**'

UNDERLYING ISSUES

shall **We** proceed further? yes **We** shall. an abundance of information slated thus far regards reasoning as to why any and all inequities occur through humanism. within the current chapter, your specific awareness shall heighten with solutions regarding what occurs within and through numerous whom continue thinking, acting and reacting to many others.

when **You** become aware that all emotionally instilled inequities are originated spiritually through **You** and others in your presence, shall **You** become aware that relying upon **God** ceases these inequities, when he allows. out with your illusion of control and in with available assistance.

the industrial revolution occurred and brought efficiency for numerous: the technological revolution remains occurring and assists countless globally whom allow as well. however, as stated previously, numerous continue overwhelmed sometimes. have tight shoulders, headache or stomach pains? take a pill. have i.b.s., high blood pressure, anxieties or adhd? take another pill remains what humanism wants from You, your money and your relative time. drug makers are ecstatic, in fact, the pain may become alleviated momentarily, however, if your liver received an ability to verbalize, it would express otherwise, 'please, alleviate your negative spiritually induced feelings and thoughts.'

'slow down, listen to your emotional pains, they are given for a perfect reason and they are spiritual, thus, fleshly induced through humans fear, negative thinking, uncertainty and discomfort within your soul.'

returning back to basics then remain there shall become solace for **You** and Yours. **You** may be asking Yourself, 'returning back to basics and then remaining there?' for all intensive purposes, decreasing clutter and distractions within your life allows wonderful calm. cell phones are useful, however, are they imperative for living? how did societies proceed twenty decades previously? **God**, through and within numerous asking. individual overwhelmedness occurs because of a plethora of culminating reasons discussed throughout your book: significant specifics regard lessening or alleviating a plethora of unneeded marketed items humans impulsively desire receiving from those wanting a piece of return on investment pie.

often, living remains congested because of how **You** fleshly choose living your life. ancestors remained relatively overwhelmed in the past needing zero medications, **We** need zero for emotional tension filled head aches, back or stomach pain either. **God**, equips **Us** with natural medications for all societies, globally: when **You** remain good and chosen with **God**, life remains underwhelmed and increasingly healthy. expounding further with many palpable suggestions. if **You** live within a large city, metropolis or **You** are hyper stimulated: upon your day off or vacation drive away from everything made from humans and then turn off your electronic devices.

once completely away from distortion, turn off vehicle and proceed outside under sun or moon with nature: consciously letting go what binds **You** most, your mind. close eyes and contemplate your navel: **God's** calm is abundantly present for You. breathing slowly, pray for **God's**, pacification and serenity for family and others. enmeshing your soul with **God's** calmness and love rather than humanism or your influenced mind,

God's adoration envelops throughout your persona perfectly well for his perfecting reason, You.

zero overwhelmedness and hyper stimulation cease. now look around upon what **God**, has given You, nature encompassed with his calmness, peace and serenity. when inhaling fresh air slowly, take heed how wonderful and calm life really is. traveling home, pray, rather than focused upon negative details or small stuff: remember, life is all small stuff, bad Spirit is who makes humanism more difficult. life becomes placated because **God's** good enmeshment flows within **You** and those **You** love perfectly well. **God** shall continually remain goodness within everything: your soul.

expounding further: **God**, desires all of his faithful offspring remaining pain free. he placed **Us** upon wonderful earth for purposes of developing and attaining peace wonderfully correlating through your heart, mind and soul, thus, progressing well. headaches, ibs, infections, rashes, sickness, stomach-aches, thus, every inequity remains ultimately from one bad Spirit through **You** and infects your three faceted self: (soul, heart, mind.)

'**Modify what You're doing and pray to Me, delete your** negative **load with Me. remaining continuously present, I, desire calming and loving your wonderful heart increasingly more when following My direction rather than your own. when You have received enough** pain **within humanism from one** bad **spirit, I, have always lived through Our soul, heart, mind and body waiting for your prayer to alleviate** negativity **through your soul and behaviors for Our peace. there is zero** hell**, this remains another** fearful **causing** scare **tactic from one** negative satan. **when deceased, love and calm embellish perfectly and I, allocate peaceful direction within My and your perfected heaven.'**

'hell **is how many live upon My earth and an abundance of** badness **shall cease when refraining from expressing** inequities **and** negativity **into others. thoughts and feelings determine life. where do they derive? earth's spiritual revolution is upon Us: an optimistic enlightenment.'**

'**Numerous humans across the earth shall become aware of this information. You are aware, many specifics within this book differ** from what humanism has been taught thus far throughout numerous offspring: together rather than dividing remain one. I shall be perfect awareness: humans once believed the sun revolved around the earth. humans shall be revealed spiritual truth, all religions were in bonds: this information shall occur in My perfect timing within the chosen. desire to be chosen? continue reading further and revealed truth.'

'This book has many purposes from Me, enlightening and bringing offspring together rather than dividing, are one. I have a wonderful plan: teaching truth and hopefulness for countless on earth whom desire calming love within Their consciousness. ultimately, I am the reason You are reading My enlightening words filled with hope.'

MIDDLE GROUND

welcome. from **God**, july 11ᵗʰ 2010. please, receive insight within this specific. through humanism, ultimately everyone thinks they choose **Their** paths or do they? yes, **You** may expound on positive or negative thoughts, therefore, your behaviors. **We** also, choose listening curiously, thus, internalizing through senses regarding medias pessimistic depiction of society, purchase unneeded items, showing others how much **We** posses monetarily with your vehicles, clothing, homes and jewelry. pardon interruption, **God**, sees prosperity wonderfully, however, also remains well aware of all human behaviors and thought processes. **God**, remains saddened because societies generally regard themselves, thus, what they idolize and receive and want rather than idolizing and receiving **God**. remember why **You** remain on earth.

God, desires **You** as his individual child loving another, remaining enmeshed with adoration, less conceit, as well as, respecting others unconditionally as **God** does: this includes who live in a lower caste or all people who assist your life working. these people and **You** are humans from **God**, attempting to live life to the fullest. because another person refrains from giving **You** monetary return, via, self serving conditions, your smile, kind word, unconditional respect and prayer remains what they need most if they blink and breath. **'pray for all, I, know what they are needing.'**

here are further solutions for an overwhelmed home. first and foremost, turn off electronic devices three evenings per week. there remains zero better interaction, fleshly, than human interaction, thus, communicating with another allows chores and responsibilities shared by everyone. accomplishing domestic tasks and contributing, yields wonderfully for offspring's self worth and esteem and assists further when they have children of **Their** own, thus, your wonderful grandchildren.

place chores on paper or personal computer as your budget and have meetings: sunday evening works well for entire family meeting together and all receive five minutes floor time: express appropriate solutions for family working functionally. facilitator, keep your tone optimistic through togetherness rather than apart with pessimism and anger: your operative and optimistic word spoken here is, together. most important, pray together for friends needing and those known and unknown. **God**, listens and answers all prayers in his time through your focused compliance. underwhelmed when responding to prayer, **God's** focus is continuously for You; granting blessings for all who seek guidance, love and listens in your time of need. **God**, desires abundance of service for **You** and Yours; taking your pain, loneliness and overwhelmedness away and replenishes your negativity with loving optimism.

God, remains alpha and eternal: beginning and there remains no end, thus, **God**, remains everywhere, at all times desiring happiness, as well as, your progression. **You** have two pertinent choices to make, remain overwhelmed within, predicated from distortions, via, negativity or relax with a good book or silence while praying for peace upon family and others throughout community, nationally and globally. when individuals come together for families and communities, this trickles down, becoming a catalyst for others desiring what **You** have, **God's**, calm and happiness. cynical readers may think these optimistic perspectives remain mostly outlandish: if **You** think pessimistically, why? shall **You** remain complacent and negative remaining off board or climb on deck having **God**, as Captain and then become underwhelmed, contented, placated, as well as, increasingly blessed and chosen. **God**, desires **You** getting out of **Yourself** and assisting others: **You** become amazed with joy, love and miracles from **God** within your life when helping anyone with less.

God, remains perfect: blessing freely through your offspring, **Yourself** and others.

psychosomatically **You** remain resolving spiritual and generational issues, as well. here lie three pertinent choices **You** shall live overcoming life's problematic areas. one: **You** may remain overwhelmed in life, thinking regarding past improprieties, receive distraction within thoughts and from others or allow **God** modifying **You** appropriately. if past, learn from your/ others received incorrectness: let go, proceed with corrected information. two: slow down and censure unneeded material possessions jumbling your living. three: receive middle ground thinking. meaning- rather than highs followed with resounding emotional, mental, thus, monetary lows: albeit, caffeine, stimulants, working, working out, shopping and over spending; focus on what remains most important, **God**, family, offspring and others. **God**, absolutely blesses **You** further.

in humanism, it's impossible pleasing all others: appease **God**, watch what occurs within and through **Yourself** and numerous known or unknown others in presence.

why do numerous attempt fulfilling themselves, through immediate gratification? your aware: feeling good for a moment briefly fulfills. allow for further delving.

sustainable decisions regarding middle ground thinking and behaviors yield less overwhelmed feelings, thus, replace these feelings with calmness, happiness, inner contentment and progress. fleshly, temporary fulfillment is inner incompleteness, generationally and then societally instilled, thus, inner incompleteness remains derived through your heart, mind and soul, ultimately from the bad spiritual entity through You.

stated previously, please, regard as emphasis. learned thoughts and behaviors are your nurturers, typically Mothers and Fathers, generationally instilled through You. all, desire implementing positive affirmations and curtail personas optimistically: denouncing learned pessimistic traits or behaviors assists **Our** wonderful progress. **God**, desires all humans positive progression above negative, however, multitudes are misunderstood and countless spiritually are remaining stagnant through **Their** flesh: also, many lack religion or spirituality, depending upon government to sustain **Them**. parable. praying only for **Yourself** rather than others keeps **You** interlocked with pain and stagnation. please proceed.

throughout history, **God's** offspring, individually attempt denouncing negativity, through **Their** obvious observations and observe pessimism as road blocks. first, behaviorally your flesh and human beliefs remain presently well or otherwise. secondly, pessimism breeds pessimism and subconsciously manifests as a big bad virus, infectiously enmeshed through numerous personas and souls then societally. thirdly, modifying others: if someone near **You** is negative, pray for **Them**, then find something more important: denouncing negativity, thus, finding function over time, they consciously become aware **Their** behavior needs adjustment and adapt. everyone shall win, behavior modifications occur from **God** through prayer. exactly as pessimism breeds pessimism, enmeshment of optimism occurs, as well.

people who come within your life, remain either there to build **You** up, from **God**, or break **You** down; humanism is predicated from spirits for succession or failures.

psychosomatic induced negativity is another splintered cog in satan's wheel of life: denounced, psychosomatically yields increased happiness, lower blood pressure, less emotional, mental and physical sickness, increasing longevity for his faithful. another solution: renouncing personal discontentment is sitting or standing erect, thus, less slouching, complacency or physical despondency that what's its name gives. implementing function and good thinking through You, **God**, is your higher focus: optimism, prayer, meditation, respect, honor, exercise, as well as, loving others as **Yourself** increases your acclimation of optimism, thus, discounts your pessimism. attending where faithful people go remains an example for offspring, Yourself, as well as, those observing your good enmeshment, thus, **God's,** perfection through You.

God, is wonderful love and the church shall always remain christ's bride.

'**Directed to church one sunday, I spoke for robert to see his pastor. She said She had received** negative **thoughts and feelings unto him. he reminded Her of God's teachings of asking Me to denounce** satan **through Her thought processes and feelings upon every awakening. She said She now has remembered. he then silently asked Me to denounce** satan **through Her thought processes and feelings and asked if I would do this? I replied, yes My son. the following sunday, She gave robert a hug and said thank You for the perfect relief, I have no more** negativity. **he said, please, thank who has given your relief rather than a vessel who remains directed well from God.'**

BIG BROTHER

previous chapter and others relates how **God**, remains **Our** wonderfulness, versus, what's its name's negativity and how good or badly infectious this becomes all, as well as, a few suggested solutions and behavioral modifications assisting **You** further. again, shall proceed with coming out of Yourself. these many specific behavioral modifications remain geared for everyone, assuming **You** are consciously, as well as, continuously desiring function and improving your persona, thus, entire being.

speaking with countless humans through previous two decades have realized how many times, especially among females, I, Me, My, Mine are used in one sentence. what happened? narcissistic humans comply.

God speaks, **'writer is speaking truth. throughout the bible I say, I, Me and My, however, I am Me, Mine, My, Ours Us, We, Them, You and Our goodness, as well as, loving others well upon My blessed earth.'**

compounded through each additional generation: societies unnatural progression of remaining within Yourself, behaviorally, has been learned upon rearing process. when working out at gym or mingling among others societally, appears numerous are within an egocentric haze with ipods, iphones or other personal components, and keep focused on only **Their** self while excluding human interaction altogether. **You** see, **God**, intends humans communicating and receiving spiritual bonds, thus, reliance with others: **You** remember previous writing regarding zero coincidences.

'Promoting goodness, I correlate good meetings continuously through private and publicly for offspring meeting one another for numerous good purposes.'

resolving problems, assistance, communication and contact information that are beneficial for personal and professional life, someone who may need a smile, your eye contact, hand shake, as well as, pleasurable intimacy naming only a few. throughout day and night time with current societal direction, why do many humans remain living within an egocentric haze and discounting others? what happened? oh yes, now 'I' remember. perceived as individual progression, however, internalized egocentric behaviors and thoughts are compounding unwell for many.

America and numerous societies globally: many remain becoming entitled. life for numerous, remains primarily focused upon outward aesthetic appearance. **We** are teaching children having fun and remaining glamorous, while others teach complete psychological, societal and technological unity: good example is china. typically, **We** teach **Our** children through societal behaviors to aesthetically appear beautiful, while china teaches focus and telekinesis related to business world: **Their** offspring receive curriculum and daily instructions surpassing Ours ten fold. **We** have pageants stating who the most gorgeous are: while aged ten, china's are learning return on investment, business efficiency, as well as, exponential growth. America remains needing to understand that **Our** children have an ability learning adult business skills while youthful. **You** remember writer's roommate, vassily. what he was taught 35 years in arrears, while ten in russia, America is presently learning in college. why? your writer remains aware and You? do business skills remain important? yes. with your awareness of why and how all progress occurs, everything heightens.

information shall be learned relatively within any age. just as pharaohs, who were children ruling societies, remaining accountable, focused, as well as, delegating responsibility for citizens; humans in modern cultures have propensities thinking, exceeding what many think they are capable of, thus, humans adapt accordingly. shall **We** remain complacent or eliminable with a wonderful balance of childhood fun and glamour or focus strengths in classrooms becoming technologically viable and current with global generations. those receiving intricate information while taught difficult tasks with a calm family life will prevail within a more blessed future.

information is power—**God's** magnificent power allows factual information flowing through You.

china and many western european countries have an edge over u.s.a. currently, through academia taught to youth, however, socialism has a plethora of subsequent breakdowns and minimizes well rounded personas. excluding the former empirically factual statement, America and other democracies are becoming more socialistic: when **You** are good with **God**, everything remains achievable and peaceful because anxieties and fear perfectly cease. **'politics remain temporal as well as spiritual through human minds.'**

big brother, cameras and government are aware of how **We** proceed in public. all of humanism remains spiritually correlated well and unwell through good direction and bad control: how **You** think/perceive through your perspective remains spiritually determined. do **You** observe specifics as 'all remains well' or control? your perspective vacillates well and unwell dependent upon a plethora of internal and external variables.

why do **You** receive more relative time and patience as **You** age? how do **You** feel regarding specifics placed upon life from the government/humanism and are these specifics control or assistance? when do they become too much?

one example. presently, citizens in germany whom wish having private gardens must receive and read a thick book from the government telling **Them** what should be planted, thus, guidelines how everything shall proceed according to **Their** rules. multitudes of negative outcomes are related through becoming socialist: freedoms are less apparent, big brother watches everything **You** do or transactions **You** make. government decides for individual families: where, what, when and how to think. observe how socialism works in past or present for russia, thus, currently works. also, regard how America has trended, especially throughout **Our** last half century. middle and lower class remain perplexed how successful are receiving tax breaks and refrain understanding who remains paying the overwhelming or 90% of taxes. 2000-2010 in the united states, 80% of the jobs were from small business and corporations, third was government.

union workers receive great pay, benefits and healthcare, yet, is far from enough. government workers are compensated well, likewise, are unhappy and want more. earths societies globally, remain cyclically, as unwell as, spiritually downtrodden, thus, many humans are overwhelmed, anxiety ridden and spiritually infected at times. when shall more humans live with the good Spirit and ask **God** to bless others, ask him questions, receive calmness internally and perfect direction?

'I am the solution: your book has been slated to reveal spiritual truth without satan's negative voice throughout all the writers of all previous religious doctrines. over My time, humans heightened awareness shall enmesh people together rather than divided. the torah remains the first five books of Moses: who do You think correlated the goodness within the minds of the writers of religious doctrines globally? all good awareness, truthful thoughts, words and the information slated upon all documents on earth remain for your procession from Me.'

'I produce function through everything upon earth: all good energy vibrations, frequencies, quarks, atoms, cells, equilibriums, feelings and thought processes remain freely given from Me. there is a reason I have allowed the scientific community to theorize an abundance. do You think it was coincidence that the higgs particle became known as the God particle, as well? was it coincidence why an abundance of scientific and spiritual information has come together in a short period and an abundance remained unknown? every question You have remains answered within this book. I have chosen this time within human history to reveal the truth of everything. what You shall learn within this book and through your heightened faith with Me, shall assist your life and over time, future generations. I have a wonderful plan for those listening well to these truthful words; with negativity absent regarding My perfect will within everything alive, life shall bless You further within numerous perfected suggestions.'

'Cancer has decreased and shall decrease significantly in America: good thoughts, feelings and life shall occur for heightened health.'

'Throughout your book, You shall receive specific prayers, from Me for the purpose of receiving positive energy within: when We allow your favor, your wisdom becomes desired within numerous others.'

PAST, PRESENT
AND FUTURE

preceding chapter was relevant with higher learning, big brother and capabilities relative with offspring who are learning more relative with previous generations. informationally, younger generations have learned more, thus, behaviorally and societally have higher awareness of life, thus, communicating progressively well. now, shall discuss personal order in **Our** lives. viewing your Mother and **Father** behaviorally doing the best they knew how rearing You, they, as well as, previous generations had enormous amounts of optimistic and pessimistic ideals instilled spiritually, thus, behaviorally, as well as, cognitively within **Their** offspring or You.

thus, generationally and societally, all humans remain hindered from observations of pessimistic ways of rearing wonderful offspring, as unwell.

past generations, males always were head of the household and supported **Their** families monetarily. taught from **Their** Fathers, numerous sons currently perform domestically, related with home repairs, yard work and adhering through **Their** roles as a disciplinarian: female roles were related to child rearing and remaining functionally domesticated. many accommodate or otherwise, thus, gender neutrality remains appropriate presently. male dominance lessened, female equality has come of age so to speak. bravo! your writer may go either way with the former sentence from **God**, however, why, are numerous females within every socioeconomic status becoming increasingly arrogant and haughty, thinking life revolves around only **Them** and how they feel? are power and control generationally, thus, societally instilled from **Their** insecurities? **You** remain aware where control, power and insecurities derive; book attempts remaining genderally neutral for everyone reading. think preceding your sometimes insecure and distorted ego.

the good and bad spirits initiate goodness and badness through everyone living upon this earth.

if **You** still believe **You** choose your behaviors, then choose only good and functional thought processes, thus, behaviors through and within Yourself.

spiritually through body and mind we're continually vacillating from good to bad. through natural selection, from **God**, **We** have become wonderfully cognitive and efficient homo sapiens. remaining overwhelmed at times, humans withdraw into states of complacency; feeling discontent, irritable and restless remains cyclically, individually and societally modifiable. many of **You** long for your sleep, achieving what remains desired most, your distortion less inner peace and tranquility within. pray and believe, then **God**, allows excessive stores of useful energy through/within You.

numerous receive solitude through sleeping and others are overwhelmed from mortgage, car payment, insurance and offspring who need new clothing as fleshly integers predicating life. why **We** have become this way remains understandably apropos, thus, foreFathers and Mothers were subjective through outside influences: they too were mortals, relying on what occurred in past, from spiritual and through generational influences.

humans, every one of **You** have periods of feeling insecure and weak some times: feeling **We** should listen outside Ourselves, allowing completeness through **God's** infinite love remains consistent. written numerous times thus far, relating various distortion in life, **God**, desires sharing his unending love, assistance and calmness. billions globally, **God**, is known and praised through daily procession, however, others believe, through life they remain owed support because they remain living: **God**, always assists You, however, **You** may remain unable observing these continuous miracles because of your modifiable, selfish and negative perspectives from satan.

thinking optimistically, attitudes and behaviors become appropriately functional, healthy, as well as, everything in life becomes increasingly fluid and wonderful. **God**, is completely aware of **Our** thought processes, thus, reciprocates accordingly for those desiring his love, as well as, blessings and making conscious efforts as wonderful examples for offspring, family, friends and others whom **You** ask **God** to bless further societally.

pragmatically looking for better ways of improving **Our** lives, **God**, desires assisting further, progressively improving your faith, thinking, thus, behaviors: **You** remain capable, continually passing learned betterment forward for others into **Their** future: most important, instilling gentle comfort and inner peace within your further blessed offspring.

'**all** negative **energy within the** arab spring, hamas, hezbollah, **the** muslim brotherhood, al qaeda, isis, boko haram, taliban **and** satan **throughout the middle east and globally shall elapse in time. goodness prevails further for humans calm, praise, prayerful and perfect direction for Our living.**'

do **You** understand, the future are years depicting good and denouncement of bad: individuals shall prevail or become despondent, dependent on a plethora of variables. your most influential remains praising and appeasing **God**, thus, receiving and yielding goodness perfectly for others. albeit, interpersonal relations through families, schools, communities and through other humans within society, **God**, desires receiving your calmness and instilling spiritual goodness, confidence, overflowing love, optimism and peace rather than anger, impatience or negativity. please, ponder what You're desiring for offspring's progress presently from uncertain volatility received through **Their** earthly vessels. humanism shall be loved and assisted well or controlled spiritually unwell: **'life shall be lovingly assisted well.'**

'Ask and do My will and life shall be further blessed. I am the one who heightens goodness within You and keeps You safe. I shall remain only good and You shall receive abundant favor following My will rather than your own. your enlightenment shall occur for My reason.'

'**Jesus speaks:**' 'thank **You** My brother robert, **You** are exalting My Father. humans new earth age shall come for many chosen from **Their** Father who created Me and **You** for his righteousness upon the gently calming earth.'

'I created jesus: the spirits revealed and predicted the future with him. the goodness shall now be predicted within the future for Our reason, hope for numerous in need, learning the process to heal one another and for the chosen to be equated with all My good within Their souls.'

'Finally, the time of tribulation has passed within the earth's weather: certainty shall replace uncertainty in weather and many consciousness.'

Chapter

BELIEVING GOD'S EXISTENCE

what **You** need to know more than anything, awareness there shall always be light following darkness, however, significant number of people are living in darkness. humans remain desiring calmness rather than on the last nerve; fleshly, unhealthy thoughts, thus, behaviors keep **You** interlocked with pain compounding feelings of overwhelmedness or **You** may live more calmly and pacified paths throughout life. the most significant factor determining former or latter are from spirits, through your accepting, loving and trusting **God** as your present savior, thus, equal praise, from **God's** continual assistance always. all good thoughts of jesus, mohammad, buddha and **Yourself** remain from, **God**. proceed, immortally to your originator, all goodness throughout life remain **God** : **We** were placed upon this blessed earth wonderfully progressing from **God's** gentle image. his good peaceful love shall be granted within Yours. thank **You God**. 'You are welcome.'

please proceed understanding, thus, learning evolution from **God's** current words. sadly there remain a plethora of skeptics in numerous of **Our** wonderful societies. as **You** remain aware millions globally believe evolution proves there is zero **God**. stated previously within book was taught evolution while attending hendrix and continuously searched for answers for **God's** existence, thus, recently revealed writings stating exactly. possibly as You, your writer has become influenced from a plethora of directions regarding **God's** existence or non-existence and presently realize why: fleshly, incorrect and distorted thought processes yields incorrect and distorted energy/thoughts into others. your writer was taught numerous different ways earlier with life regarding religious and non religious reasons for existence and empathize with anyone and everyone regarding different ideologies. following words from **God**, through one reverend remain from a christian perspective and shall allow **God** within many skeptics minds.

those believing evolution is empirically factual remain disregarding **God** altogether, and shall learn otherwise. copying and pasting text worked well here, thus, **God**, desired following writings implemented through your faithful and blessed minds: when writing this chapter, **God** correlated everything and this email arrived without seeking this information.

ergo:

herein lies a wonderful story:

proving **God's** existence through evolution

how science will usher christianity into greatness

by reverend michael dowd

1) if what one says regarding Jesus is true and understand the universe expands, so will understanding the scope, meaning and significance of the wonderful gospel.

   a) one mistake about creation will necessarily result in a mistake about **Our God**.

st. thomas aquinas (one of the church's greatest theologians)

b) the more I learn about this amazing universe, awesome, **God**, becomes.

james gramps roberts, 82-year-old farmer and amateur astronomer.

c) the disciples and early church leaders, reflecting on Jesus ministry within the context of **Their** own first, second, and third century a.d. political, judicial, religious, and cosmological understandings, formulated creeds and doctrines about him and the significance of his life and mission. since then, however, **Our** view of reality has grown enormously. whereas those alive in biblical times and well into the middle ages, believed the world was flat, stationary, and at the center of the universe, and that stars were pinprick holes in the dome of the heavens that allowed **God's** glory to shine through, **We** today know that planet earth is part of a solar system in an outer spiral arm of the milky way, a galaxy of some 100 billion stars, which is itself only one of 200 billion or more other galaxies in a cosmos 13.7 billion years old. so if Our tradition is right, if Jesus incarnated God's great news for humanity, then the meaning, grandeur and world relevance of the gospel today would reach far beyond what previous generations and the biblical writers themselves, could have possibly known.

d) it was not those closest to the historical jesus, who first gave the gospel its geographical breadth and theological depth. it was paul, who never knew jesus. impressive achievements in biblical scholarship have, in many ways, brought **Our** era closer to the fundamental events, of a christian movement than were the gentile christians within the second century. if the life and death of jesus, remains historically central, then people living a hundred thousand years from now, will be in a better position to appreciate that than **We** are. when they look back, they will surely think of **Us** as early christians living as **We** do: a scant, two millennia from the mysterious events in question. they will be right for the christian movement today is still in the elementary stages of working out for itself and for the world the implications of the gospel. there refrains slightest doubt that the greatest and boldest creedal assertions are in the future not the past. it may be rare moments that flawed and unlikely thing **We** call church even remotely resembles something worthy of its calling but nonetheless embarked as a great christological adventure.

against its institutional resistance, it is continually finding a deeper and profound implication into **Our** jesus-event. gil bailie, literary critic/historian/lay theologian.

e) **God**, who would finish revealing truth vital to human existence 2000 years ago, when people believed the world was flat and rain fell because floodgates opened in sky, would be less than generous. a living God, would be revealing truth today.

2) **God's** immanence and omnipresence remain real, as your **God's** transcendence.

a) there are two bibles: written scriptures and scriptures of nature. if ever they seem to be in conflict, the big problem, is in **Our** interpretation of one or the other.

b) the universe, remains, one story of nested creativity and emergent complexity.

c) using an analogy of nesting dolls (atoms within molecules, within cells, within organisms, within planets, within solar systems, etc.), **God**, is the proper name, for ultimate creative reality (the largest nesting doll) which embraces and includes, yet transcends, all the other levels of reality. **God**, is the great, **We** are of existence:

God is the holy one, the alpha and omega, the great mystery, the wholeness of reality, the lord almighty, thus, everything.

d) **God** is not a supreme being, **God**, is the supreme being. everything that exists does so from **God**. nothing good exists, outside of **God**.

e) **God's** eye view of the world, is not merely, the view from outside or above all, it is his view through every set of human and non-human eyes. **God**, feels pain and suffering of all creatures from the inside. **God** is love and infinite compassion.

f) what does **God**, look like on the outside? only **God** knows. what does **God**, look like on the inside? look around You. look in the mirror. look deeply within your own heart.

g) **God** has loved, created, communicated and redeemed for 13.7 billion years. what kept **Us** from appreciating this fact over last few centuries was thinking Our universe remains like a machine which essentially divorced creator from creation.

h) evolution, is another name for holy Spirit in action, **God**, created each moment.

i) the entire cosmos can be thought of as the hand of **God**, and **We** like atoms or cells in the hand of your holy one and call this perspective, 'nested creatheism.'

j) throughout the four billion years history of earth's life, **God's**, main way of communicating, has been through feelings, circumstances and relationships, rather than words: **God's** Spirit speaks clearly, as well as, silently through each moment.

k) great story or gospel is progressive and inexhaustibly meaningful. the cosmos is going somewhere and has a direction, Jesus way. We, are all part of the process.

l) humanity is the fruit of 13.7 billion years of unbroken evolution, now becomes conscious of itself. **We** are each and every one of **Us** quite literally **God's** universe becoming aware of itself. jesus, was aware intuitively, living faithfully and fully.

m) We did not come into this world; **We** grew out from it, just like an apple grows from an apple tree. **We** are not separate beings on earth living in a universe. **We** are a mode of existence on earth or an expression of the universe. genesis 2:7 is a sacred way to say the same: **We** are from nature, thanks, to **Our** immanent creator.

n) four billion years ago, planet earth was molten rock and now, it sings opera.

brian swimme, physicist/cosmologist.

o) with faith in **God**, when I trust time and trust that reality, as it actually shows, is perfect for growth and learning, aware of peace, passes all of **Our** understanding.

p) all concepts, language, and stories about **God**, or ultimate reality, derive from a people's experience of **Their** world. if **We** lived on the moon, **Our** understanding of divine would reflect the barrenness of the lunar landscape. religious differences make complete sense, from different bioregions, each religious tradition emerged.

q) in prayer, we're cells communicating with a heart of a body which we're alike.

r) to pray and work toward ensuring a just, healthy, beautiful and sustainable life-giving world for future generations of all species and to do so as an act of faith and devotion to **God**, is to embody the gospel and model real christian love.

3) Our destiny (as a species and as individuals) is to further **God's** evolutionary creativity, in christ-like ways, blessing the body of life. role of church, includes spreading the great news of the great story. evangelizing nations, thus, ushering all human families, through a process of death and resurrection and glory to **God**. in this way like Jesus the church becomes a vessel of **God**'s saving grace. **We** no longer passively are awaiting christ's return; **We** fully participate and live for this.

this remains **Our** mission, **Our** calling, **Our** great work. scriptures refer to church as both the body and bride of christ.

'Everyone alive are spiritually driven: albeit, conscious, unconscious, aware or unaware; all humans, (even atheist's) communicate with themselves for the resolution of specifics or generalities through thoughts. the voice all are hearing is God if good and otherwise if negative judgments or thoughts. what one must contemplate remains what You desire, more good and less bad or otherwise. regarding every facet of your life and those around You, the former desire is appropriate and obtainable: one- simply praise and thank God when specifics go well, (this takes a millisecond and I reciprocate). two- when any where on earth, ask Me to bless people and places and then pray for Our desire (another second and You are living in My Spirit perfectly). finally, enjoy your gracefully blessed and chosen day because life is My goodness through You and everyone around You, as well. life is good and calm when You are further enlightened, as well as, favored.'

'My writer has traversed through many zoos and other amusement parks from Me and was asked to move numerous animals through thoughts and prayers. he has always remained aware that I correlated his mind and gave the thought of moving specific direction within the animals. I shall continue correlating every goodness through humanism and weather: all of Jesus good thoughts and awareness were directed from his Father, Me, the creator of the universe.'

God? 'yes.' regarding negative energy in the consciousness causing addictions: what specific spiritual physiological occurrences transpire when humans repent?

'Comparable with all vacillations of energy within everything, repentance allows Me to negate and replace uncertain thoughts and feelings with My certainly stable energy, thus, good thoughts/feelings as well as direction.' God? 'yes.' why shall We need to repent if the unwell energy is from otherwise? 'My answer for everyone whom shall remain living, as well as, birthed in the future; humans are vacillating vessels of energy: receive My wellness.'

'All of this wonderful energy occurs continuously through and around You, while numerous continue focusing on the negative often. life is spiritual and the more You live in My spirit, the less otherwise You receive. when living through My direction, over time, You receive only goodness and this, My offspring, remains what occurs in heaven, satan has vanished, therefore, zero anger, anxieties, control, sickness nor friction and life remains good from My calm and perfect direction.'

'Following revealing how to live in and with My spirit, thus receiving continuous goodness, your writer was asked where he desired to proceed; as taught, he asked Me where? I spoke, now We shall proceed to heaven: as instructed and relaxed, closing his eyes, We proceeded eternally where life begins; everyone remains directed only well. his perspective was from 100 feet above and he received prayers of how to let go perfectly. he saw former family members, everyone whom now were deceased within the flesh and were now living only well and countless others remained unknown. in a broad field, all were walking with a consistent gate, crisscrossing one another and were separated by millimeters: everyone receives My continuous bliss.'

'All conversations remain optimistic and complimentary towards one another, continuously. all are directed well from Me alone, and this My offspring, shall occur for numerous humans I choose upon earth: awareness of My spiritual truth shall live within further blessed souls into the wonderful future for numerous. I have a blessed plan that shall resonate within numerous asking and listening to My will, without distortions and focused upon what shall arrive perfectly directed within Them. life is good and You are further blessed.'

Chapter 58

FEMALE EMOTIONAL ROLES: LEARNED BEHAVIORALLY AND SOCIETALLY

last chapter was spoken well from reverend michael dowd and **God**, showing evolution is from a **God** of goodness and has a wonderful plan. thank **You God**, through michael. 'You're welcome.' proceeding in your present chapter, **You** may understand better emotions of female persona, cave men and women, as well as, briefly touching upon homosexuality through your creator.

females have remained more emotional than males, over time, because what has been discussed formerly and shall become expounded further. **Their** role of being emotion full remains well understood and completely apropos from this vantage. thinking and behavioral feminine roles are learned from observing **Their** Mothers nurturing offspring, enabling and meeting **Their** spouses or **Fathers** palpable needs. human words are often times controlling and undesirable, yet refrain from being anticipated.

deeper **We** go. until recent generations numerous males viewed rearing children as important, however, viewed **Their** role, providing monetarily as most important.

You see, through **Their** eyes living for entire family was contingent upon what was provided monetarily: these are true, thus, correct rearing of offspring yields these future Fathers, Mothers, husbands and wives, thus, heightened emotional stability given for wives and offspring reap security and strength, thus, substantially more function, societally over time. sadly, within much of **Our** present industrialized and technological world, still remains males control much of what females say or do: let go of negative control, this disables function occurring for everyone involved.

although females have made unbelievable transitions for last five decades many still are repressed, suppressed and depressed through numerous of **God's** families: shall remain noted, females shall thrive in the future.

females often score higher academically than males. one reason why: at times, males are controlled by **Fathers** with perverse negativity, belittling and demeanment passed generationally from **Father** to son. meaning, males have an unbelievable stigma attached upon **Them** from an early age. **You** understand. males, excelled physically and focused progression athletically, rather than academically through many youths eyes. also, males are preoccupied how perceived from other females, thus, rather than excelling academically, focus primarily was and are to impress females with physicality, thus, how strong they are. general consensus remains currently, for majority of males in numerous societies. many young men continue being repressed, demeaned and belittled from Fathers, globally, via, perverse power or control bestowed upon **Them** in personal settings.

although there remain many exceptions and the negative energy refrains from occurring continuously, these behaviors remain apparent, significant and modifiable. belittled and demeaning words received when youthful, every Son remains unable overshadowing with 100 affirmations, thus, think preceding hurting offspring with harsh verbiage. again, latent insecurities through **Fathers** reflects on those closest, offspring's feelings remain generationally weak. those excelling with **God's** instilled energy remain apparent throughout societies most innovative and productive.

dysfunction within personal life upon the rearing process supersedes function through exteriorly confident personas males or females emulate publicly through facades. most youth utilize facades effectively and figuratively; feeling **Their** facade remains needed catching significant other because if significant others were aware of **Their** true selves, originally, first dates would refrain occurring for both genders.

writer remains aware, there remain numerous calm, loving and wonderful people. was making general point regarding reality of every single society upon **Our** earth.

females roles, currently unequivocally remain more and more similar with males, thus, roles expressed between male and female or husband and wife or significant others stated previously have much grey area. generally males continue wanting control of castle, however, deed states castle belongs to husband, as well as, wife. include following profound information and believed, thus, exceedingly pertinent. first- knowing thousands of married couples and mates over decades, concluding: males love genuinely learned from Fathers, they shall do anything for **Their** others. secondly, females reciprocate having wonderful behaviors for themselves as well.

thus far **You** agree with generality. also, allow predication, following thoughts are from deep inside your writer's heart, mind and soul, from **God** making sense. humans desire having **Their** lives better with less conflict, anger, tight shoulders, headaches, sadness, ulcers, thus, psychological and physiological issues. desiring confidence and worth, numerous, especially among heightened education, fleshly, throughout youthful generations, self actualization occurs often for those who are reared with calmness from **God's** love, thus, peace through **Their** parental figures.

many females are and have remained self actualized for centuries, however, were unable showing feelings of adornment, love, nonjudgmental, nondiscriminatory or unbiased thinking because they were female, viewed as minorities through others within a close minded male perspective of control and perpetual spiritual blindness.

please, receding back, extremely far back. males, have controlled females since beginning of time, when **God**, placed humans upon earth as cavemen and women. females birthed, nurtured offspring, prepared meals and remained domesticated: comparable with a plethora presently, many are repressed, controlled, as unwell as, oppressed. the bible says this unwell from what's its name.

You see, since beginning of time, numerous females followed what they were instructed to do, through males, generational control and power issues, furthering females becoming more subservient; emotionally, mentally and psychologically. fleshly reasons, most females are hyper emotional are because of many specifics. firstly, females received more emotional roles throughout time: child rearing and empathizing with children's emotional needs. secondly, generationally controlled from males. in previous and current generations, life, has been this for females, they love and adore Us, however, despise **Us** acting similar as **Our** Fathers, however, were aware of deficiencies preceding saying, I do. insecure? yes and humanism.

this specific paragraph of chapter relates personal thoughts, thus, **God**, was asked and was silent. in fact, had written many optimistic sentences stating how **God** desires, thus, loves homosexuals well. following writing many sentences stating these feelings and understanding beliefs from **God**, computer hibernated specific evening and when starting computer the next morning all good words were erased other than the quote and those following, allowing clarity from his thoughts.

'**All humans are** controlled unwell **or are assisted well, with how they feel, think, thus, behave. I made Adam and Eve rather than Adam and steve: understand that I love and adore everyone alive when they remain praising Me, loving others and doing My good will for others.**'

shall state, straight writer has had friendships with numerous male and female homosexuals over two decades: similar as heterosexuals, overwhelming majority of homosexuals are wonderful people, living life given from **God**, through Them, they receive many good experiences and bad, as all. they love and are desiring love just as You: all remain living as humans together and desire to allow **Their** gentle thoughts and voices to flow as progress for everyone.

preceding concluding chapter, **God** said, 'watch world news segment.' and did.

here was one specific causing chaos throughout society: airport security, as well as, the thinking of air traffic controllers and numerous others globally.

have known following information for two decades and presently, **God**, desires subsequent information written for others, june 28th 2011. news continues asking why many specifics keep transpiring and why airport security personnel, continue screening inappropriately elders and youth, thus, against **God's** common sense: air traffic controllers who fall asleep when working or obvious incorrect trial verdicts as o. j. simpson and casey anthony. the long answer remains extremely complex: souls, silently remain dualistic dependent upon a plethora of specifics that shall become revealed when asked. the short answer remains simple, again, the bad entity works through humanism for its agenda, thus, faithful, as well as, truth are distorted, causing individual anger and chaos, then spreads as a bad infection across society: energies received within thoughts and feelings.

COHABITATION

cohabitation works for many significant others. sharing mortgage, utilities and groceries are incredibly fair for those whom are honest through **Their** verbal agreements. auditory agreements are appropriate for numerous roommates, however, having contract, in writing, represents obligations remaining appropriate for your future, when needing a unbiased judge, deciding who owes what in events of separation. sadly, this remains what America, as well as, a plethora of societies, have become: feeding insatiable wants of being correct and having power or control over other party through egocentric and distorted perceptions from negative entity. resolution, from one biased, monetarily expensive lawyer and judge, means, agreement where ill feelings arrive between both parties exacerbating **Their** dysfunctional feelings. the roommates relationship dwindled more than likely from finances or fairness minimized through differing perspectives. having **Their** resolutions unobtainable through negotiations, they remained unable settling matters palpably themselves. learned over life, money is the root of evil. untrue, it is humans distorted perceptions. wondering if **You** noticed, thus, far in the chapter, **God**, was mentioned zero times.

God's presence within courtrooms and law processes remains palpable, viewing your specific situation and is aware of truth in specific instances, however, remains saddened with how perverse much of societies egocentric selves, images, laws, as unwell as, agendas have become. view societal thinking presently; **God's** belief, remains his law and many of **Our** law have zero correlations, thus, negativity is humanism: meaning, when **We** as humans have an audacity or overconfidence in Ourselves, thus, feeling need to rely on only **Our** fleshly selves reinforces what are contributing to America's, as well as, other societies corrosion. furthering egocentric, unethical, moral less individuals among Us, need refraining from these frivolous law suits. again, **God**, believes in your verbal agreements, your eye contact, handshake, as well as, truthfulness followed with faithful, thus, undistorted actions accordingly.

psychologically, best predictor of future fleshly, societally and spiritually are past. receiving increased love and compassion from **God**, remains, what more humans need within present behavioral, societal and economic deficiencies. pray for this. present masses have distanced themselves away from **God**, more than ever:

separation of church and state is reason why America and many other countries are as they remain. disassociating **God** from **Our** lives, what occurs? also, who is working through peoples souls and implementing dysfunctional laws for humans?

viewing others behavior, look around proceeding through daily tasks, decide for Yourself, are **We** moving forward in correct approach or away what **God**, intended? agreed, absolutely remains latter and satan, figuratively is grinning from ear to ear when its negative energy affects numerous.

God spoke, 'write corinthians chapter six in My words rather than humans: 'faithful offspring shall refrain from suing one another.'

'Dare any of You having matter against another go to law before the unjust and not before saints? do ye not know the saints shall judge the world? if a world shall be judged by You, are ye worthy of judging the smallest matters? remember, I speak through numerous parables and I am the saints, angels, holy spirit, truth, solution, as well as, all goodness within your calmness and present love for others wellness.'

'My current/future book with information shall equate within numerous agnostics, atheists as well as a multitude within the scientific community.' God? 'yes.' encompassing all of your offspring, shall there remain a significant revelation within the future? 'yes, from My words, I shall reveal all things decided for My chosen and elected to receive continual peace and joy.'

5.5.17

'The holy Spirit remains within divine humans: I choose and they receive My goodness uniquely possessing Their good minds, emotions and wills: I correlate every decision, endeavor and truthful word spoken from Me.'

'Within your foreseeable future, unaware humans shall become sentient of why My oceans, favored souls as well as atmosphere remain certainly stable from My perfect design: You're becoming aware for My reason.'

'The word christ, remained derived from cristos meaning anointed one.'

'Throughout history, humans have placed Their egocentric agendas on others. presently, needing to have awareness for parents of Their children whom attend school, before they ingest an aspirin and allow these young girls to have an abortion without parents awareness: why do You think I have been excluded from numerous factions of laws in public and governmental affairs remains because satan is working through humanism causing societies decay, thus, chaos. I, speak through robert's soul revealing future historic truth within You.'

'2017 and beyond shall remain notable for humanism. countless of My faithful humans shall learn spiritual truth: I am only good and You are further blessed doing My will rather than your own. finally, the world is better than it has ever been through the masses: life is good, so are You and You shall live in peace and harmony asking and following My wonderful suggestions rather than commandments. I am love and shall continue allowing My wonderful plan to occur.'

SAFETY AND STRENGTH

your former chapter was relative with law, as well as, perverse agendas. thank **You** bearing with writer thus far; please allow shifting gears with optimistic and functional view, without lawyers or many other processes related through law.

numerous societies with similar intrinsic unified elements are enmeshed through familial units while others are detached. whether nurturing children or supplying monetary sufficiency, individuals understand spirits and with **God** allowing further progression or **You** may digress through thinking and behaviors. from, global uncertainty, every one needs loving and caring for others. facilitating through all individuals, goodness and truth remains trusting through faith with one good entity, this one is **God**.

wonderfully, **God**, continuously leads to optimism, thus, here **You** go. all **God's** nature works well for Us. beautiful songs birds singing, **God**, says through Them, **'enjoy your wonderful day, gracefully given. proceed, through your day viewing My wonderful earth unifying further with nature and connecting with each other well for species progression.'**

flowers, foliage, mammals and humans are for commitment, love and pleasure. **You** know this. animals and insects remain aware when tension is present among individual human personas. very well this is understood.

ravens remain negative, as elephants, tigers and other mammals have negative entity in souls, at times, as You.

regarding ravens, '**they are** satan's distortion,' presently remaining from spirit. shall give **You** few examples: this information remains empirically proven true when spiritual rebirth occurred from many others visual awareness.

first, when watching parents home fall of 2009, parents were leaving for airport.

more than 32 ravens flew in, landing in trees across street: squawking very loudly and continuously until parents had driven off. Father, proceeded calling once they were on a trip within california: many black birds were there, squawking, as well. **You** see, upon this moment, writer was very vulnerable, as well as, unconfident because of generational issues, missing Son who resided with his Mother, as well as, bad entity attempted controlling susceptible psyche through weakened stages as unwell. **God** spoke, '**when weak, You are strong.**' secondly, following **God's** direction, later learned ravens had bad entity working through Them. then, walking phoebe, **Our** yorkie-poo, proceeded onto street, an enormous black raven perched across street squawked loudly and followed **Us** around neighborhood for more than five minutes continually squawked from tree to tree. from **God**, one hundred yards from home had taken phoebe off leash and prayed for this black bird to fly away. instantaneously, specifically when praying for the black bird to be gone, enormous black raven fell silent and flew away. **You** see, dependent on the writer's thought processes and prayer, these evil birds are present or gone. ravens are attempting intimidation expressed from rob, a christian pastor through squawking loudly, morning into day: until, **God**, is proclaimed more powerful and satan is denounced through mind, then they fly away. occurs through present or final editing process.

in example was thinking this was **God** showing compassion or comfort for writer, as if ravens were screaming for self's parents remaining present and showing compassion for **Their** generationally, spiritually, as well as, temporarily weak son. from **God**, through pastor rob, learned these ravens were present for intimidation purposes, thus, taking writer off a peaceful prayer full path. writer now knows ravens are present because satan had lost control of writer's soul through negative thinking and feeling need of filling void escaping life from alcohol or chemicals; giving everything to **God**, which is his already, then life becomes calmed and optimistically anew for numerous who are reading your book's good enlightenment.

our family are christians, however, have one buddha statue within back yard and talking with buddhists, they stated ravens expressed something bad shall occur. **God**, instructed your writer with asking the buddhists question regarding ravens, then following hearing negative information, immediately, asked **God** if this was true? he spoke, **'what do You believe?'** 'is untrue.' **'only good shall occur for You.'** previous sentence from **God**, is another parable for You. belief and faith in **God**, are love and safety.

here lies a wonderful place for another story. in numerous asian metropolises as America, there are roads and highways five and six lanes wide in one direction. wonderfully, **God**, has **Their** personas enmeshing very well: **You** see, they remain focusing on those around **Them** rather than themselves or **Their** electronic devices. they refrain being online or texting and occupied with focusing upon driving task. per capita, there are significantly less accidents, than u.s.a., as well as, europe. reason, focus outside themselves and penalties derived from inattentive driving.

where does humans negative decisions and inattentive driving come from? spiritually determined through everyone.

'Upon robert's age of 21 and further, I have asked him to walk alone and in the darkness within the ghettos of oklahoma city, dallas and philadelphia. when spiritually distorted **humans were approaching, he asked if they were** bad **or good? he heard, 'they are** angry.' **he asked what to think. I said for him to ask Me to bless Them, denounce** satan from Their soul and allow God's goodness into Their mind. he did over one second and immediately they turned away. this occurred from Me and I shall direct everyone well when living in the Spirit from asking and doing My good will. life and souls remain spiritually directed.'

'Viewing societies as one living organism with interrelating parts whom work together, instilling harmony, stability and equilibrium through My offspring: I, work well, for those adhering from and through good principles, as well as, following perfect suggestions.'

BOX OF CHOCOLATES

as one generation passes another comes forward, instilling within **Their** offspring, functionally positive thinking and behavior from **God** through **Them** or otherwise. with this stated, shall ask one question. when nurturing your children, have they observed expressions of interlocked, inappropriate behavior or more healthy ones? unequivocally yes and yes. individuals throughout societies, globally are angry or negative from bad rearing and many others remain empathetic and understanding: denounce satan's pessimistic control through your soul and consciousness by asking **God** for this. **God** earnestly awaits assisting **You** further. praying and thinking functionally from him through You. numerous **Fathers** and Mothers of current and past generations have viewed what had occurred negatively through nurturing, modifying **Their** wonderful offspring, thus, yielding functional instillations of calmness and empathy for **Them** and numerous offspring following.

while numerous industrialized and highly technological individuals and families are becoming less faithful regarding religion and spirituality, many disheartening occurrences transpire through thinking and behaviors within family. **You** may call specific occurrences coincidences, however upon 02.11.10, **God** said, **there are zero coincidences, they have shown themselves throughout history and the present future.'**

God, said following through writer previously and now desires quoted, thus shall, 'when **You** or **offspring refrain from praising My name, further idolize time with less relative material objects and often incorrect negative media, what occurs? more lack empathy, thus, thinking and behave** negatively **to others; fleshly, societies** deterioration **shall coincide from** satan's **presence: I patiently and lovingly await your peace.'**

many adults and youth remain unaware, calmness is from **God**, through **Them** and overwhelmed internally, thus, attempt surviving from one moment to next remains otherwise. fleshly, generational issues and personas have caused much inequities, as unwell. what's sad is, throughout history, families have publicly traversed through many motions, living facades within life as if everything remains wonderfully blissful, when reality shows itself, personal life and mind refrains being a box of chocolates.

abundance of youth rebel just as **We** did. reading thus far, **You** remain aware why all youth rebel in the first place. offspring encompassing societies have significantly increased feelings of overwhelmedness: **You** may have rebelled in youth, staying home from church sunday morning, sleeping off hangover, they too want to sleep off **Their** hangover or have been awake numerous days having zero sleep because ingesting stimulants: minds are completely overwhelmed how negative, personal and societal world has become. many youths and adults are turning focus to **God**, for solace, however, more are angry from a bad perception of **God**, or lack thereof, thus, defying altogether. here is a juncture where your words shall express, **God's** unending calm through You: **God's** presence remains continuous and overflowing when **We** follow his gentle path lying perfectly through **Our** hearts, minds and souls.

God, chooses love for **You** 100% of time, likewise, initiates your correct choices, and bad entity incorrect: regarding temptation, both are always present awaiting your unwavering commitment. question. what specific juncture, shall **You** receive an ability finding a way back receiving **God's** calm, when **You** and offspring remain overwhelmed with the bad view of society from media and human conversations? negative entity is pleased. individuals encompassing **God's** societies around earth are overwhelmed from a negative spiritual instilments through numerous families presently. albeit, hyped media or word of mouth, humans remain inundated with negativity, saturating those breathing and living **Their** technologically complicated existence: bad entity has made life complicated through humans and remains another reason for intrinsically believing, following and praising.

'Your personal heaven is possible: numerous globally, from all religions and spirituality, live frictionless and receive abundant peace because they live in the Spirit with and from Me: humans remain the only living creatures that receive an ability to reason and ask for perfect direction. when your faith heightens with and from Me, small and significant questions are answered well.'

'Life is a box of chocolates and humans are My consistent center of splendor and love. believe what You pray with heightened faith from Me: We remain one goodness. believe within My power and receive goodness while your perspective and perceptions modify perfectly well.'

'I chose jesus, upon that juncture of time to heighten other humans relationship with Me. I remain the one who healed and calmed winds through him. I heightened his awareness of what was to occur, when to remain silent and speak. I heal and heighten awareness through any offspring upon any moment, through Their willed awareness. life's good and You remain further blessed following God's perfect will.'

'Living shall remain more consistently calm and blessed following these suggestions: specific denominations have implemented negative human control rather than My peaceful love and continual goodness. countless faithful across the earth shall learn My spiritual truth: I am only good and You remain calmly blessed further every morning when awakened. Jesus eyes remained directed forward and slightly upward unless he was receiving negativity internally or externally.'

'Finally, Jesus depended upon My Spirit for questions and answers: he remained unaware where all negative information was deriving. the vacillating spiritual predictions within his soul and your mind shall remain predetermined as well: You shall learn the process of receiving continuous good for a reason: I have a wonderful plan.'

God? 'yes.' does negative truth derive from what's its name? 'yes, all bad negative energy everywhere derives from the negative energy.'

'You shall love rather than do not kill. You shall remain faith filled rather than do not covet your neighbors wife. when all the double negatives become positive, humans shall receive the word of God.'

ONE CLICK AWAY

through this chapter, **You** shall understand, numerous specifics which intrinsically debilitates family structure. first, numerous of **You** across wonderful earth remain overwhelmed with personal and public life. secondly, many are closed to society. meaning, many of **You** are dependent on having technology increasingly prevalent, how **You** proceed through day and less dependent on minds or human interaction. again, best interaction fleshly, remains human interaction; through this goodness, numerous persons are becoming enmeshed functionally, thus, spiritually together. thirdly, becoming less reliant on others helping **Our** lives work, while increasingly egocentric, we're further away from **God**, as well as, those loving **Us** most, family. less interested through others decisions for spouses refrain from being your own. when offspring are present, they wish Mothers and **Fathers** would respect and love one another.

everyone reading these words, have families whom love and think about **Them** or consciously and subconsciously wish loving and thinking of Them, absolutely more. days progress and numerous parents wish they could receive an ability, modifying these behaviors; occurring when offspring were younger, parents, were immature spiritually, thus, behaviorally, cognitively, emotionally and financially, less inept. past remains past and writer shall soon refrain, then shall work toward solutions of progress and **Our** future rather than unchangeable specifics occurring previously. parents have increased divorce because of heightened abuse, anger, control issues, chemical dependency and numerous others. why are there improprieties for life? originating spiritually, perceptions remain confused, distorted and overwhelmed from bad entity. working through humans, it, causes every one of your discountings. from **God** through writer's soul and words, shall expound deeply and further for your understanding how, **God**, works through **You** for goodness, peace, thus, love. bad is from what's its name: humans sometimes continually vacillate from good to bad thoughts.

why some act on **Them** and others refrain, remains because of spiritual control or spiritual resistance of friction from within. ergo:

having acquaintances, most within in 20's, 30's and beyond, whom are married. yes, marriage remains trying at times, this imperfectness, shall be called character or resentment building times and complex from what's been addressed previously. many females feel entitled, having what they desire through material possessions: some feel entitled and feel they have earned this entitlement, however, have they? most often, yes. **'blessed are earth's peace makers, from Me through Them, for everyone's function.'**

regarding **God's** wonderfulness through peace, life, love, marriage and offspring, remains abundantly apparent through faithful, who serve **God**, and pray for others. then satan's wrath, through anger, arguments, deceiving, impatience, manipulation, negative thinking, separation, divorce and chaos, remain less pervasive, from **God**. what occurs through your children's minds, whom innocently learn and view love for **Their** significant other from **God**, and anger from one consequential extremely relevant negative entity, who continuously works through your heart, mind and soul, wanting failure through all negative feelings and thoughts: from **God**, your negativity shall dissipate immediately or over time. desired the following information for latter chapter, however, **God** spoke, **'final** chapters shall receive heightened optimism and readers remain aware why I desire this.'

elderly remain aware through a plethora of information regarding **God's** blessings and graceful presence through rain storms: many elderly, as well as, less, many youths are aware how functionally imperative **God** remains through weather upon earth. second, profound information regarding societies today has been excluded from life's stories given to youth because generations presently communicate less with elders because of compounded fleshly specifics inundating life: every generation believes they are more advanced than prior, has been this way thousands of years.

youthful generations, disregard parents because of consciously or subconsciously resenting **Them** or believe **Their** ego, remains more strong and adaptively efficient. why have youths resented parents and been defiant, throughout humans history? are youth more advanced? technologically, behaviorally and societally, yes, for numerous, however, regarding instances attributed through masses of individuals, across continents who remain lacking **God**, satan looms, compounding weaknesses. in fact, numerous previous generations, remained well aware, how good, **God**, and bad, what's its name, are through **Their** souls: reasoning life transpired well or otherwise: every specific generation coming forward, especially, the last two hundred years, spirituality and religion decreases and humanism strengthens. why? if **You** think humans are the reason, your precisely correct- from a negative entity through humanism.

faith's decreased when humans asphalt jungles emerged, big brother watched and communication with numerous others upon opposite side of **Their** globe, remained virtually, one click away. **You** see exactly, human imperfections remain negative.

with micro chips, lasers, jumbo jets, rocket ships and globally are setting records through humanism, thus, athletics, electronics and mechanically. who needs **God**?

God speaks, 'everyone living and breathing Their good existence. how might You receive brilliance, inventions, love, as well as, maintained anything absent My good? I remain why Jesus received an ability to think upon one sentence as well as observe the surroundings while receiving another sentence of direction upon the same moment: I shall continue answering any questions, give perfect direction and remain the calming splendor within your soul. remaining everything, absent negativity, I have a wonderful plan through blessed direction within your mind and calmed physical movements through your body. I asked robert to write this book for numerous reasons: awareness of how every generation has occurred and how the future shall become more favored for numerous globally: receive My perfect peaceful love, enveloped through your direction for others to emulate, are a few.'

NEGATIVITY AND INCORRECT THINKING

discussed through book, **God**, blesses more who think well, are praising his name and loving neighbors or other humans as themselves. because fleshly, individuals generational and societies imperfections stem spiritually on every continent and many love themselves less than others. throughout rearing, many heard repetitively, 'You are always wrong? You are so ignorant. your stupid. You suck. bad job. why do You always screw things up? i'm pissed off at You. use your brain idiot.' discouragement, thus, negative verbiage through demeaning or inappropriateness, occurs intermittently through rearing process, then life. why? aware, following was previously discussed and presently feel comfortable with expounding further. from **God**, parents rearing was fleshly instilled with confidence, encouragement and optimism through Them. shall **You** proceed deepest thus far? yes **You** shall. remember, truth has zero negative agenda: please, receive additional information.

ergo:

from **God**, there remains calmness and comfort, through your optimistic thought processes and everything marvelous encompassing earth, however, satan looms. **You** remember percentage wise, **God** vs. other one, how **We** cognitively are swinging upon a pendulum, deviating from optimistic to pessimistic thoughts, happiness to sadness, feel and surrounded by calm lucidity to confusion and overwhelmedness. doctors of psychiatry, label this bi-polar or manic-depressant through humanism, however, deeper reason, revealed from **God**, **'euphoria, shows the potential of your mind: receiving an ability of thinking upon many complex specifics at once, remains from Me while** bad **entity seeks your** demise **through** negative **feelings and thoughts: I have allowed humans to understand how specifics occur through Their physical bodies, however, humans remained unable to comprehend how Their consciousness works: all consciousness, well or** unwell, **remains spiritually driven.'**

minds vacillate and many highs become less, causing incorrect negative thoughts. doctors attempt controlling or numbing **Our** spiritually induced souls from **God**, or satan, through numerous unnatural medications and all have side affects. unnatural energy yields negative energy for some.

expressed numerous times previously, media, society, rearing, thus, environment influence fleshly who **You** are, however, who **You** become depends upon following ideas, thoughts, thus, these words from **God**, through **Our** loving prayer and praise.

'If You are desiring offspring or Yourself becoming less overwhelmed, **refrain watching movies and playing games with** inappropriate **themes and** violence: **all processed through your senses when living are filed then retrieved, thus, from your mind through current and future behaviors, thoughts and beliefs.** anger, negativity, overwhelmedness **and** violence **observed through minds or personal family life, subtly or profoundly** damage **offspring whom are sensing.'**

why would persons deliberately produce negativity through media for consumers? your aware. first, living egocentrically, they are wanting a return on investment, thus, curtailing to many impressionable humans stimulation through visualization. second, they are aware or unaware of these repercussions transpiring for viewers. from originator to producer, shock value or heightened sensitized anguish and the fear and despair, visually and auditorilly through media are overflowing with kill or be killed, gloom and doom negatively affects desensitized younger generations.

You may think, these are games and movies, thus, zero harm, zero foul. really? adults, writer's age or mid 40's, had these games and many others into 1990's, yielding numerous of temporarily stimulated emotions, feelings, as well as, minds.

think for one moment, when had society begun snowballing through overwhelmedness? this is one specific correlation, 3-d computer games produced within early 90's, called doom and heretic. inception of graphically violent games, blood and destruction became paramount and **We** deceased aliens rather than humans. if memory serves correctly and does, preceding 1990, was dig dug, asteroids and centipede, rather than mortal combat, grand theft auto and many others: 'satan **influences My youth, life and dreams.'**

your aware, numerous offspring currently, remain desensitized from the violence, inappropriate behaviors given to females, disrespect for parents or others. **God**, remains saddened and satan becomes stronger, through every violent game, affecting thoughts and behavior instilled negatively through many youth and adults presently.

satan has a plan and remains happy presently through human influences, affecting and altering thought processes of impressionable young minds through societies: **God** remains sentient or aware, in time, goodness triumphs and prevails over bad. all is well. consciously and subconsciously, overwhelmedness are what many parents refrain desiring, however, purchase appeasing **Their** friend, rather than denying offspring. truth has zero bad agenda, likewise, shall **You** sit comfortably back allowing your offspring contributing with societies manageable future or unable to focus because of flesh filled attention deficit disorder or attention deficit hyperactivity disorder? one side note, please. following reading writings regarding plethora of negative influences, **God**, was mentioned zero times, other than he remains very saddened. from **God**, via, calmness, love, patience and thoughts, thus, numerous behavioral ranges, select wisely for **Yourself** and your offspring heightening peace upon earth. **God**, reveled previous information, july 2010; on editing desires quoted 04.21.11.

'**Throughout humans last four decades, numerous** regress, **moving backwards with** inappropriate **technology, likewise, what occurs through** blackouts, **lost cell service,** viruses **on computer remain from** satan **alone or through many souls. what remains occurring through** badness **upon My earth, also, remains from** satan, **through your influences, thoughts and behaviors for others societally. writer knows many details regarding life and he shall speak further for Me.**'

CATHERINE AND
CYCLICAL CORRECTION

leaving preceding chapter, writer remains aware how to proceed, therefore, shall. listening to one friend, whom remains married and in the word of **God**, numerous interesting observations, thus, stories are shared. first, allow predicating briefly regarding who he is: interjected in former chapters, sean, remains one extremely close friend and his Son kyle is closely affiliated with the writer's Son from **God**. sean, mentors young men and adult males regarding life, as well as, emotional or mental support: sharing healthy processes for young males who need assistance. what remains extremely relative for book, his observances of male friends whom confided in him with marital issues, apparent through many overwhelmed lives. first, these male friends being married for two decades have marital discountings. secondly, females are more emotional, spoken previously because of observances through senses during rearing and behaviorally inscribed roles instilled through interpersonal relationships, via, society: and these learned societal roles through media and life exacerbates feeling of entitlement. societies progression modifies and compensation becomes many: meaning, as a cog in the wheel of life, **We** adapt accordingly from personal comfort and societal beliefs viewed through humanism.

herein lies one relative and palpable example, please receive numerous parables.

catherine, Mother of two children, age is forty and married 18 years with lennon. they met in 20's just following college: love at first sight and became better when **Their** spiritual, thus, emotional personas enmeshed brilliantly and lovely thereafter. catherine completes lennon and lennon completes catherine's persona, as well.

years progressed and they remain inseparable and having children intensified love for one another: observing his great work, **God**, blessed both of **Them** accordingly. **Their** relationship remained flowing with much marital bliss, however, over time, catherine became complacent; shall be slated, complacency was through both. specific story, catherine was most complacent, thus, began anticipating love and expecting more, until one day life became modified within most unpleasant way. society was receiving cyclical financial correction, specifically with stock market; catherine's husband, lennon, received word his vocation was downsizing the employees sustainment: privately difficult, numerous societies became overwhelmed, as unwell. manifestations, were culminated through many families enmeshment, community, thus, societal discontentedness, lennon, thought and pondered his palpable future. unaware when this downsizing would occur, thus, affect **Their** wonderful family; naturally for **God**, lennon, received comfort through his lovely spouse catherine. enmeshing **Their** personas, both of **Them** had began feeling overwhelmed from life: catherine, feels what lennon feels and vice versa, they are one from **God's** love, however, through both **Their** souls, thus, hearts, an infection enveloped **Them** both.

they read newspapers, watched local, national, international news and internet: showing societies, were within patterns of relative chaos, thus, numerous humans viewed imminent demise through societal structures and earth's natural disasters.

catherine, feeling increasingly lethargic, as overwhelming majority of individuals throughout societies remained completely sluggish through **Their** days and nights. catherine and lennon, began praying more, thus, confiding in **God's** wonderful love and support; **Their** depressed minds began feeling energized at **God's** speed. from **God**, lennon's job was spared and life became solid for this blessed family. prayer works, well. **God**, is everything wonderful, what remains needed from **You** are believing and prayer. many feel powerless through life, love and themselves.

your aware where negative feelings derive, has been this way throughout history.

when **You** have two beakers of water: speak negatively within one and then speak gently into the other. freeze the particles and the negatively received beaker remains fragmented/distorted while the positive remains perfected: this remains the same as all of nature and the flowers within your residence. light oscillating within a diamond remains termed brilliance for perfection.

before procession further, allow your writer, placing another good understanding.

remaining present through all humans, **God**, assists through everyone's guidance, love, miracles, calm, good, healthy, perfection and optimistic energy through Us. one atheist girlfriend when nineteen, stated, 'God, remains a crutch for the weak.' upon specific juncture was impressionable; similar to college professors wanting distrengthaning **God's**, adoration and faith within, subconsciously She was also.

presently think, thank **You God**, all mortals are weak at times needing your crutch. **God**, continuously remains a pillar of unwavering strength through those desiring. from **God**, your wonderful peaceful thought processes and tranquil feelings occur, then receive calmness, pacification and eternal salvation now, as well as, forever.

creating and correlating goodness in life, **You** remain offspring from one perfect **God**.

chapter was received from **God**, second quarter of 2010. upon editing, **God**, desires quoted, october 14th of 2011. **'throughout history, every individual through every generation has received** incorrect **information from numerous. wanting to** weaken **others faith or beliefs has affected millions,** unwell: **You shall receive correct information when You ask and live in the Spirit of correctness and perfect lucidity.'**

'Finishing another chapter, here remains another suggestion: when You consistently do My will, negativity, **thus,** distortions **dissipate through and around You, awareness and focus heightens and You realize the duration of the day is perfect because I gently bless You and others around You well; life will become heaven on earth within numerous: the book of revelation/bible shall modify gently further.'**

Chapter

65

FEMALES TOO

welcome within another wonderful chapter related with females. writer, is aware feelings and thoughts were discussed previously, however, presently shall become impressed upon more thoroughly through a wonderful heightened enlightenment.

ergo:

God's earth, progresses further through females: they remain significantly professional and many males are perplexed having prominence and power reduced and less control. past generations, female influence were domestic, bearing, thus, rearing offspring: **God's** intention, originally regarded females significance, bearing and rearing **Our** offspring and they did exactly, it was so. females, nurtured and enabled others in society and through family unit while males hunted and became great conquerors.

aside, from bearing and nurturing offspring, females, roles societally were micro, while males were macro in the grand scheme of life, however, rearing offspring remained most important, thus, developing these numerous future male personas. complimentary remain human roles, both are imperative with what **We** call life. over generations female roles became increasingly proficient outside of residence: societally, males remain observing females perseverance, in many specific cases, outside of **Their** control, while females are showing they are viable and significant. dissimilarly, numerous males maturing into young men, observed Father's control, appropriate or consciously and generationally suitable for **Their** spouse, as unwell.

your aware, where all negativity derives throughout **Our God's** universe.

You see, while numerous reading, may feel as though they are increasingly feeling denied many of lives pleasures or consciously aware they are receiving more than most deserve, please, respect your solace from, **God**. currently, **You** shall proceed with societal views of living, loving and attaining **Our** perfect joy, thus, happiness. progress further, through your family unit, becoming more influential, regarding providing monetary sufficiency, females are sustaining **Their** significance in **God's**, world and males, shall regard past power and control issues, as past. therefore, numerous males within **God's** families shall be increasingly humbled through life. becoming reliant on two incomes of progress for future, many males intrinsically oppose, however, upon what juncture shall **You** embrace **God's** current intentions? after spouse has gone with offspring and **You** become alone, then decide to work for one common goal, life and love from and with **God**, through your great faith?

some, remain progressing further with **God** as **Their** captain, he also views females evolving through patterns unfounded. allow specifics spoken before proceeding. specifics, transpiring in **Our** past, generationally, individually and societally, shall remain past: progressing further, seeking calm feelings internally, **You** shall desire viewing your past, through religion or spirituality, as one good broad example or instance, imperative for offspring's progression, hence, future societies progress. presently, numerous husbands become physically ill, because emotions, viruses or significant other desires and presumes male role within familial units monetarily. **You** see, females are having heightened worth, because of exactly this, wonderful! feeling wonderful, contributing for **Their** families, providing monetarily, presently, females strength is typical in family units. there are a plethora of females, across **God's** globe, whom contribute numerous other ways in families and communities. if this may be You, congratulations, for those domesticated, rearing offspring and keeping family units strong, absolutely remains societies most important function. wonderfully appropriate, those assisting others are functionally designed by and from **God**, thus, working perfectly well through emitting affection and love for all.

plethora in last paragraph, progress through societal function, thus, remain aware, **You** contribute furthering societies and modifying **God's** earth through betterment. individual humans from every walk of life have potential in themselves exceeding criticism endured from many others, thus, some feel overwhelmedness personally. powerless or unable, assisting through your family units, females remain desiring peace for family and others, as one of many wonderful blessings, **God**, gives You. therefore, love and be loved, while showing empathy upon those less fortunate. earth proceeds having **God**, as captain, then your calmness shall proceed, as well: **God**, remains calmness, loving and patience, encompassed throughout humanism. many females progressing in future, realize individual behavior and thinking have calmed, empathetic and gentle: gone are outdated thinking, that hostility and anger are needed, however, some still contribute negatively from bad entity through Them.

while **We** become less worried with global wars among major nations, as previous generations, numerous, have internalized **Their** lifestyles. fleshly, reason for this. first, egocentric behavior, as well as, thinking. meaning individually, **You** believe thoughts and behavior are correct: or nonobjective regarding spouse is paramount. secondly, **Our** insecurities are instilled upon rearing process: meaning, **We** receive generational pain, subconsciously, suppressed pessimistic feelings regarding self worth, esteem and pessimism are internalized and instilled, spiritually, through Us. outwardly expressed, through subtle or perverse behavior, these pessimistic latent insecurities, profoundly affects, who love **You** most: family, offspring and others. third, **We** bring function and dysfunction into **Our** unions preceding saying, 'I do.' all want control, power and influence, yet, **God**, desires all functionally together. **God**, desires all blessed and wonderful offspring working together, enmeshing **Our** personas for life, loving families, as well as, another, rather than conflictual as negative entity wants, seeking **Our** demise through finances and personal dysfunctions.

spiritually, negative thoughts, behaviors and words, through Us, remain why many are hurtful to others and Ourselves and are needing an intimate reliance, with **God** for your wonderful future.

MARRIAGE DISSOLUTION
WITH SOLUTIONS

next page through finishing book, **God's** quotes and miracles remain You, the reason this book of answers remains slated.

divorce has become prevalent through previous two generations and many remain aware why, while others, unaware. following reasons sound rhetorical, however, these generalities are why each single pessimistic issue occurs through humanism: letting past improprieties go, shall minimize listening readers future discountings.

first, power, control and egocentric thinking: meaning- thinking your thoughts or behaviors are only correct or nonobjective regarding your spouses view, at times. secondly, latent insecurities instilled in rearing process then outwardly expressed: meaning- all humans have generational pain and subconsciously suppressed latent feelings regarding self worth and esteem: fleshly, these feelings, remain obvious through behaviors towards others outwardly expressed and Yourself: personal latent insecurities intensify with subtle or perverse behaviors expressed to family. insecurity and how **You** feel internally and expressed outwardly manifests intensely. meaning, individual pessimistic behaviors and thoughts affects negatively others, specifically your spouse and offspring: these internally compounded pessimistic emotions, thinking and behaviors expressed, enmeshes unwell. oscillating and reverberating externally through offspring, as well as, others as one bad infection: goodness shall prevail, life remains modifiable.

insecurities, anger, selfishness, negative control and power are humanism, however, deeper than humanism is spirituality, thus, when You, offspring or others remain negative are because negative entity, continuously through souls turns peace to friction. encompassing **God's** assistance through calmness, gentle love, optimism, passion, stability and truth, life is wonderful through the positive affirmations instilled into offspring and grandchildren. through faith filled prayer, **God**, sometimes calms immediately: good infections encompass souls, thus, minds rather than contrarily. remember, **God**, knows what **You** shall think and if good, he gave it You: from praying for others, he, modifies others thoughts and behaviors well, for You.

God's shown this to writer, thousands of times over numerous years from prayers.

when in public or private; he would say when others would become negative or angry and then said, '**pray, God, works through all and they become positive.**' regarding writer's Father, prayer, refrained working through him until this final rebirthing; following numerous of his angry and vocal moments, **God**, would say, '**every morning upon awakening, ask Me to denounce** satan **from his soul and allow God to envelop his consciousness for good: then pray for his calmness.**' over time, writer's **Father** became increasingly more calm and patient for everyone.

likewise; **God** said, '**pray for his blood pressure to lower.**' now it has lowered, as well.

Father says this is from medication, however, **God** said, '**reduction is from Me.**'

back to story. unhealthy, inappropriate and pessimistic behaviors seem entirely directed from a significant other and infrequently from **You** or your sometimes distorted mind. many cases, males and females remain impervious related through accountability. fleshly, accountability lies through both the parties regarding 95% of dissolutions. **You** know this. please, communicate and enmesh with one good Spirit within You: when **You** receive an ability of letting go of Yourself, **God**, reveals an inordinate amount for calmness, ideas and assistance through your wonderful lives for living.

desiring approval and respect from others through specified boundaries, if asked, **God**, shall lovingly bless ways of bettering your spiritual lives, thus, flesh, as well. **You** recall previously, **God's** assistance: please, regard next sentence as emphasis.

albeit, finishing homework, mowing lawn, giving speech, calculating quarterly or fiscal earnings or facilitating the students class work, **God**, desires **You** praying for assistance continuously. desired respectable boundaries become understood and reciprocated from mate: life becomes better, through **God's** way rather than Yours. life works well: believing your way is correct over others often remains incorrect. meaning- traversing through life believing your ideas remain the only appropriate methods and expel other ways of thinking as incorrect are narcissistic and closed.

once receiving ability to listen, while refraining from speaking negatively, **You** find your individual perceptions were distorted and other methods may, in fact, be wonderful. over time, **You** desire becoming objective through better ways directed from **God**, through another's wonderful mind. **You** may think, 'there isn't enough time, I, know what's best.' why is your thinking distorted? secondly, there is much time when **You** rely upon **God's** assistance through **You** and others, rather than Yourself. predicating how others shall act and react, **You** remain further discombobulating truth from fiction. **God**, desires all becoming objective with others thoughts and ideas transgressed through other methods. proceeding through day remain aware, **God**, instilled best interest direction, sometimes through others souls, thus, minds. what remains healthiest for all present, are letting go, thus, allowing **God** to direct **Our** wonderful paths correctly within each specific occurrence for all things good.

when allowing **Yourself** higher spiritual awareness rather than living only in flesh, **God**, figuratively smiles, thus, blesses **You** further allowing wondrous occurrences transpiring further: frequently and simultaneously relieves many negative inequities. living in flesh vs. the good Spirit shall become expounded upon further in your book:

God, continuously yields your good, **You** too, shall desire sharing love with others.

concluding chapters shall bring increased calmness, thus, good and positive souls. **'life is good and I love You continuously.'**

one friend was asked regarding a voice through him for safety. paul stated that a voice spoke one day for him to 'not' go home. the spiritual voice was for his safety because his home was being compromised by an armed robber and information kept him safe. second, paul was traveling in front of a school, the voice told him, **'slow down'**, he did, in a few seconds a boy ran in front of his vehicle: paul stopped his vehicle within a few feet of the youth.

the word 'not' remained implemented within the sentence heard because 'not' remains commonplace through his consciousness. your writer received not, can't, won't and other negative verbiage throughout life for safety until **God** taught the process of receiving heightened awareness through optimistically modified verbiage. positive and negative voices/thought processes correlate exactly how **You** receive/perceive through your spiritual consciousness.

God was asked upon this juncture if there was too much **God** written in writings? he spoke, **'with more of Me in lives, thus, society- everyone shall reap what I sew or continue disassociating truth, as well as, good away from society and continue observing** digressions. **who worked through humanism for My exclusion throughout history and presently?** satan **affects everyone** badly: **reading thus far, Our readers**

comprehend the truth and You continue to ask why negativity remains stated? I have taught You repetitively, do My will and You shall receive abundant favor through your feelings and thoughts. continue slating My truth, I have a plan perfectly through You and numerous others.'

PRESENT GENDER ROLES

proceeding into future centuries and past humans lives throughout **Their** histories, countless feelings, thought processes, as well as, behavior progressed delightfully. information following are directed for all individuals and those desiring increased contentedness from **God's** perfected healthy and appropriate guidance within You.

ergo:

societal functionalism, received significant modifications over time absolutely for humans betterment. **God**, assists further modifying all of hindrances or inequities: earth remains generous, gentle and full of promise for who listen to his direction. days of a **God**, filled with anger, brimstone, fire and wrath extinguished long ago. again, pessimistic thoughts and behaviors through humanism, remain satan's work. **God's**, presence, through **Our** three faceted heart, mind or soul, regards happiness, love and optimism for every human believing, praying and praising his direction. **God's**, unending passion and compassion remains crystal clear through everyone following good function, progress and loving kindness are continuously available.

while governments are less angered and revengeful from international grievances, **God**, views your goodness well: as nations are less interested destroying another, thus, functionally unifying with each other, **God**, observes this favorably, as well. **God**, speaks, **'I always have and shall.'** aware of exceptions connected through jealousy, power and control originating spiritually through religious differences, who want harm upon others because, one negative entity directs **Their** distorted souls.

'Life is praying for peace. simply ask God to denounce satan **within these men and allow goodness to flow through Their souls. remember, from numerous prayers within those I** choose, negativity **alleviates in My time. all remains well.'**

'over time, all followers invoking peace on earth shall proceed harmoniously.' especially your heightened recent anger, insecurity and inequities remain internalized. becoming less involved worrying, regarding having innate needs met or surviving day to day because of threatening world wars, numerous remain abolishing **God**, among masses taking insecurities out on those who love and adore most, family. also, among majority, humans remain praising, thus, praying, only when needing. christian bibles, thus, clergy say everyone are sinners and numerous consciously psychosomatically behave similarly thinking thoughts or behavior are understood. bible also says, forgive all **Their** deviant behaviors, they know not what they do. what? fleshly, **We** remain aware or unaware what is appropriate or inappropriate, thus, cognizant **Our** individual behaviors are bad or good? **'most yes some no.'** reading thus far **You** are brazenly aware, numerous past and present are unaware. most humans are perplexed by others actions and unaware how powerful, bad Spirit affects abused children maturing into adults yields badness in **Their** souls. **God** speaks, **'deviants remain** controlled **from** satan **through temporarily** infected **souls.'**

denouncing satan's control over **You** and consciously praying for **God**, disallowing satan controlled negative thoughts, thus, through anger, anxieties, discontentedness, impatience or overwhelmedness shown through behaviors of illegal activity, harsh treatment of spouse, offspring and another, individually yields healthier societies. your behaviors remain paramount and life's compassion from **God's** love through **You** is intrinsically wholly, thus, ceasing subtle or grandly inappropriate behaviors for family affecting more than only your offspring through following generations. thank **You God**, working through readers understanding why life remains volatile. **'You are welcome, this is why I remain redundant and I have a plan through You and those reading these emphasis filled words.'**

'Through My calmness and love within, your future absolutely shall become functionally contented through wonderful decisions, prayers and thinking. dissimilarly, your negative **feelings, thoughts, beliefs, words and overall persona, from rearing and life, affects Yours and others as** unwell. **when You choose Me, every** negativity **remains admonished: this occurs every morning when I awaken You and proceeds through your frictionless life when living in the spirit.'**

from present generations, regarding blurred dark grey rather than black or white: relating roles through family units; females and males shall work together, place power and control issues aside or remain as many, oppositional, thus, absolutely fueling satan's unrepressed conflict hindering and stagnating everyone's potential. especially, innocent children societally whom become instilled with inappropriate negative thinking and behaviors furthering dysfunction generationally, as unwell. spiritual and functional thinking and behaviors traversed gently through offspring: think prior to punishment: behaviors and words affect countless lineage in future. desiring humans from conception of time working together through life, **Our God**, remains functional for everyone whom believe, live and love others as themselves. numerous whom remain living presently have brought efficiency and progress for societies as former generations, likewise, upon what specific juncture shall **You** become less concerned with fulfilling egocentric completion and more interested relieving and sustaining others who are less fortunate with and through **Their** lives? presently blurred societal roles among many remain dissimilar regarding what has been instilled into prior generations and learned domestic and professional roles: what **You** have learned dysfunctionally through rearing shall be past, fleshly and clearly remain your spiritual or futuristic decisions let go, **God** flows through You.

first quarter of 2010, **God** spoke, 'when letting go and following My direction through your soul, your anew. commences every evening, specifically midnight: then how You desire living, loving others, praise and praying are dependent upon your will from and with Me.'

God, mechanically then verbally revealed former quote early 2010, how revealed shall be disclosed for **You** when **God**, speaks through soul from his loving grace.

'Listen to My good suggestions, thus, thoughts and life shall be good.'

Chapter

WIND SPEEDS

God, showed and spoke following information november and december of 2009.

every individual was made in God's image, thus, great joys shall lie within your fleshly future on earth, when conscious choices remain appropriate and functional from praising and thanking God, consistent and continuous throughout your lives. accentuating calmness, evening winds throughout morning intrinsically reflects general emotions and behaviors through humans personas ultimately from God, or what's its name. inconsistent winds are less calm through daylight hours because of Our thinking: humans remain angry, bitter, confused, conflictual, thus, stimulated negatively. distorted perceptions cause uncomfortable emotions and stress through numerous situations related through residences, schools, work, thus, individual enmeshment.

notice winds occurring upon athletic events regarding contact sports or otherwise. when humans are aggressive or energized, winds increase absolutely accordingly: specifics accord through altitude and other spiritual factors when humans are absent. **'when I revealed this to My writer, he understood multitudes of truth from Me upon the same moment and remains aware: now his mind has calmed perfectly, thus, focus upon My will. I have a plan.'**

receive awareness of wind speeds watching contact sports live or upon television. **You** see, players, coaches, as well as, fans are excited, therefore, half of spectators remain absolutely for one team or otherwise, therefore, conflictual or oppositional. secondly, massive amounts of cognitive functioning through numbers of humans attending exacerbates these wind speeds, as well. differentially, regarding golf, winds typically remain calm, because these spectators and athletes remain calmer, as well. societal calm within occurs in communities, culminating once the day has completed: stressors lessen and **You** proceed forward seeing your spouse and offspring, loved ones, friends, personal time, therefore, receive an increasingly relaxed comfort zone. personas relaxing, culminates with others through neighborhoods and community. from **God**, through Us, calms your communities and the earths winds, thus, what a wonderful feeling working with a calm **God**. optimistic, placated and functional personas through You, yields comforted feelings from **God**, and enmeshed human personas throughout present and future living upon a more wonderfully perfected earth.

ultimately, almighty **God**, maintains the calmness regarding **Our** light winds, refreshing rain storms, as well as, high and low pressure systems. humanism has become significantly proficient through **Our** plethora of various technological instruments, predicting specific soothing rain storms, from **God**. he gives daily progression, functionally through weather and creating rain where needed and gorgeous skies reflecting peace herein. regarding human nature, **God**, continuously places good hearts, thus, adoration, calmness, contentment, love, patience and your optimistic praise as perfectly apropos from his loving view, together through your splendors.

upon this specific juncture, **God** spoke, '**share information regarding your first stage or experience, I, had shown You related with calming winds.**'

one month following rebirth, september of 2009, there were fast swirling winds: speaking continuously with **God**, asked how he desired the fallen leaves to be gathered. previous seasons always used leaf blower. realizing now, he desired asking him. '**use broom to save gas, keep leaves off other lawns and silence in My nature.**' thought winds are fast and swirling, should use leaf blower, '**trust Me,**' he said. proceeded to garage for a broom. when walking slowly and calmly to sidewalk, **God**, shared what vehicles, people and animals would travel by and what people would say and how to reply, then said, '**silently, pray for Them, because I, know what they need.**' very well, proceeded to sidewalk, with winds swirling, asked how this shall occur with a broom? he spoke '**pray continuously for others.**' did. swept first pile and then asked what now? he said, '**make another pile.**' thus absolutely did. mind You, winds swirled over 40 m.p.h. upon body, hair and trees, however, leaf piles remained motionless. praying for everyone known over life over milliseconds, **God**, was giving these individual and wonderful thought processes perfectly.

following sweeping eleven piles, he said, '**walk to garage praying for others.**' doing what he instructed, thus, getting dust pan and trash can, returned: observing motionless piles, however, the tree branches were whipping frantically to and fro.

he spoke saying, '**pray for others and calmly sweep up then place into trash.**'

upon this juncture, eyes were wide open and he was giving continual information through soul, thus, mind regarding what shall occur within humanism and weather locally and globally preceding specific occurrences. he asked, '**how would You like perfect vision for three months?**' or, '**You have photographic memory.**' every morning and throughout day, would pray/do all spoken through mind. the following fall, after calm winds occurred from prayer: sweeping leaves into piles on stagnant day, made eleven piles, brought trash can and dust pan and this time, walking calmly to sweep piles, spirit, spoke saying, **'think how great You are.'** thought, have traversed over one year thinking or praying continually for others. shall do as **God** desires. thinking how great your writer was, immediately, winds came abruptly from stagnant air: these piles exploded onto street, as well as, grass.

asking why this occurred, he spoke, **'was a lesson, talk with Me and pray for others suggested, thus, follow My will, You shall be cared for well: earth's spiritual revolution shall occur and You shall teach others what has been spoken through You. I am and have been only all goodness throughout history and most assuredly within the future.'**

continually conversing with him asked what he desired: then doing as instructed. he, showed writer through electronics, human behavior, mechanically and nature, countless miracles. few examples: few weeks post rebirth, he said to take bicycle rather than walking. while riding bike, talking with **God** and praying for others, he said, **'would You like to change gears?'** yes. **'pedal faster, pray for your son, then slow pedaling, pray for next gear.'** did, immediately gear changed. continuously ask him what or who he desired writer should pray for: **God** spoke, **'this was for Our book to teach others to rely on Me rather than themselves.'** second example: **God** spoke, **'walk your dog phoebe.'** did. walking, he said, **'pray for anything desired.'** prayed silently for peace, heightened love and **God**, working through militaries for peace throughout middle east and dictators to fall.

'Good. now, pray for phoebe to move to right side for five seconds then left.'

immediately She did. **'now, think the word** satan **and phoebe shall defecate: presently, I correlate your soul, You think the word heaven.'**

asked why this occurred? **'My good energy and the** negative **energy within ecosystems affects everything upon the earth: My readers shall desire continuous good energy within Them for others. now You shall learn to think only good thoughts, My son, for others.'**

your book becomes very good: enjoy reading and including your blessedness.

'Humanism shall continue to modify: the present society remains the best time to live compared with any other for countless whom I choose: there is a reason. I shall continue working My plan: numerous remain consciously aware and countless others, imperviously unaware: awareness of truth transcends negative boundaries, all remains well. upon every specific occurrence You share goodness with others, this is Me through You. when You do My will, significantly, less negativity occurs for You and Yours. be careful with what You read and observe, because, life is psychosomatic and what You believe, affects You well and unwell. when You live cognitively aware, I direct your senses perfectly, thus, You disregard irrelevant distortions, thus, receive abilities to focus and prioritize relevance. I am only goodness, so are You and life is good.'

GOD'S PEACE VS. SATAN'S WRATH

adoration, calmness and unity through **Our** families shall become more wonderful. **You** see, progression occurs throughout your day and personas emulate feelings: if feelings are filled with pessimism, confusion or stress, they exacerbate upon those present, via, enmeshment through human's verbal and non verbal communication. why are overwhelming masses of humans, encompassing numerous societal tiers, remaining complacent and stagnant through personal, family, thus, societal roles? long mortal answer remains what **You** have read thus far and trumping humanism upon deepest level, satan seeks demise and failure in your mind, thus, giving in and up.

humans are learning truth presently: diminishing is the belief regarding **God's** wrath, gone are days of him showing angered bitterness, impatience and vengefulness. **God**, revealed through your writer, thus, ultimately for individuals, '**throughout all of human history, I, have regarded merely functional love, peace, optimism and unity and I share through You.**

You are made in My image, however, wrathful, vengeful, full of anger, hate **and** spite **are far from Me and You.'** God, creates humans and everything seen and unseen, yet, satan, remains looming. all creatures, thus, humans and animals are sometimes angry, confused or hostile. all living mammals upon **God's** earth have spiritual, thus, generationally instilled pain within **Their** souls, thoughts, ideologies and theologies shared through others. receiving these optimistically calmed, **God,** like lovingness or negative angered propensities remains interchangeable throughout **Our** specific continual moments: occurring sporadically through **Our** day and night, culminates inner goodness or badness through behavior, feelings and thoughts encompassing **Our** lives, are life. enmeshing your persona with positive, functional and joyous humans whom have good through **Them** from **God,** or angered, dysfunctional and negative individuals who receive difficulty from satan, some times. humans desire optimistic wellness, however, many feel they are needing to vent to another regarding problems, thus, hopefully receive prayers from others for these temporarily weakened souls.

confiding, listening and sharing hope, love and strength remains **God** through all. writing offspring, all these pertinent and relevant thoughts from **God,** are through your writer and conveyed for your receiving a better understanding regarding life. upon conceptualizing your book, preceding editing, attempted to write relevant to negativity of satan; upon specific stage was unable to think relevant with looming negative entity, then progressed over a short time more for **You** from **God's** guidance. received from **God,** this ability to proceed deeply with specific harsh loomer of anger, chaos, distortion, impatience, misery, pain and sickness within all, at times.

observing earth controlled pessimistically, via, human nature through emotions, feelings and thoughts and negative fatal physical irregularities occurring on earth remain only satan's wrath. proceeding deeply immediately. high and low pressure systems, rainbows, calm winds, tides from moon, seasons and gentle rain showers are absolutely **God's** perfect nature, however, avalanches, earthquakes, hurricanes, lightning, mud slides, tornados, tsunamis, volcanoes and other natures anomalies affecting humans negatively remains satan's responsibility, rather than **God's** wrath.

biblically, when Abraham was told supposedly from **God**, 'offering your Son issac shows **You** unending faith.' shall quote **God** more upon another juncture, **'voice heard through his mind was** satan **rather than Me, because suggestion remained** negative: **I, spared isaac with good direction through Abraham's soul: same voice through your thought processes, however, through awareness You shall differentiate between good and** bad. **writer's of all religious doctrines globally remained unaware as** unwell. **I have chosen to heighten your awareness for a reason, season and life: living becomes effortless when We allow Me.'**

writer and countless mortals have sometimes continual conversations with **God**, instructing functionally appropriate behaviors and thoughts. cult leaders, as well as, preachers who proclaim **God**, has spoken for **Their** congregation following **Their** dysfunctional, demeaning, emotional, physical and **Their** sexual abuse from **God's** name remain hearing satan, rather than **God's** word. these pompous individuals receive pleasure controlling weakened souls from satan's distortion of perceptions. serial killers, know what they are doing and remain controlled from satan through **Their** souls, as unwell. adolph hitler, said he spoke with **God**. hmmm. satan was correlating his power of telekinesis affecting 60 million lives. **God** spoke this on may 11th 2010.

'I remain God and would refrain from seeking, emotional, mental, physical or sexual submission **upon any of My offspring: when feelings or thoughts introduced through You are healthy, I, speak; if** hurtful **and** negative **this remains** satan. **when feeling** incorrect **through soul, heart and mind—your** pains **are easily remedied.'**

from You, another blessed mortal expressing calmness, love and truth functionally, satan is looming, aware of wonderful repercussions optimism shall have on future generations and wants individual failure, unwell: consciously resist negative temptations, over time, **God** alleviates **Them** completely. (zero negative thoughts, feelings and behaviors because **You** remain aware where thoughts derive.) the illusion of free will has been revealed for a reason, your continual progress and peace. writer has viewed satan's wrath, on many occurrences in humanism, spiritually, when writing your book and life. **God**, restores confidence and self worth, while satan sees **Our** fresh found strength and yields **Our** discontentedness and unhappiness introduced through every soul, via, bad infectious thoughts seeking unhealthy behaviors and fleshly weaknesses. has occurred throughout history; satan, wants failure and unhappiness, however, **God**, instills wonderfulness, therefore, hopefully over time **You** remain weary of pain and misery, thus, desire sharing with others his restoration, spreading good enmeshments across societies within humans faith filled future, with **God** as captain.

throughout 2010, cumulatively, more humans became deceased, 250,000, from natural physical earthly disasters than terrorists had caused previous four decades. 2011, globally, how many record natural disasters occurred? what does this say? biblically, people are aware. when masses of humans have egocentric behaviors and think negatively, physical occurrences transpire from bad entity. view the earth, negativity shall be denounced further through numerous prayers and '**natural** disasters **shall alleviate**.'

God spoke, '**every human receives the illusion of having positive and** negative **powers, life remains spiritual,** negative **thinking correlates as to why physical** disasters **occur and known or unknown** negative **spiritual individuals having power over other souls affects My earths weather** negatively **for faithful offspring: I yield the earth and humans relief. remember, My good energy shall trump the** negative, **in time.**' **God?** '**yes My chosen son?**' is any good energy from humans? '**within Their minds, yes: where do You think the illusion of good correlations and energy derive from your perspective?**' absolutely **You God.**

2010, **God** spoke, '**watch movie, regarding roman empires demise, equating the** negative **thinking within Their society and** earthquake's destruction **of parthenon. follow My will rather than Yours and You shall receive continuous optimistic thoughts and feelings: life becomes only good and so do You.**'

many surviving disasters are faithful, thus, praying for **God**, sparing **Them** rather than relying only upon themselves or numerous fleshly others. **God**, knows and is exalted; working through everyone rebuilding life for reasons understood, in time.

prayer refrains saving some, while restoring others, however, absolutely there are numerous, unknown variables and unanswered questions, regarding why specific individuals whom, outwardly are known as faithful servants of **God**, perish, while others proceed further in life. writer asked the question to pastor rob, early 1989, was acute following car accident, 'why do bad things happen to good people and good things occur for drug dealers?' fleshly, was answer. when writing chapter, **God** spoke, **'ask who knows everything, good and** bad, **throughout the universe.'**

did. **'negative in life, is satan, who gives power through individuals, seeking your fleshly** demise **and is histories** digression; **countless are aware, I, always have had a plan, all humans shall reunite ultimately upon My higher linear plane.** funerals remain ultimate celebrations **because then they receive continuous direction from Me alone.'**

having occurred throughout history, earth has had natural occurring disasters, cavemen times through present: in time, they learned occurrences were **God's** wrath, showing discourse with how **We** lived. view occurrences in **God's** world past and present and assuredly in future, these natural or unnatural disasters remain taking an abundance of good, **God**, loving humans. **God**, had your writer ask why from numerous religious scholars with minimal consensus among Them, **God** then said, **'ask who knows.'** revealing, information making complete since, **God's** answer remains quoted and ends with one extremely pertinent question for **You** and Yours.

'I, the supreme Father, share wonderful powers with the magnificent mortal world: healing, loving, creating life, optimism and babies coos through all My humans. naturally working through rainbows, seasons, sunsets, sunrises, water falls and every wonderful moment transpiring through life: I work very well, however, satan **does** loom. **cognitively through souls,** satan **remains working and envelopes**

within/through limitations, **thus, causes** weaknesses **throughout your persona:** distorting **senses temporarily or durationally longer occurs when listening to** bad. **shall You denounce** satan **through faith, hope and goodness from Me? yes.'**

wonderful answer. You, may have noticed, satan has refrained being capitalized from your writer's perspective because negative entity receives zero respect and remains denounced every morning upon awakening. denouncing satan, allows your procession through day filled with calmness, contentedness, functional and optimistic thought processes. with this said, as day progresses, an occasional pessimistic or inappropriate thought enters mind requiring praying optimistically to **God**, for one millisecond, for bad entities denouncement further. over time, negative presence becomes less: **God's** good enmeshment asphyxiates badness. consciously praising **God**, praying for others and thinking optimistically, negativity, in mind lessens and remains how your thoughts and will remain affected optimistically from **God**, rather than from what's its name. these good thoughts derive through writer's soul, thus, herein lie two parables relating how negative entity's dysfunction and distorting perceptions causes further displeasure in heart, mind, and soul relating generational and societal dysfunction through earth.

in first example, **You** may replace alcohol with any specific causing **You** or another in family, emotional or physical discomfort, thus, excessive shopping, over eating or substance abuse contributing to individual, thus, increasing societal digression.

ergo:

driving home, john realized how his life was becoming increasingly wretched: remaining feeling discontented, irritable, overwhelmed and restless, because his personal and professional life were diminishing rapidly. wife lisa and two young Daughters catherine and kate, loved john immensely, however, remained feeling temporal, generational and societal pressures, also. working in the same vocation for two decades, john, remained aware of downsizing in company and his work was reorganizing for heightened efficiency and corporate restructuring. unbalanced, realized he may become placed upon black list in near future or rather next to go.

You see, john, proceeded home this evening for his wife and children, suddenly an overwhelming weakness overcame him: fleshly and spiritually instilled within, satan was aware, dysfunctionally placing a thought through his overwhelmed mind, regarding one specific liquor store, cyclically, becoming increasingly frequented. for purpose of escaping discontented and overwhelmed life, john, was aware how he would feel soon after beginning drinking. pleased and remaining triumphant, bad entity knew exactly what would occur following johns over consumption of alcohol.

following first drink john feels a sense of calmness and contentedness, numbing or slowing overwhelmed mind, however, lacking moderation, sometimes many inequities infect his consciousness, the bad energy grins. hung over following morning, johns distorted feelings, thoughts, thus, behaviors were reasoning for another families fleshly demise.

victorious, bad entity triumphantly relaxes and is completely satisfied as detrimental intentions remain working perfectly. feeling shunned, **God**, views this amazing family dissolving because of john's thinking, stemming from satan's wrath; distorting and perverting his thoughts, thus, inappropriate, justified and rationalized behaviors.

proceeding with your second example, relating dysfunction on physical earth and **Our** occasional sadness. traveling very deep. percentage wise, **God's** wonderful and underwhelming wonderful existence vs. satan's dysfunction and misery through **Our** lives remains magnificently unparalleled. from spiritual, **Our** fleshly personas percentage continuously vacillates from good to bad, dependent on faith in **God** or lack thereof through positive or negative thought processes, choices, behaviors and former lineage. former lineage? **God** remains aware of your entire existence: parents, grandparents, great grand parents and so forth, therefore, dependent upon what has occurred throughout **Their** lives: relative with thinking, good behaviors, having faith and praying for others; **God**, blesses numerous offspring's functional and optimistic thinking accordingly, thus, compounded throughout **Their** nurturing. (shall be noted: this too is easily remedied.)

very well, think of someone living downtrodden who takes ill care of themselves. they are receiving unhealthy nutrients, lack exercise, ingest illegal or prescription medications and remain negative: smoking and sleeping little, seems they should have horrible disposition, however, remain living with a very healthy complexion. wondering, asking why **Their** complexion beautifully transpires clearly for Them? **You** have friendly conversation and part ways preceding back within current life, possibly living in moment or flesh only. proceed directly to the point immediately: **You** asked **Them** a question relative with lineage and faith, herein lies your answer.

God, loves and assists generationally and genetically blessed individual offspring. from **God**, **You** shall receive propensities through emotional, mental or physical, accomplishing more achievements than parents and grandparents have, thus, **You** shall become wonderful future lineage, your children then grandchildren aspire.

You remain well aware, **God**, has power over everything existing, through earth. once **You** receive an ability, living within his spirit, rather than remaining merely in flesh; through guidance from **God**, assisting your mind sufficiently well, receiving underwhelmedness and love, life, remains wonderfully calm, magnificent and gorgeous as desired.

blessings in life, come continually from **God**, **You** may refrain seeing an abundance because images and thought processes of **Yourself** temporarily remain distorted or overwhelmed at times, thus, lacking **God's** wonderful potential, through You. regarding prayer, numerous prayers are answered immediately, dependent on your thinking and behaviors: all prayers for **You** and others remain answered from **God**, in time. when distortions through your day have ceased preceding sleep, proceed under gorgeous moon and stars, breathing deeply in through nostrils and out through mouth slowly, praying for calmness, peace and unity in **Yourself** and those nearest: infectiously good becomes **You** and many prayed for: what **God**, abundantly gives, remains calmness for sleep and then, excess useful energy for your following awakened moments when needed.

'I, remain good and female, as well: earth was given for humans and remains wonderfully pacified or otherwise dependent on your perceptions and faith: atheists express otherwise, however, shall learn spiritual truth in My time. I shall continue working My global plan through You and numerous others willingness.'

allow your perspective through anger, control over others, depression, impatience, negativity or through God's continuous goodness, calm and function through You. please, embrace calmness enveloping your heart, rather than pessimistic prejudice. denouncing pessimism and negative human behavior while enmeshing optimism, calmness, hope, love, thus, peace integrated through life, God, showers You with abundant blessings of love, calm and patience, then follow Her love above all the others.

discussed previously, satan remains present in God's world through catastrophic occurrences: transpiring through a negative energy within nature; lightning, hurricanes, mudslides, tornadoes, tsunamis, shifting plate tectonics and earthquakes causes chaos and negatively affects countless. God, is present through humans perfect nature and optimistic thought processes, thus, behaviors, healing and restoring humanism with peace from him. oppositionally, from God's broad or specific awareness of Our thoughts and behaviors for others, satan does, as unwell and unbalances balance, stability, harmony, thus, equilibrium, decreasing your faith, hope and love. very well, You comprehend spirits in Us all and life remains good.

You ask why satan has powers or why, God, as an overwhelmingly more powerful entity refrains denouncing it, figuratively, keeping bad or horrible entity, in check? here remains another answer from God, for a previous question regarding why he allows badness occurring for good people. compounding through life, there are consequences for You and lineage inappropriate thoughts, thus, behaviors from satan, thereto, remains one intrinsic and viable deliverer of love and wonderfulness, whom redeems and relieves, via, your optimistic thought processes and behaviors, for **You** and your offspring: shall **You** call him **God**? acts 17:24-28 yes, **We** shall.

satan's here to heighten your belief, faith and trust. from and with **God**, every negative occurrence through consciousness, humanism and weather decreases through and around **You** perfectly when reasoning non impulsively.

herein lies appropriate place for another empirically true story. was a young boy, three years of age in enid, oklahoma, visiting maternal great grand Mother and a yellow jacket had bothered sister: She relayed information, immediately into your writer's mind. before She shared information, voice in mind said where a broom was and picking up a broom, voice said, 'hit the nest.' proceeded toward specific conifer tree where nest loomed, thus, began striking yellow jacket nest with all the force of small boy. suddenly, an enormous swarm descended upon **Their** attacker. shall leave details aside, however, was placed in bath tub, packed with meat tenderizer, from head to toe with over 200 stings. entire body swelled, comparable with a balloon: when writing this in book, became aware, satan yielded these impulsive thoughts and feelings and without reason, was directing your writer in harms way; **God**, was who saved self. this moment forward, stinging insects were terrifying to writer, sensing this they descended throughout life stinging spiritually tense, thus, fleshly, tense persona.

please, forward 37 years. following spiritual rebirthing was cleaning back yard, one wasp landed on arm; rather than flailing arms uncontrollably, while running swiftly, felt completely calm. with **God's** calming presence completely in body, mind and spirit, **God** spoke, '**place middle finger specifically under this wasp.**' wasp, who always was terrifying, walked onto finger and following direction in soul, from **God**, proceeded further moving hand slowly six inches in front of eyes.

calmly, watched this wasp with amazement: **God**, had taken all tension away. specific story remains a parable for calmness given if **You** let go, then listen and trust **God's** suggestions through your soul, negativity ceases. further, in book, **You** shall become aware of enormous miracles occurring through nature, technology and human behavior from **God**, when writing offspring, ultimately for his chosen reader's awareness of every mystery.

here remains another miracle from **God**, occurring upon the summer of year 2010.

communicating with **God**, prayed for others while mowing six acres with sean. had finished, **God** said, **'get off mower and walk into field.'** did. in field, the voice said, 'step two strides to left.' did. sean, had driven around directly in front and mower went over a fire ant pile, 69, flew onto bare legs stinging at once. **God** said, **'pray for** pain **being insignificant**.' thus did. had minimal pain, was uncomfortable though. **God** said, **'wave sean down,'** sean came around again, stopping and pointing down to stings, he said, 'oh, I bet that hurts!' immediately and psychosomatically pain overwhelmed writer. parable, choose words wisely when negative.

following occurrence, **God** said, **'was a lesson for Our book. what shall occur with 50 plus fire ant piles?'** thought, they were satan and prayed for **Them** gone. following week, mowing again fire ants were gone and next season walked out, **God** said, **'walk to one pile and look down.'** queen was coming out of the hole. asking **God**, what to do next he said, 'step **on queen for She has** satan **working through Her.'** thus did, praying for fire ant piles gone, throughout edmond then country and earth. they vanished as known through three places here in edmond. two years later when first edition of offspring was published, douglas stussi said, 'the fire ants are gone throughout the central u.s.' **God** had your writer open the book to this page and showed him why. in humanism, it was because of your writer's prayer, however, ultimately the prayers are from **Our** creator.

following reading the previous story, **You** may have wondered how to discern the good voice/thought process from the bad, because 'take two strides to the left,' may have been good? answering this question, this was a learning time following the rebirth process, as instructed and earlier in life, always had faith and did exactly how directed most often, however, there were a few profound exceptions.

here remains one: again, written with emphasis 08.16.15

2003 when visiting the white river in arkansas, walking across a tall bridge and holding evon who was a toddler, a voice spoke, 'throw your Son over the rail and into the river if **You** love Me.' without reasoning, had turned towards the side of the bridge: **God** spoke over a millisecond, **'refrain: why would You do this? he would** die.' confused and telling no one, reason had showed itself, the dualistic battle continued within your writer's consciousness until the final rebirth in 2009: finally became aware, from Abraham through present humans and enlightening others of truth.

'Upon book God's offspring's third revision, I spoke for You to write this and additional stories for others. continue to ask and do as I direct You: whom I work through shall receive My future wellness and truth.'

another story. predication first. continuously elated from communications with **God**, was fall or winter of 2009. **God**, was asked and was silent and then spoke, **'write story upon final editing, others shall remain aware when this occurred.'** as everyone reading, your writer sometimes forgets and has distorted perceptions, thus, influenced from bad entity because throughout life, your writer, has vacillated with having the whole armor of **God's** splendor, therefore, spiritual awareness to having zero in the blink of an eye: **God** said, **'when You are** weak **You are strong.'** more information: learning mysteries of **God**, why earth works well or refrains, had feelings of enlightening bliss and knowledge to sadness: who is your writer? **'proceed one of My sons, your human and spiritually influenced as all others. when your following My directions, life is good and when your adhering to** negativity **in humanism, from** satan's bad infection, **life is sometimes bad:** infectiousness **through souls causes feelings of** weakness **through your minds. stay faithful, I, shall bless You countless miracles within your life for a multitude.'**

very well, relating through your parable, **God**, has spoken. life, remains spiritual through humanism. now, your aware why Jesus had become angry, thus, toppled tables of many others treating sacred walls of the temple as a joke for **Their** prosperity: temple as a joke for **Their** prosperity. **'if Jesus was God as a man, he would have thought for Them to be** gone: his thoughts would've occurred and he would have refrained from becoming angry. the reason Jesus became angered was because throughout his life, his prayers from Me occurred and when his prayers refrained from working he became angry. he remained unaware of the illusion of power as all writer's of religious doctrines and spiritual vessels. robert was revealed this information for your and My future: awareness of truth, spoken for enlightening numerous of My chosen.'

returning to story. following God's advice, he said, 'walk outside each morning,' embellished upon fact Their were continuous ravens squawking loudly, until God, was pronounced more powerful than satan and then they fly away. God asked, 'what shall You desire occurring with these loud ravens?' unable focusing on prayer, thought, 'desired the ravens becoming deceased.' that evening God, said, 'watch and pray for world news.' newscast regarded thousands of black birds or ravens fell from sky in bebe, arkansas. God spoke, 'You were unspecific.' perplexed, had prayed for Them specifically gone here in edmond, with no avail.

if You remain only a good God, asked why. he spoke, 'remember, it's My will, rather than Yours.' thank You God, writer concurs with your good through life and shall follow your will rather than own.

he spoke, 'You're welcome: all your prayers and praising are from Me perfectly through You and others whom are willing, I have a plan.'

God? 'yes My son.' how much longer shall your writer wait for many to be transformed? 'are relationships with all of your family members and friends frictionless?' yes. 'is your Son blessed further and doing well at school and home?' yes. 'are You aware, specifically and generally, how the world works?' yes. 'has negativity been extinguished within your consciousness and minimized within those around You?' yes. 'are You aware of what I have promised?' yes. 'continue doing My will and all is well: this is My decision rather than Yours: remember, this information occurred upon this juncture for many reasons. one, remains to heighten awareness, thus, numerous chosen humans shall receive continual goodness, as well.' thank You God, all is well and You are praised. 'You are welcome.'

'The final significant denounced oceanic weather anomaly that shall affect the land of north America occurred upon september of 2015. I asked robert to pray for this to decrease to a tropical storm when affecting western mexico. he did as spoken: pamela, traveling to puerta vallarta the following day, spoke with him regarding the significant hurricane approaching. he said to pam, 'all remains well.' every good and true word Jesus spoke was from his Father as well.'

'2016: I spoke, pray the eye of the hurricane remains off the south east united states: it did. previously, I spoke, pray for it to weaken and dissipate before haiti: uncertainty continued: My Son ask Me why?

I said, everything is My decision: proceed further, You are elected.'

'Humans shall learn truth: where We shall proceed into the future. numerous currently are learning to refrain from relying on media and politics for truth: from uncertainty, many will receive certainty.'

STILL WAVERING? YOU HAVE EVOLUTION

progressing regarding evolution: these uncertain thoughts were discussed earlier and shall delve deeply answering some questions from **God**, enlightening further. through recent times within schools of higher learning and conversations through families or colleagues throughout societies, **You** or another were taught evolution. evolutionists believe, everything alive through natural selection have causational existence and how **We** evolved over time. over millions or billions of years when one cell splits repetitiously. **God** asks, **'elephants are related with mosquitoes?'**

upon year of 1990. arriving on campus at u.c.o. in edmond, was speaking with rehabilitative services regarding receiving some assistance for books and tuition. following conversation with a counselor, **God** spoke, **'pray for Her and others when leaving building.'** voice then said, 'walk across campus and into specific building and one classroom already in progress.' voice said, 'sit within back of classroom of thirty students' and stated what the professor was to say and how shall be replied. professor asked the class to give an example of something non-empirical: without hesitation, replied, 'God.' nodding accordingly, he said, 'your exactly correct.' now, realize was incorrect, voice heard in mind, thus, throughout life, sometimes was bad entity distorting the real truth through millions of souls, therefore, minds within humanism.

here is another factual story through another experience. as expressed formerly, have and shall refrain telling untruths, neither shall speak sarcastically for sarcasm remains unresolved anger, thus, what comes from lips, rather from fingers on these pages shall remain empirically factual from origination through concluding words.

upon final editing, **God** continues to ask, **'are You ready My chosen son?'**

'yes, if this is your will and plan.' **'good, why do You think I had You write this book?'** for your truth. **'I have qualified You throughout life.'**

God, remains working through humble writer, then Yourself, effectively resolving many of life's questioned specifics and instilling functional stability, harmony and equilibrium for You, offspring and others who need solace through awareness, continuous love and continual direction.

ergo:

attempted culminating evolution with **God's** apparent presence, thus, enmeshing spiritual and evolution, performed research online. mind You, **God** was asked and spoke, **'look up information online.'** copying and pasting excerpt from charles darwin's origin of species, was desiring to convey origin of earth remains from **God**, through evolution: another perfect miracle had occurred through technology. copying text then pasting writings in book, **God**, booted word perfect application. proceeded pasting text onto a blank document for editing evolution working with religion; subsequently implementing **God's** spiritual origination of earth through evolution, attempted copying and pasting document within book. what occurred this time?

yes, was booted out of word perfect, all together, again. **God**, worked splendidly revealing another question regarding evolution and had proceeded exclaiming his profound and undeniable thoughts through writer for your perfect enlightenment.

'I had You look up the information online because I was aware what would occur.'

'My good world given unto humans, countless are treating as if it were a machine. My offspring, remain aware, throughout history, I, have watched those whom attempt disproving **Me and the ideas that have been allowed within your minds: receive My truth and what shall occur. rely on Me, in time, everyone shall learn My and Their factual truth.'**

God, remains the cosmos creator and wonderfully unites humans within every nation. those with solid faith or millions of others having nil and believing in zero more wonderful than themselves and disbelieve, **God**, is the reason **You** are: remain blessed and enlightened further for a reason.

mentioning further, those who dishonor **God**, altogether through acceptance, **God** has a plan and others shall find him upon **Their** own. because **You** are reading in depths of these pages, **You** may be interested and searching for answers: searching, **You** become aware there remains one entity a quintillion times greater than anything existing around You. writer upon vulnerable junctures, pondered something other than **God**, as unwell. learning evolution upon an impressionable age, many years after, psychosomatically believed humans evolved becoming taller and increasingly intelligent, your writer questioned religion. confused, for **God** spoke of future occurrences continuously.

God calmly speaks, **'unless You are able proving otherwise, your entire existence and everything good that remain seen and unseen remains joyously and calmly perfected from Me, a good God of love and peace.'**

You see, especially with current behavioral, generational, economical and societal circumstances, may **You** find him now. your quote from **God**

regarding evolution, 'there remains healthy, unhealthy, intelligent, less intelligent, aware, unaware, tall and short living presently, same as Abrahams day and numerous generations between: I chose Them.'

empirically factual is God. numerous attempt disproving good entities existence, many more are viewing God's love, present within Their lives: in fact, those who know his empirical factualness, dance, live, love, sing, run, sleep and think better. rather than disproving God's, reality upon wonderful earth; seek, devotion, faith, hope, love, optimism and peace. increasing faith-praising and praying: energy, monetary sufficiency and relative time increases—God's functional productivity arrives enveloping every blessing through every faithful life: always has and always shall.

providing education through others and generational healing, God, in You, reveals wonderful and enticing occurrences transpiring: generational issues are formidable regarding feeling downtrodden, via, thinking for personas among masses globally. inequities: attributed through anger, chemical dependency, crime, domestic abuse, impatience, obesity, low self worth, image, theft, thus, numerous other behavioral improprieties are fleshly related significantly through generational discountedness, instilled through souls, spiritually from satan. denounced, life becomes filled with affluence, calmness, inner contentedness and disallows egocentric thinking, thus, behaviors: refocus your good life, from God's, optimistically wonderful direction. wonderful or problematic, good or bad thinking originates from God, or otherwise. You may think, modifying the human psyche is complex or exponentially varied: entailing intense therapy, culminating modifiable variables preceding healthiness. mortals, over time, need further instruction regarding individual therapy sessions, confiding with other humans and medications for generational solace: medications come with a cost, side affects, time away from family, as well as, professional life.

let Yourself go and follow your continuous, available and free direction; your creator works alone and through others perfectly well. any specific inequity shall be released through your willingness and over God's time.

herein lies one exceptional place for further delving. stated within previous third sentence, most mortals shall need further instruction or remains specifically where **You** shall be instructed otherwise, **You** are an individual rather than most mortals. **You** are beautiful, calm, exceptionally intelligent and a wonderfully adept individual: what remains needed for calm and comfort in mind shall be an entity, whom intimately has known your desires, feelings and thoughts your entire life, this remains **God**.

ask Yourself, 'shall I spend My time, money and effort fulfilling psychiatrist's beliefs with unneeded medications or follow the direction freely given within your heart, mind and soul for your spiritual relief?'

countless believe they must rely upon others for resolving inequities within **Their** bodies, when reality shows itself, the originations remain spiritually directed through and within everyone living, as well as, breathing well.

denouncing pessimistic psychosomatic labels, as well as, generational discountings heightens function and awareness: focusing on letting go of everyday overwhelmed feelings, through prayer, life remains splendid. **God**, blesses **You** with calm, love and wonderful strength, through your heart, mind and soul, when following his suggestions rather than your own. **God**, listens and relieves all personal discountings, and **You** proceed forward appropriately, thus, progressing Yourself, family and society. numerous reading, are completely aware of **God's** good, wondrous presence and miracles occurring continually: stated previously, he is present for all on earth who are needing solace presently. **God**, shall always be present. what **You** need is believing, praying, receiving and thinking optimistically for your future rather than infectiously remaining negative and saddened.

everyone reading and abundance on every continent have pondered who **God** is, what role he has with present, however, perceptions differ related through beliefs: every human has an intimate and personal **God** in Them, amongst every religion. many humans encompassing previous cynical generations believe **God**, made this world, as well as, everything within, however, also believe his presence through current life ceases existing. meaning, many faithful believe **We** are conceived and nurtured from parents, then life progresses and **God** gives good free will and thinking determining what **Our** lives ultimately become. writer, typically amongst masses, culminating past and present, comprehends the reasoning humans rely significantly on others only and **Their** existence are less certain absent others assistance. individual's learned thoughts/feelings occur from man.

in fact, aware of one specific worldly, successful and intellectual human, in his 60's believing satan rules earth. saying, 'many priests and preachers believe this.' statement explains thinking and behaviors throughout life. man is writers Father. expressing august 14th 2010, when your writer was directed to initiate one conversation regarding **God's**, love and optimism vs. satan's bad infectious pessimism and overtaking numerous human souls.

Father said, '**God**, has halted his love and peace today.' completely incorrect he remains, thus, was this satan working through his soul and discouraging his son's enlightened and correct perception from **God**, through your writer? following his negativity, asked **God** and he said, '**absolutely yes, many** defy **My optimism.**' shall be stated: Father, over the last six years has become increasingly calmed, quiet, gentle and more optimistic from continual prayers/ thoughts for him from your writer.

having a third complete rebirthing upon 40 years of age, shall express similarly. many reading, feel likewise with what shall transpire in the later paragraphs, thus, writings are freely given for countless who currently remain unaware of **God's** presence through all pleasure filled contentedness, happiness, optimistic occurrences and thought processes experienced. desiring your higher comfort, solace, strength, increased faith and praise, **God**, reassuringly reciprocates through and within countless individuals continually for humans future wellness, from and for the **God** of humans.

allow enlightenment, here lies another perfect and appropriate place for a factual story relevant through **God's** specific wonderfulness and loveliness for goodness.

ergo:

involved in discussions with adult bible study january of 2010, **God** said to say, '**God** remains function through all existence, specifically calm winds in nature.' without pause, actually disallowing last few words expressed, one well respected retired professor in class room remarked, '**God**, has no relevance with wind, high or low pressure systems, they are Mother nature and **God**, has zero significance.' replied, **God** is Mother natures goodness. time for classes dismissal, allowed debate to lie calmly, for his belief or distorted evolutionist perspective remains respected well.

immediately professor's shoulder began twitching. **God** spoke, '**ask Me to bless the u.s.a., then ask Me to alleviate his** twitch.' did exactly. twitch immediately resolved.

allow proceeding deep. following church while remaining still and quiet, began consoling **God**, intimately: conclusion remains, allowing atmospheric anomalies through high and low pressure systems and every gentle gust of wind are from **God** and prayer through **Us** from him. stated previously on the subject, **God** has ultimate control over everything seen and unseen, through past, present and future lives; those faithfully following his will shall receive heightened awareness and perspective.

upon this juncture, **God** said, '**read and write galatians 1:11. 'but I certify to You brethren, the gospel which is preached from Me is** not **according to any man.**'

God, your writer is a man? **God** replied, '**yes, these words are from Me and I have qualified You through your willingness and love for all people: I decide when good individual and societal paradigm shifts occur. I have a wonderful plan, time has come for others to be revealed My mystery; the door of utterance has opened wide and those who rely on Me shall receive continual blessings of safety, as well as, favor.**'

completely present through Us, **God**, allows **You** emitting conscious and subconscious present feelings, emotions and prayers: living in the Spirit and doing **God's** will repetitiously, winds and your mind calms from specific prayers. life remains good and **You** are increasingly connected.

humans, have more of an illusion of influence with **God's** wonderful world regarding **Their** living auras and nature than they are aware: **God**, speaks through writer's heart, mind, soul, thus, love for You.

God speaks twice:

'You intrinsically hold keys in your human lives that shall further You calmly or otherwise; cherish lives and families, pray and think of calmness, patience and loving one another, whilst praising My calm, good and righteous name.'

'Idolizing technologically inscribed devices or methods, affects lives: embrace calmly, for I shall dictate all of Our good communication.'

having abilities to purchase unneeded material items, assisting and becoming more organized and efficient, numerous are living within flesh and sometimes, idolizing **Them** above **God**. hmm. bible says this. many remain unable purchasing unneeded items because of generational improprieties within **Their** soul and this hinders **Their** functionally blessed thought processes and feelings, thus, success.

while everyone, sometimes has stagnantly compounded relative pain, **God**, remains expressing compassionate thoughts and feelings for all his offspring; **God**, from and through loving grace, remains whom encompasses everyone on a beautiful blessed earth, seeking peace within **Our** souls.

individually, life progresses well when correct thinking occurs: when your perspective remains faithful from **God**, through You, then life remains wonderful rather than otherwise. viewing your successes and failures in life, three pertinent questions are apparent.

first, how have **You** accepted pain from others and received an ability from **God**, learning from your past mistakes and allowing the past to be past? secondly, relating with significant other, how foundationally solid are **You** fleshly? third, are **You** spiritually one together? yes, this process occurs perfectly when living with **God** rather than Yourself.

aware there remains a plethora of criterion why **You** are contented with life and these questions remain relative: specific questions remain imperative because how **You** feel and think remains programmed silently throughout every persona from **Their** rearing: life remains instantaneously modifiable, then your actions and reactions, for and from others, remains consistently appropriate.

love others through wonderful heart and think optimistically through your mind: remember, all humans are **God's** offspring and **We** are living upon earth for peaceful togetherness. societies are complex because many have made life this way throughout history from negativity within differing religious ideologies, egocentricity and indifference of others: **You** remain aware where egocentric thinking has derived.

'In My perspective all are related; I, desire You living and loving others well and observing how good life is because You are abundantly blessed further from Me.'

spoken and written previously regarding some people seeming to have everything working well for **Them** through all life's facets and others refrain catching a break. upon a fleshly level, humans remain aware how others think only from what they verbalize and how they behave, therefore, how they think relates to how they feel.

following two years of heightened spiritual awareness, as life, then received none: zero worked well, prayers refrained from working at all, winds continued fast and ravens followed writer everywhere squawking loudly: disheveled, asked **God** why.

God spoke, '**I have enlightened You regarding humanism, spirits and weather, now You are doing your will rather than asking Me what You shall do for Me. live within My good Spirit and ask My will. I taught You, pray to receive the questions and answers I desire: follow My good will and numerous shall receive perfected direction through and from Me. I have a plan through You and others elected whom listen well to Me.'**

asking his will, life worked well, ravens flew off and winds ceased from prayers.

feeling hopeful and spiritually enmeshed from words, it was so; what a wonderful feeling remaining lovingly intertwined with **Our** creator's frictionless direction rather than controlled negatively.

when **You** feel particular ways, this corresponds how others treat You, how frictionless your moments traverse, how sporadic your thoughts and behaviors, how grounded and prayer full for others, thus, optimistic and focused on **God's** direction within your three faceted self. **God** said, '**there remain more chosen people than others and vacillates individually and then societally: your willingness lives in Me.**' majority of humans whom have calmness, patience, kindness, frictionless drives, vehicles requiring less maintenance, calm personal and professional relationships and healthy families are chosen when **God**, envelops **Their** good faith, positive communications, as well as, behaviors. reciprocating continuously through countless humans, **God**, desires enveloping your frictionless Spirit as well.

how your fleshly life transpires, why numerous good and bad experiences occur within your life are spirituality through You. **You** may think, if i'm unchosen why try?

God lovingly speaks, '**when** lethargic **of following** pain **and** uncertainty, **follow My direction. countless offspring globally, have gone from** unchosen **to chosen in a blink of My eyes: when desiring abundantly more favor, love, pacification and time, You shall receive My potential through You. remember, life becomes consistently pleasurable and then You shall ponder why You refrained from receiving continuous blessings earlier in life. the past has passed,** negative **thoughts from the past are far from Me and the future is continuously present for any whom desire peace.**'

'**I have asked My writer to ask Me to heal atheist's in europe, muslims in pakistan, agnostics where I choose, as well as, numerous christians globally because they are all offspring from Me: I have a global plan.**'

Chapter

CORRECT CHOSEN PATHWAY

throughout history, societies are influenced from **Our** creator through **Our** caring, loving and wonderfully optimistic nature or from satan through angry confusion, impatience, verbal and physical abusive nature, **You** understand. look around **You** upon one another's behaviors, politics and societal discountings. in a macro scale of **Our** existence, **God**, is goodness and satan is badness, **You** know this. throughout history, humans feelings, thoughts, agendas, beliefs and behaviors are predicated from **God** or otherwise. numerous living elderly, understand this premise exactly: they idolize zero ipods, blackberries or technological devices, thus, know more regarding spiritual life's presences within Us, more than most youthful generations.

remaining very aware, observing through **Their** hearts, thus, minds what remains occurring presently, however, feel helpless because youths dismiss elders thoughts because youths think themselves have correct information, this remains untrue upon a plethora of deep levels of thinking.

think for a moment, new generations come forward, they become more interested with **Their** temporal material possession, outward appearance, glowing white teeth, rock hard abdominals, as well as, plethora of many egocentric enhanced variables, rather than having soul cleansed from a holy spirit: why speedo needs capitalized while heaven and the holy Spirit refrain upon word perfect, behooves your writer. humanism remains surface, thus, impressing others through images as paramount. why? oh yes, now 'I' remember, it's all about 'Me,' is it? the latin word for ego is 'I'. **'life is praising Me, prayer and love for others, then You shall receive peace, harmony and your perspective modifies perfectly for what You have always desired, My hopeful direction, thus, stability and serenity.'**

as a child, remember, Mother would say: 'it's not what's on outside that counts, it is what's on the inside?' countless heard this appropriate statement in youth also, however, within what juncture from life had offspring began believing otherwise?

possibly when the majority began realizing stigmas associated with aesthetically appealing persons remained accepted from peers in school and throughout all of **Our** medias. remain completely aware, writings are for a good purpose: thinking outside the **You** box: there is reasoning **God** allows **Us** to function and live, upon the same moment **We** remain enveloped and living in the Spirit with **God's** perfect feelings and direction. **You** are an individual and status quo remains irrelevant: how **You** judge, criticize or behave, affecting others negatively, remains derived from soul, heart and mind. from **God's** love enveloping your wonderful soul, human lives work beautifully. shall **You** proceed deep? very well, **You** shall. from **God's** macro perspective, through human thinking and behaviors presently occurring upon all continents: many are moving and becoming further disassociated from **God's** original desires. commencing when masses of humans depended less from his word in **Their** mind and abundantly on **Their** own will and ego—this is the paradigm for which specifics seem unsolvable—and this sets in motion the paradigm shift, which shall occur individually and societally well.

having less awareness within minds through history, humans viewed themselves more powerful than they previously had thought and began feeling powerful rather than powerless comparative to **God's** splendor. **God**, so desires your humbleness. throughout human history, mortals have enmeshed **Their** good and bad behaviors, agendas, beliefs, desires and thoughts with others showing brilliance and otherwise.

discussed previously, **God**, yields prevalence for those who believe and praise his name accordingly. those who desire, feeling happy and able contributing through charity and good deeds among humanity with time, energy and monetarily for less fortunate remains reciprocated from **God**, through **Their** thinking and continuous blessings, thus, individuals are compensated well through these good deeds: **God** remains all goodness.

wonderful occurrences transpire for those functionally living through **God's** way progressing forward assisting others: jealous, exclaim **Them** lucky, however, lucky is incorrect, they remain blessed from **God**, through **Their** living upon earth and then forever eternally.

there remain zero coincidences: when individuals win the lottery or other significant amounts of monies:

'I desire **Them** using money through charities and helping others; when satan **alters Their thoughts and heightens a** bad **agenda through** chemical abuse, sexual impropriety or dysfunction, what shall they and society to learn.'

throughout history, countless have desensitized themselves away from **God** : what prerequisite shall be required for receiving solace and contentedness again? actually, there remains an extremely simple solution and quite easily remedied. turning your will and life over, following **God's** direction, praying for others then your needs are provided for: **God**, is inner peace and many continue searching for solace through humanism. remember definition of insanity? having the same thinking and behaviors, yet, looking for a different result each time.

believing your a healthy thinker receiving progress through your egocentric mind, disallowing **God's** calmness, thus, reproaching psychosomatically ingested pain. meaning, individual insatiable minds think egocentrically and abide to pessimism: resist temptation. psychosomatically adhering, through other's negative views of humanism, how shall **You** become proficient, progressing for **Yourself** and your wonderful family?

traveling so far, all humans, living through satan's subtle or profound disasters on **God's** physical earth, yet, still many minds remain undeniably impervious or resistant. meaning, succeeding through your life, **God**, remains completely aware and he, coexists through and with **You** when having healthy choices, ideas and behaviors: **God**, gave **You** Them. when listening to him, self indulgence lessens and a plethora of negative thoughts and feelings alleviate, thus, **You** have more time and a favor filled drive to receive perfect direction and peace within your soul, then heart and mind.

exceedingly, countless of humans defy **God**, thus, recede backwards and act as if, they remain increasingly more powerful than they really are or have been. if this remains You, unequivocally life passes **You** further. **God**, placed **You** on his earth, becoming one wonderful thinker, thus, desires **You** following his suggestions. offering your three faceted life, **God**, assists placing **You** on his path, relinquishing your will and following his perfect direction rather than your inconsistent own. ask and listen well.

once **You** allow **Yourself** letting go and **God** takes away specific hindrances, holding back the potentials of your mind, shall **You** proceed experiencing what has been desired for **You** before **You** were conceived: peace, splendor, an optimistic mindset, elation, a bold and confident self image, wonderful relationships and continuous contentment. life's good, then **You** wonder, why numerous in society continues living in humanism; anxiety ridden, overwhelmed and stressed, when life in **God's** good Spirit is vastly available and calmness through your differential advantage.

'There shall be a global revolution through numerous blessed vessels receiving My love. twas industrial, then technological and Our future revolution shall be spiritual for those who listen: desiring less friction **and** negativity **with heightened and abundant blessings, I am God and You are Mine.—here is the global plan.** life has been is and **shall remain spiritual: numerous humans think they have the power, likewise, Our good feelings, optimism, thoughts and health remain derived from Me within Us:** enjoy your heightened awareness of My **unwavering commitment, truth, love and goodness within your life.'**

God? 'yes.' who is the anti-christ? **'if there was an anti-christ, would You look him boldly in the eyes and ask Me to denounce him forever for all?** yes, your good and infinite power prevails over bad. **'good, proceed safely My son: I have a wonderful plan that shall occur; I am all humans truth.'**

God? 'yes.' was Jesus aware of all human thoughts and feelings? **'are You?'** no. **'are You God?** no. **'this remains My and your answer for all vessels.'**

'Countless humans throughout history have received information within the bible and Their minds yielding a sensationalizing bad **consciousness, thus, emotional, mental and physiological** inequities **within Their bodies. You learned spiritual truth from Me in 2009, how healthy have We been?** zero emotional, mental or physiological illnesses/ inequities. **perfect, this is what shall occur through numerous chosen whom live within My spirit.'**

PAINFUL AWARENESS
INTO CONTINUAL LIGHT

preceding age two and through life, writer has received visions and voice in mind instructing where to go and what would be said through conversations with others. regarding circumstances through private or public life, voice in mind, sometimes continuously would say how people would move or what would be said, before movements or words spoken. preceding, space shuttles columbia and challenger disasters, voice, on lift off for one and reentry of other said what would occur and when: all writer could do was watch in horror, praying it would refrain occurring. over life, millions of specific subtle and enormous occurrences transpired with writers awareness preceding **Them** happening: here are a few of millions of examples.

when watching movies or television, was aware what would occur, because voice who **God's** writer has sometimes continuous conversations, expressed through thought processes, now remain completely aware, this one voice heard was **God**, when yielding heightened awareness. regarding mt. st. helens, was aware to millisecond when eruptions would occur, branch devidian compound in waco, texas, was aware preceding a.t.f. agent becoming shot through second story wall by two seconds, then, voice would say, 'tell no others.' before writing any writings in book, asked **God**, what his desires were, how to structure or proceed and he spoke on numerous occurrences, '**I, shall write through your soul, for humans to understand who good and** bad **entities are and why good or** bad **occurrences have transpired over life.**'

writer's life has been filled with joy and elation, to depression and sorrow nearly continuously throughout life, as possibly You. preceding the final rebirthing, always thought good and bad voice was **God**, however, following july 19th 2009, learned from **God** over one year what had occurred through life over millisecond clips in mind, showing when good thoughts, thus, behaviors were from him and the bad thoughts, thus, behaviors were otherwise. january 11th 2010 at 1:11 pm, learned from **God**, profound information related to christianity:

'**Forty apostles who had written of My goodness, yes, were hearing My voice, through Their souls and also heard** satan, **relaying information of** controlling **wife, females should attend church silently or** fear My **wrath, thus,** negative. **I, have always given desired calmness, love and optimism through everyone.** through mohammad, what he heard negatively **through mind when writing quran, also were from** satan. **I, impose zero** control **over or through anyone: when praising Me and asking God to bless others, life remains good; your peace lives within.**'

hearing earlier, in 2010, allowed information resting with permission from **God** ; then asked repetitively for one year, thus, confirmation after confirmation realized why humans behave as **We** do: knowing and had written regarding this previously, thus, shall allow resting, however, bible says **Fathers** shall be against sons, Mothers against Daughters and chaos, thus, conflict is inevitable. what if the bible would have said positive words from **God** only? God, said upon your books conception, '**humans would still have** satan **working through Them and causing** conflict; **thus, Our blessed book shall modify society and generations wonderfully into** the future: if thinking You have no control over others, this is true, however, I may modify anyone at anytime from your faith with Me.'

learning and hearing optimism throughout your life, changes everything better for offspring and Their lives becoming fluid and filled with a joy rather than pot holes.

plentiful useful energy comes from God, desiring Us striving increasingly further. let go of life's negative thinking, constructively alleviate fleshly bad hindrances, thus, having faith and believing God's, unending love for You remains paramount; rather than discountings instilled in Yourself, through others from negative entity, who distorts minds and behaviors, shall, inconsistent darkness become continual light.

SINNING AND SATAN
INTO GOD'S GOODNESS

current chapter remains relevant with sin and satan. first, encompassing societies, in fact, two billion plus humans upon **God's** earth presently, christians, learned through rearing process reading bible and attending church, all mortals are sinners. psychosomatically hearing this repetitively, bad behaviors are understood over life. herein lies one pertinent question. are **You** weak and sinful because **You** heard repetitive negativity in your rearing through mind generationally, then societally? human imperfection remains factual, yet, being sinful remains entirely outdated. consciously, humans determine to behave appropriately or inappropriately through mannerisms, thus, desiring pleasurable fulfillment in life or otherwise remains **Our** choice or does it? goodness comes from **God**, and Jesus dying for **Our** sins on a cross 2000 years prior remains the most significant occurrence for christians globally.

when in spirit, writer remains sinless because **God**, has taught through life there are consequences for negative thinking in humanism, thus, why should **We** all be labeled as sinners while numerous have outstanding dispositions, personas, thus, gentle thought processes through prayerful, thus, optimistic self actualizing lives? 'condemned **as** sinners **has taken hope from many of My offspring who heard this** negative **statement and who said this to apostles? was far from Me.'**

'negative **thought processes are far from being** sin, **they refrain from You initially: when earnestly focused and behave** badly **You become** controlled **from** satan.'

screaming and stealing humans remain aware these behaviors are inappropriate. all consciously whom remain behaving badly, receive understanding where they shall go, how they shall behave and who they are with, or do they? most yes, yet, some are unaware. minority believe they are controlled badly and remains factual.

upon this juncture, **God** spoke, write ephesians 6:11-12. **'put on the whole armor of God, that You may be able to stand against the** wiles **of the devil. We wrestle** not **against flesh or blood but principalities or the ruler of** darkness: **You have learned where your good derives.'**

satan is controlling more and more thoughts and behaviors, because many remain unaware of **God's** direction and believe **God** is also negativity: living through humanism, overwhelming a multitude of lives when badness occurs, numerous believe they happened to be at the wrong place at the wrong time: again, there are zero coincidences. (culminated energies: thoughts and feelings)

please, allow one story: james is humbled writer. **'write this story.'**

james, had received multiple driving under influence arrests through two decades. james, remains good most often, from **God's** blessings, however, with his heightened negativity, immaturity and overconfidence, james, sometimes was away from **God.**

directed spiritually, preceding age two: he was praying for others and received specific awareness from **God**, and was also controlled from satan: lives are spiritually determined.

learning philosophically within another way and refrained to live **God's will**, thus, fell deeply from temptations. observing, satan manifested deeper through writer's soul and worked through others; **God**, spoke truth regarding years 1987 through 1988. **'unknowing, You refrained following My good will, You listened to** bad **and questioned Me; soon, car** accident **ensued that was far from an** accident, **your Father's business had burned to the ground through a vision and your Mother had broken Her femur because You were doing mushrooms: your femur broke because** satan distorted **your thoughts, thus, presently You have been taught spirits power through your goodwill for everything and living in My Spirit from questions yields blessings of continual favor, direction and safety.'** is negative from your writer? **'they remain spiritually directed correlations through all: alone and within My writer, heightened peace occurs within human minds.'** do humans have the power to bless the goodness and denounce negativity through other humans?' **'yes, this good power remains dependent on My willingness through You.'** how shall others know if they receive this illusion of power? **'when they live in the Spirit with Me they shall know well.'**

following hearing and doing this, began thinking and feeling only well.

james, attended alcoholics anonymous meetings through his adult life, therefore, was fleshly taught after returning to drinking again, this was just a slip in aa's eyes, 'keep coming back, it works if **You** work it,' they say: this was far from a slip, for he knows what shall occur when drinking unmanageably, above **God's** positive direction in soul.

consciously taking another drink, allows satan strength through your uninhibited, temporarily weak and overwhelmed soul; badly, thus, infectious, satan, proceeds distorting your thinking with dysfunctional, egocentric, inappropriate, narcissistic and sometimes harsh verbal treatment for those loving and adoring, your family. sometimes there are fine lines in mind among perceptions, appropriate or otherwise, functional or dysfunctional, optimistically loving others and negatively depressed.

each moment **You** remain good, having best interest thinking, thus, praising **God**, and loving others your three faceted self heightens, thus, bad entity weakens and has significantly less power upon your occasional, vulnerable and negative perception.

from **God's** heightened, wonderful and optimistic thoughts flowing through your soul or otherwise; spiritually, these generationally inherent qualities or discountings are instilled through your soul. how **You** act, react, relate, think, what interests You, what **You** hear, see and feel, consciously and subconsciously through specific moments of your past, current and future life, determines ultimately how your fleshly life transpires. your aware, palpably well.

these are why sometimes, **You** receive abilities thinking perfectly well upon one moment, and then upon next have a brain freeze, thus, forgetting why **You** went to a specific location, appointment, deadline or room. life's, spiritually good or bad and **You** shall receive alleviation of negativities.

fleshly your life, remains culminating specific moments occurring simultaneously through senses, cognitively then behaviorally creating every persona through life. within your previous statement, every human directly or indirectly influence **Their** feelings, thinking, thus, interactions of others and themselves when alive in spirit. once culminated feelings, emotions and occurrences internalize, **You** precipitously remain making decisions predicated upon specifically what has transpired thus far.

when your feelings regard calmness, comfort, peace, as well as, love: this remains **God** placing contentedness through your wonderful heart. when embracing function throughout your wonderful senses, life is good and **You** become enmeshed with **God's** glorious plan desired within You. remember, your heightened awareness of truth occurred for a reason: for **You** to joyously share what's learned with others for **Their** awareness. your perfect spiritual enlightenment proceeds divinely through your soul.

while countless humans derive **Their** fulfillment through fleshly/temporal stimulation, numerous others are completed from spiritual enmeshment. progressing throughout your day, receive perfect direction through your consciousness, thus, ideology from **God** rather than material or Yourself. feelings, thoughts and behaviors become wonderful when **You** envelop a divinely guided and reciprocated grace from, with and through your soul. praising **God** and loving others remains the perfect reason for living well.

God remains the good energy within everything and alleviates negativity: he creates every individual and uniquely manifests goodness within your consciousness for his ultimate desire, peaceful unity within all offspring. when **You** rely continuously upon the goodness living inside your blessed soul shall **You** become cognizant of what **You** have desired all of your life. choosing your soul, heart, as well as, mind remains **God's** perfect desire.

when your worries, internal and external distortions continuously remain alleviated, **You** receive favored and peaceful sustainability, for all others. when this occurs, **You** shall receive pleasant certainty within, as well as, direction, thus, a calming peace within. You're living rather than existing.

when **You** receive the ability of allowing your ego and control to diminish further while asking and receiving perfect suggestions, shall your humbled blessings heighten well: remember, good enmeshed energies remain **God**. rely upon the goodness **You** have learned throughout life from reading the bible, **God's** offspring, as well as, communications with others, life is good: overtime, trials and tribulations dissipate - **You** have received a softer way.

'**I create all living creatures and dwell throughout Their good energy: allowing many individual humans to think they remain responsible regarding a release of Their** sometimes **negatively influenced souls, I am God and desire You to live within the perfected Spirit from Me.**'

'**Life shall remain spiritually predetermined: always loved, individual humans whom comprise the united states, as well as, governments abroad, shall receive an enmeshed ideology and desire serving My good will for the masses rather than Their own** egocentric **agenda.**'

'Jesus was different from My chosen writer: I spoke for robert to slate truth for future generations and humans shall receive My slated truth. when asked to remain silent, he shall, when asked to speak, he shall. as Jesus and revealed an abundance of what would occur around him, robert would refrain from calling any female a dog or the men on the boat cowards: I have enlightened robert well of where the origination of negative thoughts, feelings and every humans expression derive.'

'You have been revealed humans truth and My great mystery of why specifics occur well and unwell: what shall occur through and within Yourself? I remain aware and You aware of the good occurring for Us.'

God? yes My son? this information proves You are the reason for good: 'everything has occurred for a reason My son: We shall teach future generations, I remain peaceful love upon My glorious earth, I have a wonderful plan and shall reunite humans together as one for good.'

very well. regarding the book of revelation. 'yes.' what does this regard related with the present? 'the bible remains true within good respects: 1000 years of peace shall occur preceding My Jesus anticipated return. You remain created to speak My future will of good rather than bad.'

God? 'yes, My son? what shall occur? 'I shall heal numerous, calm the winds around You when I desire and unite humans globally from Me.'

what does this mean? 'You remain the chosen one, teaching humans the door of utterance spoken in the bible: I have told You this when equating your mind with a multitude of good occurrences within life.'

'I remain profoundly good: every famine, drought and negativity within everything are from satan's negative energy rather than God's energy. My words, as well as, actions through You shall prove My existence. the truth of everything shall be revealed within whom I choose for a reason.'

shall your chosen believe this information? 'when they become aware of My truthful predictions, through You, of a decrease of global weather anomalies, **numerous humans shall listen well: I have a perfect plan. remain humbly faithful My son: I have revealed specifics and general information regarding all humans consciousness and weather globally within You for others awareness; My and many future humans truth.'**

'**Do You know who You are?'** everything with You. '**yes, are You ready to prove My existence?** You are proving your existence: '**what I desire occurs: My writer remains available for others when ever I desire.'**

do **You** have a gentle plan for numerous who shall live in your present?

'**Yes.'**

'**The present is the future: ask and follow My perfected suggestions, life shall remain favored within You and those around You for Me:**

The instruction manual for life has been slated for future offspring.

Our book remains what shall be desired, learned, as well as, taught within My chosen offspring's souls, hearts and minds for the future.'

God? '**yes My son.'** regarding the book of revelation and the negativity spoken. what shall remain truth and what remains the fear causing farce?

'**You've written how good shall occur for others. how is your faith in My door of utterance?'** good. '**I have spoken well regarding everything: do You receive any** fear **or** anger?' no. '**do You have any** anxieties?' no. '**have all** inequities **been denounced within You, My perfect son?'** yes.

'**Ask Me and follow suggestions: My chosen humans shall learn truth.'**

SOUL, THUS, HEART
AND MIND

your current writings remain relevant with your inner three faceted self, therefore, body, mind and soul are centrally enmeshed through all of your feelings, thought processes, actions and reactions through your emotionally inscribed spiritual life. first- shall proceed with intellectualizing (mind). present societies are accessing abundantly more information, than **Their** fore **Fathers** and Mothers received: former generations received significantly less stimulation through information overload. were they less intelligent? life is relative and many had an edge with this respect. keeping life simple yields zero psychological medications or overwhelmedness: compounded unhealthy feelings remain plentiful throughout humanism presently.

with this stated, **God**, views **Our** intelligence wonderfully: he gives this to Us, thus, desires Us, further sharing **Our** correct knowledge with others assisting **Them** well. **God** believes in offspring's succession, thus, attempt viewing life as time passing, day to day, through less overwhelmedness or anxiety, from a plethora of incorrect or unneeded information instilled in all. there are countless myths and one truth. progress remains less dependent upon information overloading minds and feeling appropriate action remains intuitively felt through everyone's (hearts), thus, bodies. your heart feels what shall remain inherent and more assuredly correct, preceding, often times excessive intellectualized interpretations through many racing (minds).

here lies one palpable example: and there are two interjections, from your writer. first, your outside with nature upon the earth. second, the sky remains clear and sun filled from **God**, through blessings. distantly, **You** observe one unknown individual: examining visually and sense through **Their** non verbal communication, gate and behavior, something feels incorrect through **Their** distorted demeanor.

they walk closer, **You** are noticing **Their** eyes are filled with anger, nearly raging: looking elsewhere, **You** avoid eye contact or may turn away from **Them** entirely. **You** see, within this example, preceding receiving ability with processing further intellectually through (mind), your senses, (heart), body remain already aware. numerous humans label this as intuitiveness, while writer knows **You** may need a **God** ly verbal expression, **God**, desires quoted, '**I, bless all through Their senses.**' enveloping humans for your protection, **God**, works through senses, in all specific situations throughout **Our** blessed lives further encompassing **Our** heart (body), **God**, protects **Our** lives through subtle or dangerous specific occurrences from one satan.

your senses and heart (body), are working precipitously before intellect (mind), therefore, body and mind are imminently predicated from **God**, via, your (soul). throughout history, **God**, knows what **You** shall become, how many hairs are on your head, your thoughts, feelings and desires for offspring, **Yourself** and another. remember preceding chapters and through your good life hearing **God**, is love? **God**, remains love, always has and shall: now **We** go further, love is **God**, as well: living through all offspring, continually sews goodness through everyone of You. **God**, places himself into your (soul), **You** receive one perfectly intelligent (mind), thus, emitting **God's** wonderful love, through your (heart) and senses or body. what a wonderful and correlating three faceted self **You** possess.

emitting these delightful feelings of calmness and pureness through your persona, life is underwhelmed or eloquently flowing and more manageable than imagined. your peaceful serenity within **Yourself** reverberates and oscillates encompassing those near You, optimistically enveloped becomes everyone involved: when societies, become generationally calmer, functional and healthy from **God's** spiritual awareness, life is a pleasure. offspring's soothing living view becomes abundantly placated and healthy.

thank **You God**. from **You** and within your favored offspring, life is continuously good. '**You're welcome My son.**'

viewing society, **You** shall ponder strengthening a personal relationship from **God**, through religion or spirituality into You. globally, among technologically unified countries, there are extreme fluctuations of overwhelmedness and sadness through humans feelings within themselves and infectiously enmeshes into many other souls. stated two sentences previously, regarding strengthening a relationship with **God**, and what shall occur remains this: **Our** christian bible's ten commandments and other functional ways to progress forward with life, **We** view much of what **God** desires as generalities. thou shall not kill, do unto others as **You** would have **Them** do unto **You** and love neighbors as Yourself, remains your wonderfully healthy handbook and collection of functional instruction within your consciousness for everyone following his good.

feel **God**, when attending church, enmeshing souls with **Our** public religious good infection or receive continual spiritual fulfillment, communicating daily with **God**. once individual faith and love heightens **You** shall receive your spiritual humbleness: truly believing truth through your optimistic ideas and information **You** are receiving from **God**, life's perspective, thus, awareness heightens regarding many miracles. occurring continuously around You, others shall desire having exactly what **God's** perfection is through You, your offspring, family and other faith filled lives.

while these generalities scripturally remain wonderful through your soul, humans unique and spiritually manifested consciousness feels abundant energy upon one moment and lethargic upon the following. one reason

You feel this way corresponds with how You receive your consciousness. once You remove the facade and become real, rather than an inwardly absorbed model, shall You desire living with God rather than existing.

receiving solace from God, through Ourselves, desire loving life with others as a welcomed yearning rather than another chore, life becomes contentedly wondrous.

secondly, desiring something more, remains what God shares through You: more adoration, assistance, love, patience, peace and prayer for others, then abundantly increased healthy thoughts are reciprocated for You. many individuals throughout history feeling egocentrically empowered and filled with arrogance or deception; immodest egos are perceived from others as weak or insecure, thus, unbecoming. 'You're desiring modest contentment, through My calmness and abiding love: bravo, i'm living throughout your soul, heart and mind perfectly optimistic.'

filling your heart with caring, hope, joy, love and prayer for others remains well respected by God, he gave You this, however, masses societally remain stagnant and complacent: numbers increase exponentially within many labeled have not's. why are they have not's in the first place? You remain aware, unhealthy through thoughts and behaviors exacerbates generational pain; psychosomatically instilled personas through rearing, originates from the loomer of pain seeking Their demise. earth's societies, many are having spiritual voids from creator with repercussions. weakened souls enmesh bad emotion through Us then remain outwardly expressed through Our verbal, as well as, non verbal communication and behavior for others. preceding digressing further through God's societies, what shall occur and when? intrinsically possessing absolutely your higher faith with God, therefore, negating satan, affects all individuals, thus, societies throughout humanism and weather well.

You see, humans living through flesh only, thinking and focusing on present tense and repeatedly pondering unchangeable past occurrences, thus, abundant negative information given in life, psychosomatically hinders achieving your full potential. stated previously, God, desires all of

Us, making one appropriate spiritual choice, calmly living **Our** faithful life and as a fleshly example for his following offspring. education, faith and rearing are significant factors learned from spirits through Us: if reared within family, inundated through behaviorally inappropriate occurrences, transpiring through majority of awake hours, consciously **You** behave accordingly. **You** know this. there remain many exceptions, achieving more than how reared. **God**, chooses souls, desiring an increased higher return upon human investment. absolutely **God**, desires progress and prosperity rather than complacent stagnation: your aware, society has overflowing divisions separating haves and have nots: stagnation sadly looms through feelings, thoughts and behaviors of all involved. societal deterioration remains spiritual through Us, always has, however, also may be altered optimistically through awareness, faith, praise and **Our** loving prayers. enjoy the frictionless ride.

over three decades, the spirits spoke regarding murders upon television: '**they are spiritually** infected: **pray for the family of deceased and Their friends. he also hears, pray God heightens peace within the future.**'

satan works through drug dealers, gang bangers, hackers, terrorists, murderer's and thief's minds for his agenda and You're aware what this is. those living in downtrodden inner cities, are complacent because government enables Them: feeling hopeless, they desire minimal achievement through themselves, attaining or striving further within life: coupled with drugs, gangs and violence, remain altogether shunning **God's** desire: lacking **God's** assistance spirals **Them** downward, possibly generationally forever. individuals living anywhere, **God**, desires **Them** getting off **Their** buttocks and from watching television, ceasing ingesting chemicals, masking discountings originally instilled through **Their** souls, thus, persona from satan, wanting demise and failure; thus, another capable individual from **God**, who has much to offer a great society.

similarly, writer, preceding **God's** third and final profound intervention was also in satan's grasp, consciously using chemicals primarily for escaping life and filling a spiritually incomplete void. stated previously, occurring often in writers depressed and overwhelmed soul, thus, mind, here was another lost life cyclically numbing discontented feelings inwardly through chemicals then outwardly through another.

from **God's** guidance, escaping altogether has vanished. from **God's** wonderful calm, patient and unending love, taught your writer to rely upon **God**, rather than wasting precious moments attaining a fix through many unhealthy behaviors and material distortions which fill the internal voids through soul temporarily. listening, thus, following **God's**, suggestions alleviates egocentric, temporal fleshly fixes, thus, negative perception in mind and **God**, allows happiness and forgiveness within your gentle love.

proceeding upon your wonderful path if **You** let go, **God**, instills thought processes for healthy behaviors, optimistically for **Yourself** and ultimately for your offspring. spiritually progressing upon this road, immediately or over time leads to calmness through your mind: feeling overwhelmed vanishes, thus, thoughts for all others becomes pleasant while **You** become miraculously calmed and contented within. when **You** heighten your goodness, thus, consistent thinking and behaviors, living functionally productive from **God** through You, remains most healthily attainable. life returns, enveloped and overflowing with your consistent calmness and peace. insatiable wants diminish, emotional, thus, physical pain lessen and focus returns: joyously **You** remain feeling wonderfully blessed or increasingly more from **God** : **You** are because **You** live through a focused faith and a loving prayerful embrace.

optimism, saturates every pore of your three faceted self, with **God**, through your awareness as well as truth. **'10th grade, robert came home from school and I directed him to run to his neighbors home. when arriving there, paul, who was three years of age, had fallen into pool. directed well from Me, robert dived in and saved him, the pool liner was enclosing all around paul.'** life remains your good awareness.

'Do You believe it is humans control why most movies and television shows are negatively **named and enveloped with** bad? **I, desire You experience only goodness.** psychosomatically **believe in this** negativity **or believe in something greater, My loving calmness through your**

perfected goodness and love. all religions globally have had satan infecting minds through negativity: much of religion remains control. I correlate good magnetic energy within the earth with living things. all religious ideologies have implemented My golden rule and this remains from Me because this was and is good.'

'Religions remain cultural interpretations of spirituality: I directed Jesus through countless suggestions from Me. I healed and directed numerous within his good presence: there have been and shall remain zero coincidences for life. Jesus was directed from Me, preceding organized religions egocentric control and doom from satan's negativity. Jesus received heightened direction from and with his Father/spirit.'

'Many christian preachers remain incorrect: when You speak with the deceased, as life, You're speaking with Me rather than Them when the information remains helpful, good, blessed full, as well as, truthful.'

'I spoke for Jesus to say to others in his presence: heal those in need: albeit instantaneous, gradual or proceeding to heaven, God decides.'

'The term rapture was man made, no where in the bible is this stated: specifics regarding the rapture remained manifestations from a human within Her dream and spoken to a priest in the early nineteenth century. who do You think distorted Her dream and following listeners thoughts?'

'A transformation of human souls, thinking and feelings shall occur well. zero new heaven shall be created: it remains perfected and directed.'

Chapter

SCIENTIFIC
FACTUALIZATION

shall delve briefly with scientific facts, informationally overloaded and expressed. scientific community says there remains 150,000 genomic sequences of stroke and cancer risks among a plethora of indefinable variables through sequential instances. first, allow awareness, these facts pertaining within genomes, isotopes and other controlled variables are inconclusive and fallible through a plethora of indefinable spiritual thus human manipulation. genetic disorders are caused through many of these specific types of sequential variation; fleshly exemplified molecular genetic disorders remain necessary establishing **Our** causal link among particular genomic sequential variants, as well as, the numerous scientific diseases being investigated.

many scientific studies constitute realms through molecular genetics: likewise, carbon 14 dating, showing the age of fossilized material as certain remains proven empirically inconclusive. **God** had shown how all data remains altered well and unwell. numerous think humans become more apposite having increased education and sensitized through science and technology, thus, further desensitizes humans from reality: **God**, remains reality of everything good. specific information coupled with differential variables remains irrelevant, what's relevant are how **You** praise, have faith and love calmness within many humans.

before proceeding, writer remains completely aware, scientific communities only intention are helping others through assisting with palpable life preservations and sustainment: the overwhelming majority globally remain aware of **God's** good presence and direction within Them.

may **God** continue blessing **You** further. was making a point from **God**, related to society and what remains most important for the good sustainment of humans wonderful progression.

thus, life remains quite simple and underwhelming when allowed: when all of your thought processes, ideas and feelings remain originated well from **God** or unwell from otherwise, **You** become palpably aware, choices in life remain another spiritual illusion. individually, remain aware, **You** hold keys lovingly for **Yourself** from **God's** grace. **Our** sustainability shall remain blessed and unwavering, with **God**, for several following generations.

thus far, your writer has discussed a plethora of differential reasonings related why **You** and others behaviorally act, react and think as **You** do. within offspring **You** have traversed behaviorally within conscious chosen and generational instilments, psychological and sociological methods intertwined through humans or ultimately stemming from a hindering negative Spirit through **Our** souls, thus, hearts and minds.

progressing, please allow your writer discussing further how an outline remained irrelevant and minimal research was performed other than vocal communications with others, life experiences, situational observances and **God**, through senses for writing book offspring. influencing writers thought processes and all sentences throughout, remains **God**, who is a pillar of confidence and gentle calmness within good functional physical movements, feelings and thought processes deep inside your calm and calming three faceted personal family and offspring's future lives.

'September 11, 2009: My Son arrived home following working evening until dawn. he was unaware what was occurring and mowed the lawn. his wife molly stopped him and said, come inside and watch the news. proceeding slowly, he had gone inside and saw the second airliner had hit the second tower. he asked what he should pray? I said, pray for all, there is another airplane being hijacked west of washington d.c., he asked Me what to think and pray. I said, pray for God to work through a few onboard to storm the cockpit, alleviating future badness, he did.'

'Our book reveals truth, how I have thwarted some negativity within u.s. through My writer; over time, i've asked him to assist Me globally: I give blessed thought processes, prayers and wonderful correlations. every morning and throughout the day, he asks My perfect will and I thwart terrorist activities where I choose, My goodness occurs and You remain becoming aware of what Jesus had received from Me, for many others.'

if writer was a betting man, would smile while your heightened awareness becomes more constant with every page turned, satan is becoming less and practically gone. if You are having any problems with life, spiritually implementing denouncement of unhealthy looming negative entity remains completely apropos through your prayers; having ultimate power, God, figuratively places negative loomer away from your and other souls.

remaining continuously present throughout your soul 24 hours a day, seven days a week and 365 days of the year, God, is all good occurrences through this wonderful earth.

optimism shall prevail increasingly further for You, one of God's calm, blessed and viably favored offspring. God has a plan, perfectly through You as well.

God rebirthed your writer and discerned all religious texts, humanism, spirits, weather and the human consciousness for a reason: over numerous days, through conscious visions with unbelievable clarity, **God** revealed what buddha, jesus, Moses, the disciples and other significant humans had experienced and what spiritually was occurring through **Their** minds and then would speak when and what to write for You. **God** decided now is the time for others to learn truth. continue with enlightenment: proceed favored, advance humbled and assisted well into your optimistically blessed future. life is good and your purpose shall be revealed, as well, when **God** desires. remember, all goodness remains **God's**, humans whom adhere to these words shall receive a soft, gentle and optimistic progression. life is good and so are You. **'thank You son, for slating My truth, I have a plan.' You** are welcome **God** : how shall **You** be served? **'ask and follow My perfect suggestions and life shall be good within numerous others.'**

76

OUT OF YOURSELF

present writings, numerous reading are aware, having instillations of **God's** love, in plethora of specific junctures with life's blessings occurring often around **Them** and many others have refrained having a spiritual enlightenment, thus, less aware. if **You** live in former instance, please proceed to next chapter, however, **You** may read further, thus, receive specifics and communicate with any human behaviorally, emotionally, mentally, physically or spiritually challenged whom are desiring less pain and heightened awareness, therefore, countless individuals upon the earth.

here **We** go. stated previously, numerous religions on **God's** earth remain correct. how **You** were psychosomatically taught, trained, how **You** act, think and deepest beliefs in your heart, mind and soul remains imperative, thus, viably significant. throughout humanism, egocentric interpretations through fleshly control, coupled from satan distorting perception and wants failure, life is more difficult for humans. writer learned christianity primarily, however, believes what buddhism teaches relative within present theologies through **Our** intellectual and optimistic mindsets. **God** is **God**, one **God**, now and forever. remember Abrahams two sons isaac, as well as, jacob? **God**, had spoke appropriately and perfectly to his son, Abraham.

'**I am God of Abraham, God of isaac and God of jacob: I shall always remain a God of all blessed humans living upon My earth and ultimately, everyone shall live perfectly within heaven.**'

taught jesus, shall expound accordingly with christianity. similar as the majority of this book, writer shall use **God**, because all good occurrences are from him and Her, as well. '**son, there remains a reason You receive My words: I chose You to slate My book and relate with all humans.**'

shall proceed with a palpable question: what leads christian behaviors in homes, good actions or a wonderful theological virtue, faith? first, faith in **God**, remains what saves **You** from overwhelmedness; the instances from christianity, buddhist, islamic, judaism and the one good Spirit through Us, positive thoughts replace pessimistic. second, when praising **God**, your offspring and your calmness comes intuitively and naturally. remember, all of **Our** good intuitiveness, nature-alness and coincidences are **God**, working perfectly through offspring globally, therefore, **You** and Yours as well.

christians, believe optimistic thoughts and behaviors for family and others remain paramount, thus, empirically proven true repetitively for two thousand years. **You** reap what **You** sew. also, many christians desire giving charity through time or monetarily for less fortunate remain viewed viably important by **God**, as well. are **You** seeing a wonderful correlation here? yes, one **God**, yields everything for **You** when remaining faithful, thus, contented within. **God's** goodness, envelops all emotionally, financially, mentally and physically when remaining out of Yourself. as faith grows, everything does, as well, everything. stated briefly previously; please regard as emphasis, numerous of **You** coming out or away from pessimistic situations and within more calm, optimistic and peaceful ones remains simplistic.

comparable with removing a suit of armor weighing **You** down, causing movements becoming slowed and heat in the suit saturates every skin cell, because You're having to battle and fight, day in out for good sustainment. for others, this process becomes more difficult, how simple or difficult life's process becomes depends how much You're willing to let go, praise **God** and give **Yourself** to others from his will in You.

these specifics may seem extraordinary within your complex mind, however, **God** neither judges nor condemns your past improprieties if **You** repent and mean this. this remains why Jesus died: as a symbol for the relief of your transgressions and **You** shall receive a pure new life.

'Live in the Spirit with Me and You shall receive zero transgressions **nor a reason to need repentance.'**

satan, on the other hand and through many mortals, yields anger, anxieties, control, deceit, depression, jealousies, manipulation, pessimism and spitefulness, at times. **God**, awaits all with open arms, thus, desires giving assistance and peace of mind; once optimistic behaviors, feelings and thoughts enter soul, a thorough restoration occurs, then **We** desire giving Ourselves to others through good actions and helping **Them** find a gentler way from **God's** calmness and patience received through Us.

preceding proceeding, shall acknowledge one who has influenced writer's feelings and thought processes. following the rebirthing process, **God**, with zero coincidences, remained aware your writer had matured enough, gone through significant emotional, mental and physical pain from bad entity. **God** has given your writer an ability to receive higher awareness of a multitude of specifics occurring at once, as well as, relate or empathize with numerous others: writer would receive many inequities within body and mind over several months with information of how to relieve **Them** through specific prayers from **God**. writer was unaware why, however, **God** spoke, **'all these specifics were occurring for a reason and all shall be well over time.'**

fall of 2009, soon after the final rebirth, **God** placed a family friend here in edmond with his wonderful and blessed family. through spiritual conversations, writer received information regarding one divinely inspiring book. this book became the only book your writer had read in adulthood because preceding doing anything in life, **God** taught to always ask if this should be done. **'I shall discern this book as everything for your experience: trust Me, have faith and You shall be revealed My perfect will for all lives.'**

influential books title remains, mere christianity, author ~ c. s. lewis. reasoning lewis, remains mentioned through specific occurrences preceding and following writings in book shall be noted: praise shall be given to **God**, for yielding lewis's wonderful thought processes, writers, Yours and **God's** numerous chosen offspring following.

please note, specific quotes from lewis shall become paraphrased because lewis's writings remain from a half century prior and relate male function from **God**, only.

stated briefly previously, please, regard as emphasis: placing optimistic thoughts through your wonderful mind continually for progress, **God**, does everything well. one pertinent question: are optimistic thoughts, thus, behaviors from **You** or **God**? before answering, think, **You** and writer are well aware, your parents upon rearing process and the bible, taught You, all have free reign, thus, choosing your will. answering question, optimism arrives directly from **God**, through everyone's thoughts and behaviors: deeply understood and expounded upon when finishing your book.

quoted from **God**, shall end this chapter, **'ponce de leon, christopher columbus, george washington, john Adams, as well as, other great persons on earth as You, remain affected well from My good spirit.'**

'Every goodness within and through You remain Me. I allow everyone's functionality, happiness and optimism- shining brightly through Yourself and all offspring. I, remain triumphant as well as everyone's God : loving and adoring through everything.'

'2013, the final significant hurricane, affecting masses, was in the gulf of mexico. asking and receiving God's continual direction, My writer asked, what shall occur? **from the Spirit he said to sean, the** hurricane **shall dissipate soon: this occurred perfectly. My son, pray for global**

anomalies to weaken further. did. energy shall become certainly stable within the near future globally and determine My perfecting peace.'

'I have allowed scientists to theorize relativity and quantum physics: scientists have taught many, specifically what comprises My universe. physics refrains from revealing why there is gravity, what assimilates the strings of vibrating energy together for mass or why life remains everything rather than nothing: become aware of My absolute truth.'

'Do You understand, life is good for humans through Their specific awareness: becoming sentient with a good perspective and perceptions.'

'Write deuteronomy 1:11 in My words:'

'I, God of the universe, shall allow You to be a thousand times more, when following My direction rather than your own. I shall bless You further and yield what has been promised. I am God and We are one.'

Chapter

HOPE

current chapter remains another theological virtue, hope. adhering God's desire, **You** receive an ability of escaping negativity received through humanism: as negativity decreases, from **God** through You, your awareness heightens and **You** shall find something **You** are truly meant to be. throughout history, christians, and other religious individuals, because of **God**, have all thinking away from the past, within the present and upon a much higher level, the wonderful future. through broad instances, 'those whom built up the middle ages, roman empire or english evangelist abolishing slave trade,' individuals, rosa parks, eli whitney, george washington, john Adams, albert einstein, Mother teresa, gandhi and countless others, 'left impressions on earth because **Their** minds were from **God's** divine intervention, conscious or subconsciously focused on a higher linear plain.' living impulsively dependent in present **We** have become less effective thinking spiritually, on a next higher linear realm:

'**Your book occurred for a perfect reason and I have a marvelous plan: societies shall modify well, in My time, thus, beliefs, faith, praise and culminated prayers shall remain predetermined, sooner or latter.**'

humans who live in the flesh, with **God**, may live within **God's** good spirit, as often as they desire: praying for direction, then listening and feeling **God's**, guidance or when attending church, a spiritual good enmeshment saturates and **You** feel **God's** Spirit through your soul. when focused upon a higher plain, earth, becomes moist chocolate cake following its perfect icing: focusing on the past and present only, sometimes many of **You** are receiving one stale doughnut.

health remains another blessing, if focus lies upon health as a main objective, **You** have a propensity of becoming upset with **Yourself** and 'imagining there is something wrong with You.' **You** are likely receiving health provided **You** desire other things: work, school, better career, games, joy, vacation, mountains, oceans and open air.

similarly, **You** shall refrain saving civilization if civilization remains only specific objective, **You** shall desire learning something deeper and further within your soul.

'The former sentence was another parable for You and your writer, remain patient from Me: let go of Yourself and I shall work perfectly through individuals and societies, well.'

'those proceeding through life, thinking if I would have tried another significant other, had gone on expensive holidays and other fleshly specifics related with past, I would have found something desired. numerous bored, outwardly contented and wealthy mortals remain this type. they have spent **Their** entire lives trotting from one human to another through divorce courts and from continent to continent thinking the current significant other becomes the real thing and remain disappointed in the end.'

'Why would You become disappointed **in the beginning or the end? refrain from imposing your** negative **feelings as well as thoughts into others, over time,** negative **feelings and thoughts cease from Me.'**

for relationships, school and life working well, **You** shall let go of personal wants, allowing 'the real thing,' working through **You** and others for peace and harmony.

God said to write this story: when Jesus was upon one boat and suffocating winds breached many passengers and they became anxiety ridden and thought the end was near. awakening, jesus, prayed for calmness and this occurred. **God** spoke, 'satan **gave these** inequities **through humanism and weather: Jesus was My vessel, I am who awakened and directed him to pray for the** winds, **as well as, the** anxieties **to cease. I do all goodness in the blink of My eyes throughout everything upon earth.**'

GOD'S WAY

'creatures are not born with desires unless a satisfaction for desires exists. babies feel hunger and there is food, ducklings desire swimming, there is plentiful water.'

following writings remain paraphrased because lewis's writings encompass only males desires, thus, because **You** may remain female and societal constructs have modified, shall continue equating writings through gender and spiritual neutrality: humans rather than males receive primal and innate sexual desires, there is sex. if **You** find within **Yourself** some of these desires which zero experience upon earth or another satisfies, the probable explanation is **You** were made for another world. if your earthly pleasures are far from sustainably satisfying, this shall exceedingly remain distant from proving **God's** good universe as fraudulent, more than likely earthly pleasure refrain from satisfying and only arousing, suggests the real thing.

please focus: if this is true **You** must take care, on one hand, keep from despising or unthankful for these earthly blessings or others, please, refrain mistaking **Them** from something which are only one kind of reverberating copy, echo or mirage.

You see, **You** must keep alive within **Yourself** and desires for a true world which **You** shall refrain from finding until deceased. disallow **Yourself** getting snowed under or turned aside and make **God**, the main object through life, pressing forward into **God's** next world while helping others find the exact same: inner calmness, faith and peace, numerous believers have through **Them** and **Their** wonderfully favor filled lives.

'Praise and love Me, then You shall desire praying for and loving numerous others: humans prevail perfectly through the countless speaking My name of calmness, goodness and contentedness they blessedly receive as life becomes better for My numerous chosen.'

one additional factual story related within **God's** wonderful power through writer. conceptualizing these writings, **God**, had taken your writer upon another journey: this expedition was with evon, sean and kyle. remaining blessed through **God's** adoration was his, second stage of splendor and embrace, calming winds. traveling across edmond, with ski boat following, sean, an ex professional sailor gazed upon a flag and stated, 'looks as if white caps are inevitable this day, there are 28 m.p.h. straight winds.' saying zero, focused upon **God's**, will. **God** said, **'pray for everyone seen, there shall be 23 vehicles on next intersection and 40 on following.'** when speaking, **God**, also explained why certain instances where occurring, locally, nationally and globally regarding governments and economy. desiring peace for all his nations, your writer understood thousands of words of information clearly spoken through a few seconds. **God** spoke when writing this from/with him, **'I shall do everything.'**

preceding lakes observance, **God**, said these words through writers mind, **'have sean pull over, join hands and then You pray for calm upon the lake,'** joining hands, writer simply prayed for calm upon the lake: continued over last hill, with lake coming into view, it was magnificently calm nearly flat. on lake, writer having wide open eyes, stated to son, **'You** know son, the faster **We** go, larger the waves become.' this occurred, and when slowing, winds calmed further through continual communications with **God**. he spoke, **'I place the good thinking within You.'**

months passed and miracles occurred continuously, throughout awakened hours: asking where to walk and what gate, as well as, prayed for **God** to allow his will, thus, who needed his prayer. next occurrence or third stage when cycling within ymca here in edmond, **'look upon monitor.'** fall 2009 were three approaching hurricanes south and east of yucatan peninsula: **God** asked, **'where shall they traverse?'** thought away from the united states. then he asked, **'specifically where?'** prayed for two traversing through mexico, third up and away from atlantic coast: **God**, having supreme power over satan, did. writer began feeling powerful, yet, humbled. asked **God**, why he desired these boastful statements? **'You are far from** boasting, **this is My truth through You and I gave the good thoughts, prayers and correlations.'**

'Following My writer's third and final rebirth, he was taught and now You, to rely upon Me rather than humanism because I envelop the thought processes and feelings of everyone upon earth for goodness. throughout the previous six years, My writer has learned how to discern the good and bad **voice/thought processes, he receives only good presently and lives within My good spirit: he asks and follows My suggestions upon all awakened moments. he is asked to watch global news and does what I suggest through his mind, therefore, countless minuscule, as well as, enormous good occurrences have transpired globally. I choose specific individuals for My greater good. many times his mind remains correlated with what shall occur and many times, occurrences transpire from his prayers; all of the good occurrences remain originated from Me. albeit, denouncing** satan **from the consciousness of governments, as well as,** terrorists **for the purpose of releasing** hostages, **decreasing** crime, bad **friction as well as gun** violence **in the u.s. and where I decide for reducing major weather** anomalies **globally: My specifics occur because I am God and have a wonderful plan for those whom listen well to these spoken words. My Son was chosen and trained from birth to perform and reveal spiritual truth for whom I desire. within humanism, it is My writer from My**

will: similar to jesus, robert remains aware where all goodness derives. I asked for this quote to be slated on january 14 of 2015 and in My time, those whom desire shall receive absolute truth and wellness. I am God and shall empirically prove My mysterious truth through him: free will shall remain an illusion and spiritual truth shall arrive for whom I work through well. life is good and so are You.'

there remained numerous emergency sirens here, summer nights 2009:

God, spoke saying, 'would You desire these sirens gone for your chosen son?' thought yes. 'pray, I, denounce satan working through edmond souls, sirens gone in evenings.' did. zero sirens upon the evenings, weekends nor new years eves for seven years and counting. God is good.

only one of countless examples of how God works through masses well.

february 2010: God desires quoted regarding how the bad entity works through blessed souls relying upon Their sometimes distorted consciousness,

'Priests and preachers whom molest children; who might You think controls Their thought processes and behaviors? all mortals, on My earth who cause pain on others at times, remain temporarily infected: revealing historical awareness of truth within many humans thinking shall the masses receive the ability to discern My goodness within or otherwise from otherwise.'

preceding mowing with sean in 2010, was learning to discern the negative voice/thought process from the good. the voice said, 'the stock market shall drastically collapse today.' in two hours, sean stated, 'market lost 600 points.'

global markets, august 2011, are roller coasters from fear and uncertainty; where might fear, uncertainty and volatility come from? bad Spirit infecting human souls.

upon editing 03.04.12 God said, 'write when You asked Me to denounce satan within those working in u.s. stock market and Me working through Them for good decisions.' your writer did this early 2010 and God asked, 'what number shall it arise to?' thought 111 because of son's birth and God said, 'this is good and shall occur. now, pray what is spoken through your soul and watch world news this evening.' did as spoken and he had market close up 111. 'six months previously, I spoke for your writer to ask Me to bless humans working with agriculture, as well as, technology globally. I did.'

'Writings are from Me through one son. time has come for numerous to receive countless blessings from and with Me: I, patiently have awaited My truth told from robert through numerous I desire chosen. I, work through everyone's grace, perfection, performance and peace.'

numerous concerts attended throughout life, the voice, would say, 'electricity is going out in auditorium.' did. through mind following blackout, thought what now? God spoke, 'pray for the electricity returning.' doing what was instructed and immediately electricity returned. occurring sporadically throughout life, when roller skating as young boy, playing video games, computer, electric garage doors and parents home alarm system turned off and then back on. snow skiing, voice would say, 'chair lift is stopping in three seconds.' God, would then say, 'how's your faith?' 'good.' 'pray, chairlift begins in five seconds.' praying as said, this chairlift proceeded perfectly following precisely five seconds: almost continuously have been aware of many things at once.

correlations within human minds are from the spiritual world, the good are from God through You for progression: when You look in a mirror, demeaning thoughts and words You receive are from otherwise to decrease your self worth and image.

fall of 2009, was running around lake hefner, here in oklahoma city, with sister preceding daylight. as life, voice was speaking continuously of what to do or who to pray for. mind, was spinning and received thousands of words of information in seconds through soul. after running and praying for thousands as directed, sun had refrained from rising and **We** were driving up to one intersection. **We** were stopped at a red light, what seemed like numerous minutes: neither directions had a green light, thus, moving. sister, was impatient and became angry. communicated silently with **Our God's**, good spirit, voice said, 'light is stuck.' now aware bad entity was who stuck light. asked what to pray for, **God** spoke, '**pray for anyone other than Yourself.**' did. prayed for sister's patience: **God** said, '**pray for the light turning green.**' did. light turned green immediately. asking why this had occurred, **God** said, '**I have power over everything when I speak this shall be written.**' 1.5 years later, **God**, said to watch transformer movies and completely related through what occurred.

'**All goodness within life are from Me alone and through others for heightening of awareness. I have a wonderful plan and desire your participation.**'

shall make this brief. countless athletic events observed in flesh or on television, **God** spoke, '**whom do You desire winning?**' praying for **God**, to work through these athletes energy, continue to ask what **God** desires and they always win. writing book for and from **God**, had arrived to church one sunday morning of february in 2010, torrential rains came down. '**it is raining in the front and the back of the church: the congregation shall arrive within twelve minutes: what shall occur?**' prayed for rain staying in back of church, thus, people would refrain from becoming wet. immediately rain continued in the back of **Our** church and subsided in the front. **God** spoke, '**go tell your pastor dawn.**' did, told Her it was raining in the back of church only while the front became dry. felt zero need saying this was from prayer and continual communications with **God**, it was so. following church had gone home to work upon your book, however, lightning had affected power to residence and computer was off. upon juncture was worried much editing was lost. asking **God** - turned on computer, praying text to be saved and 15 pages were erased, however, what were edited and unsaved were there. perplexed, thought to go through book finding what was gone, **God**, clearly spoke, '**why** waste your precious time, Our book has been edited: proceed.**'

what is wonderful, following reboot of computer, **God's** writings were saved: he asked, **'do You trust Me to save the text I desire for others?'**

replied, 'yes, what is your will?' many times preceding sleep, he asked, **'when might You desire awakening?'** when the chilean coal miners became trapped: asked **God**, when shall they be rescued? he said, **'pray for Their safety.'** did. he then spoke, **'good, when were You born?'** thought 1969. he spoke, **'there is your answer.'** thought, 1,969 days is long time. received zero reply. on day 69, they emerged alive! praising **God**, continually prayed for others good.

edmond, is the number one suburban city to live within America. why? **God** speaks, **'upon awakening You are asked to bless edmond residents, You then denounce** satan **from Their souls and You ask if I will do this and I always reply yes. repetitiously, You ask and do My perfect will.'**

God, revealed thousands of memories through life; relating sometimes continuous communication, **God** would ask, **'what shall occur and countless times when.'** listening and doing as instructed, prayed for an abundance of rescues for people lost from mud slides, hurricanes, tsunamis, tornadoes, tidal waves and accidents occurring from bad entity, globally: 95% of time, would occur specifically as prayed.

after evon's birthing **God** said, **'turn to a specific channel on the television I direct You to regarding local, national or global weather.'**

progressing through stages, **God**, asked if storms shall dissipate or rise then where they shall traverse. when spoken to watch live footage of tornadoes, writer asks **God's** desire, **'pray what is received, then pray for** tornado **rising immediately?'** praying what's spoken, tornadoes rise immediately: life miracles occur for others. sometimes receive zero awareness, however, observe the significant decrease of hurricanes, tsunamis, typhoons and tornado deaths globally over the last few years. excited to see the goodness that shall occur for numerous in the future.

first and second quarter of 2010, voice continuously spoke of natural disasters that occurred globally with specifics of numbers of people that were lost and deceased: writer replied, 'how may **You** be served **God**?' instructing what shall be prayed, thus, had thought **God's** words verbatim, 'praying **God** works through the rescuers souls for **God's** good agenda, life.'

'**I, initiate all goodness, pray for all My desires rather than** negatively **controlled; directing goodness, I, shall modify earth through My followers spiritual and chosen lives well: following robert's direction to publish God's offspring, I shall show My power within him in time.'**

from **God** through writer, february 11th, 2010: following relearning information, asked him why these thousands upon thousands of miracles and rescues correlated sometimes to the second or day?

'**I know past, present and future; be joyous for I shall yield, as well as, correlate the thoughts and feelings of those chosen further: affection, blessings, optimism, patience, peace, prayers, suggestions and good ideas within wonderful thoughts and feelings remain from Me alone and through other humans for good.'**

'**When your writer was youthful, I initiated countless instructions for him: when I desire, he receives lightning speed direction continuously. upon the ages of 12-39, he received similarly, likewise, the miracles vacillated from humanism to weather. I instructed him to tell zero others because prayers refrained from working every time: he remains aware all goodness occurs in My time and he always does as instructed, if good. My writer continuously asks and proceeds as directed: he remains highly aware and became profoundly** depressed **through life** because of future negative **awareness. upon conception of this book, your writer was receiving continuous** negative **global awareness of what would occur through humanism and weather. I spoke, do You desire this** negativity **gone from your thought processes and feelings?' overwhelmed, he thought yes, please zero more** negativity. **I spoke again, ask Me to denounce** satan **from your soul and pray for God to envelop your thought processes and feelings. he prayed this verbatim and all** badness **ceased instantaneously. he prays this every morning** when awakened. what relief he finally received: over four decades, his negative awareness has ceased. I speak for those reading, negative awareness within your feelings and thoughts that allows your and others safety are from Me and otherwise is otherwise. (consciousness) live within My Spirit and life shall be a pleasure for You and others.'

'Numerous human within the civilized world remain misunderstanding what remains occurring through who receive visions of enlightenment. within the indigenous world and far away from electronics, as well as, other temporal specifics, people see Them as gifted rather than delusional. why shall numerous family members and psychiatrists remain distorted through Their thought processes and want Them to receive medications? this question shall become resolved within your mind and allow You to understand whom I work through for many others wellness rather than individuals within societies affected from Their distorted consciousness.'

'Presently and for writing this book for You, My writer receives information slowly and fast upon any given moment. I remain always present for questions and yield yes and no answers, as your faith heightens, I sometimes give suggestions through sentences for your wellness: the suggestions may be different from what You desire, remain patient, in time, You shall understand why. I remain aware of what is in everyone's best interest. through your and My writer, receive heightened awareness, spoken and suggested for friends and family: these suggestions shall prepare You well into a certainly blessed future. remember, one of many purposes within offspring remains truth for You, as well as, negating a plethora of friction full and negative ideologies, learned through humanism. You remain further blessed following the creator of all goodness rather than Yourself and others. life remains wonderful and You are Mine.'

Chapter

FAITH

much of this chapter are from the book mere christianity and **God** asked his writer to modify the text when directed. lewis's writings are quoted.

present chapter, shall remain referenced what **God's** people, call faith in **Our** lives. specific word faith, shall be used in two senses or planes, thus, taken respectively. through first sense, faith simply means believing, accepting and regarding factual doctrines of **God's** perfect word as truth. this remains simple, however, puzzles many of **God's** offspring thinking and regarding **Our** faith are from virtuous senses.

how could faith remain virtuous, believing or disregarding statements? sane humans accepts or rejects a set of statements, because they desire accepting or otherwise because **Their** evidence seems optimistically or pessimistically solid. when **You** become correct regarding goodness of evidence, **You** shall consciously desire remaining good, thus, realizing **You** are more intelligent than **You** first anticipated. if your evidence was bad, thus, forced **Yourself** believing, this would be illogical. thinking **You** shall procure the former view of goodness. what many refrained seeing before and numerous disallow observing currently was and remains the following.

assuming your mind accepts specifics as truth, **You** automatically proceed regarding as true, until empirically proven untrue, thus, reasoning reconsiders showing itself. many assume **Their** minds are completely ruled from reason and this remains incorrect. example. reason, remains perfectly believing and convinced with good evidence, anesthetics asphyxiates and surgeons abstain from operating if **You** are conscious. differing from altering fact, 'when they have **You** lying on an operating table and clasping sMothering mask over your face, a mere youthful panic overcomes You.' becoming afraid, what if I choke or they might proceed before becoming anesthetized? **Our** intellectualizing from reason and faith becomes less, thus, thoughts supersede what **God** gives, calmed and focused direction working through the surgeon and Yourself. (soul enmeshment)

preceding operation or other subtle or cathartic occurrence: pray for **God**, to work through the surgeon and other minds, thus, your entire process proceeds perfectly. from **God** through others, his blessings of peace and tranquility envelop everyone. **God**, is goodness in and through everything. writer shall return within your story.

why do humans emotions become distorted sometimes: between faith and reason from one side and imagination from the other? thinking of this, **You** may commence viewing a plethora of specific instances having occurred previously. 'males, know gorgeous females,' very well, currently males and females alike through every aesthetic form typically 'express non-truths, unable keeping secrets and should refrain from being trusted.' when finding **Yourself** with one who appeals to senses, your mind disregards faith from a minuscule amount of knowledge and think formidable desire, shall behave differently this time: confiding, your said specific should have remained concealed. feelings have ruptured your faith through what **You** already were aware were true.

writer believes when asked questions **You** should always remain honest, thus, zero explaining later or others faith lost in your word. returning to faith upon a higher sense remains a most complicated specific attempted. approaching then returning back with subject of humility: first step related to humility is realizing **You** remain proud.

adding next step remains practicing christian virtues. if You're attempting one week, this refrains becoming minimal enough of a duration, similar to relieving negative impulses of halting drinking or smoking, sometimes occurs well upon first week: attempt stopping negativity for eight weeks. traversing higher from point where **You** began, **You** shall uncover numerous truths, as well as, learn how positive life becomes when calmly optimistic. resisting negative temptations, awareness heightens and viably **You** are living through **God's** continual optimism.

'**You** find out strengths of russian army by fighting against it rather than giving in and become aware strength of wind by walking against it rather than lying down.' one who gives to temptation after only five minutes, remains unaware what shall occur one hour in the future, thus, remains why bad people, in one sense, are less aware regarding bad; they have lived sheltered lives, always controlling, cheating, deceiving, lying and manipulating others. resisting **Their** unveiled strengths within from **God**, thus adhering to the bad processes rather than goodness through **Them**.

'**Resisting** temptation, **christ, became all of My earths most complete realist: directed to speak well and** unwell, **he continuously asked to do My will. he spoke regarding how humans would behave in the future.**'

please focus: faculties **You** possess- health, positive thinking and good movements throughout your wonderful body, as well as, a sound mind remain freely given from **God**. if **You** devoted every awakened moment of life, exclusively to **God's** service, **You** would refrain giving him anything personal or already his within the first place. when speaking of one mortal doing and giving everything to **God** ; writer does and shall share what this remains comparable with. throughout life, asked **God**, what his desires were on most awakened moments and then followed every suggestion.

now aware, suggestions were sometimes bad resulting in negative consequences: resist all negative suggestions given, in time, they remain admonished.

numerous continuously receive spiritual communication or transformations from **God** through Them, therefore, living life outside themselves; assisting others, many wonderful miracles transpire when your faithful, thus, believing in Her and him.

asked **God**, how he felt referred to as Her. **'I gave You these thoughts.'**

'Remaining Her and him, as well as, all goodness through blessed hearts and minds, I am the blueprint for living well: receive My grace.'

Chapter

SPIRITUAL TRUTH

You may have refrained from receiving a wonderful rebirth from **God**, continuously, remain living with **God**, desire calmness and blessings or skeptically disobedient. succeeding any of these paths, **You** are blessed because **You** live rather than which denomination your affiliated, how and when **You** pray or other definable variables expressed through humanism. **God**, desires blessing **You** anywhere and needs You, in fact, all of You: out with bad behavior, emotions and thoughts and in with good.

'I, love and adore You through your consistently humbled wellness.'

countless remain aware, **God**, is personally available; yes, a **God**, assisting with specific fleshly desires and ultimately allows your eternal life, into perfect heaven.

only specific or definable variable, related living on wonderful earth, more calmly or chaotic, remains your heightening religious or spiritual focus, beaming, **God's** wonderful joy rather than negativity. sounds simple, well it is, as life, with **God** as superior rather than **Yourself** or other humans, life absolutely becomes glorious. mortals, fail **You** repetitively over time, while **God**, has failed zero humans ever: failure and other negative behaviors, influences and thoughts affecting **You** and Yours are attributed from what's its name, always has and shall. **God**, always forgives, desiring wonderful offspring praying for children, another and then themselves: embracing **God's** loving calm, patience and peace, through You, allows prevailing triumphantly over bad entities demise within your heart, mind and soul throughout your favored life.

youths lives remain wonderful for several years, many things remains about **Them** as offspring, then a limbo transition of finding themselves occurs perfectly. one instance, lives modify rapidly through offspring's birth and life regards Them. life's pendulum figuratively swings to and fro through negatively abrupt and fluid transitions; many, thoughts and behaviors remain abrupt or fluid, as well. **God** remains your fluidity.

with awareness of **God's** calming presence, through Us, your impulsive thinking, negative thoughts, behaviors and mood swings are extinguished, fluidity comes. the pendulums of life becomes centered, focusing on what matters: faith in **God**, loving others and certainly numerous present and future enlightened offspring's lives shall proceed utterly well.

wonderful readers, again, remain aware, all **Our** stimulation flowing across senses instantaneously in **Our** minds, remains stored then retrieved for your future recall. males, having been labeled visual and spatial, psychosomatically act accordingly. previous statement remains relative for males, likewise, numerous females also are visual spatial creatures: plethora of **Our** humankind are, rather than only males. stigmas differentiate males and females when solace and peace becomes achieved through **Our** prayers.

perspectives modify, your water glass is neither half full or empty, it runneth over. dependent from two spiritual factors, plethora of males as writer remain athletic, confident, emotionally, mentally, physically, as well as, highly spiritually selected: through continual blessings by praising **God** and assisting others with **Their** enlightened awareness of truth, all is well.

human's thinking remain cyclical, as global warming and ice ages: anyone notice, when global warming summit occurred many years prior; ice and snow storms, enveloped the n.e. u.s.a.? this summit was postponed. asked then, God said, 'humans shall patiently adapt and overtime shall refrain spending billions on global warming research and educate whom desire education while feeding My hungry.'

expounding with God's quote march 11, 2010, 'conditionally and individually from Me through You, seek a better life for Yourself and others, from My continual direction of wisdom, peace, progress, behaviors and thinking of chosen ones: whom I choose, shall become chosen when consistently following My good direction through Their soul: let your ego go, praise and ask Me to bless people, as well as, places—You shall be cared for well and consistently favored from God.'

You remain aware, fleshly, whom You enmesh your persona with, shall become imperative with who You become: think about, either remaining content with what You have or what You shall. receive awareness before proceeding: when these writings commenced formulating, a wonderful rebirth from God, occurred. depressed, overwhelmed and had unfocused mind, perceptions of writer remained distorted and weak: satan, controlled all these unhealthy thoughts, seeking failure. God, at God speed, then allowed letting go of temporal bad thoughts, and teaching spiritual truth.

one week, post spiritual rebirthing, God, spoke through mind one morning saying, 'john is in his front yard, go to him.' when there, God calmly said to tell john, 'christianity, traditional religions and spirituality are correct, thus, praying to God remains correct.' and did. following morning when john came outside, 32 ravens flew into his yard squawking loudly. God, calmly spoke, 'walk over, silently pray, God, has power over satan and Them flying away.' they did. upon juncture, thought God, was giving powers to your writer: over time, learned these powers were from God, through his writer. week later, following God's direction, expressed information regarding praying to God for sean; aware what would occur, stated, 'numerous ravens shall descend upon your trees the following morning.'

awakening following morning, **God** said, '**go outside,**' heard 69 black birds squawking 0.11 miles away, asked what shall occur. **God**, spoke over one millisecond, '**stay in yard, pray, God has power over** satan, **for Them to go for his family.**'

prayed verbatim, as **God** had spoken and silence occurred following three prayers. only when asked, **God**, gave instruction through your writer performing miracles, through silent prayer with continual communications from **God** : helping others, from following **God's** direction, thus, the dissipation of hurricanes and tornadoes, as well as, prayers for calming winds, healing cancers, seizures and tumors globally without laying hands on **Them** because **God's** gentle relief remains within every human on earth when living in the spirit. over time, learned all of these correlations and prayers were from **God** for Us. **God**, through writer, shall graciously expound regarding millions of miraculous occurrences within life. what shall occur well in the future shall remain from **God's** direction.

God, We have spoken for over four decades. why have **You** disallowed your writer from receiving the illusion of assisting humans previously? '**one, You have over your life and two, the time has come.**'

thought, time has come? '**for offspring to learn, Their lives are given to praise, love Me and lovingly ask Me to bless others: I, give good ideas and alleviate** badness.'

'**Humans whom desire continual peace shall follow My directed and good suggestions.**'

'**You shall do everything I desire My son, because I, work through You perfectly well and have a wonderful plan for numerous chosen.**'

2010, **God** said, '**turn on television.**' he had channel already on to watch. **God**, said, '**listen.**' 'We wait for superman to save Us.' **God** said, '**is absolutely You.**'

your writer remains a vessel who receives your gentle wellness for others. **You** are why, how and when every goodness occurs.

'this is true.' humbled and excited replied, 'when shall occurrences transpire?'

'Speaking truth; discerning humanism, spirits and weather within book: ultimately, all decisions are Mine. calmly continue asking Me and proceed how You are directed for others: I have a gentle plan.'

faith filled souls shall rely upon **God** for **Their** questions and answers. **God**, shall allow whom are chosen, perfect direction, rather than **Their** own.

'Heaven on earth is possible when following My perfected direction— receive patience, life is a wonderful process: countless offspring shall receive the illusion of finding Me when My masses desire peace upon the earth from living in the Spirit with Me. matthew 5:48 is from Me: be perfect, God throughout all of heaven and earth remains perfect.'

'All My offspring's meaning of life, remains, for receiving significantly more positive thoughts, feelings and beliefs through Their souls, hearts and minds. You remain aware where they derive. in time, having increased optimism because of your heightened praise for Me and prayer for others, I, shall work through You and others around, thus, feel safe and secure: when numerous perspectives and perceptions modify, the future shall become blessed for My following generations.'

'Understanding all, I, equate everything good given through You and others. I, remain the reasoning humans love and respect one another perfectly well. listen to these words- life's good and You shall become perfected within your soul. everything spoken through your book are true, I, am God and love You well.'

God, is your writer jesus? **You** have taught the process of healing anyone on any continent and calming storms where **You** desire. **'I have chosen You for this specific time in history: your favored life and this book occurred**

for a perfect reason. continue speaking My hope and truth into others from My goodness. Our book, spoken for numerous current and future offspring, reveals global spiritual truth. countless remained and remain unaware from where the information they receive derives: chosen humans shall become aware of truth and receive My goodness.'

what was Jesus aware of? 'all he revealed was from the spiritual world. Jesus repeated what I had spoken when he said, no one comes to the Father except through Me, as well as, I am the truth, way and the life. he was unaware of an abundance revealed within and through robert: he believed he was healing and calming winds/storms because he was told this. over a short time he was revealed, every goodness remains from Me through human vessels: humans egocentrically distort truth.'

'Within My/your writer, I shall slate a few more quotes within book.'

'The reason may 21st 2011 shall pass without Jesus returning, taking believers to heaven and leaving others in chaos as numerous christians believe, remains because of what they have in Their minds; what the mayan's believe shall occur december 21st 2012 and pastors stating time of tribulation is here are untrue. satan, has worked through blessed souls throughout history yielding untruths. from thoughts throughout book, You shall desire rethinking agendas and behavior, thus, rethinking personal faith and love for following generations.'
'atheists, everything from nothing remains ludicrous: deeply they are aware. humans belief, behavior, prayer and thinking determine your lives notably. when humans, I desire, become sentient of the truth of everything and My perfect awareness heightens; terrorism, anger, distortions and negativity shall pass: trillions spent upon defense shall be directed well for My blessings. I, have asked robert on numerous occasions what shall occur for terrorists. upon first question to him regarding this, he asked Me what should occur. I, replied, who do You think works through Their souls? loving God or satan? as instructed, robert prays that I work through the soldiers altruistic blessings, safety, direction and eliminate evil: I have asked him to pray for Me to

modify Their ideology and denounce satan from Their consciousness countless times. this occurs in My time as well: I have a plan.'

'Why are dictators and terrorists being extinguished upon My earth? why shall there be significantly less hurricanes, tsunamis, typhoons and tornado deaths in the future? Me, through many chosen individual prayers: ask and follow My will and You shall be chosen.'

'From Me through robert, I, shall show humans globally who remains most empirically factual: unbelievers shall learn truth. disbelievers are blessed, I, provide Their wonderful useful energy, intellect, love, optimism, thus, peace. remaining one facet contributing with societies disbelief, many atheists are good moral people who love others, this is good, however, those who remain attempting to lessen others faith, observe societies and the earth You live on. numerous, remain naive from satan's agenda through many centuries; discrediting My good name works unwell for numerous living upon My glorious earth.'

'God, family, chivalry, compassion, ethics, focus, love, morals, optimism and honesty are how numerous humans shall faithfully proceed through My loving grace.' You may think, yes, in a perfect world exactly this remains desired for everyone. with anyone, growth begins from faith through every single wonderful individual. You are God's planted seed- growing then blooming into one healthy example for spouse, offspring, families, friends, neighbors, thus, societies significant progress.

time has arrived for closing of your book. shall depart with sentences regarding feelings from soul, heart, thus, sequentially mind summarizing what book entails with questions. every human was given free reign through Their thought processes or were they? individuals living upon earth, initially choose Their thought processes or do they? observe any of societies profound good, bad and your soul before concluding. who directs optimistic thought processes, as well as, behaviors? negative ones? if You still think Yourself is who chooses your will of staying positive or negative, then simply choose joy, love and continual optimism and refrain from negativity.

reflecting on **God's** truth, how shall families receive more blessings, favor and optimism throughout life? simple answer.

'From what is written within this book and through all offspring's faithful praises and prayers. follow Me and share what has been written for My readers: I am all universal goodness and shall yield joyful calmness and blessings through You.'

on 02.23.2012 he spoke, 'write colossians 4:1-6 for readers from My words.'

'Masters, give unto your servants that which is just and equal; knowing that You have a master in heaven and on earth. continue in prayer and watch in the same with thanksgiving; with prayer also for You that I would open for You a book of utterance to learn the mystery of God, from which countless were also in bonds, that I, make manifest what You should speak. walk in wisdom toward those without and convert in time: allow Me to enlighten your speech always for grace, seasoned with salt and aware how You may answer everyone alive.'

'My and your book God's offspring remains the door. there remains zero mystery: goodness remains from Me and badness is otherwise.'

having supreme power through everything, **God**, minimizes bad entities influence through You, modifying many others negative thinking, thus, behaviors around **You** in time. offspring's lives receive less overwhelmedness, therefore, his, future generations shall receive higher optimism in chosen minds and good occurrences for all societies. with bad Spirit weakened, earths weather becomes increasingly calmed from **God**, through prayer.

God, desires **Our** happiness, as well as, progression with acknowledgment of where every specific goodness derives, thus, praise accordingly, then life becomes comforted and calm through your good soul, thus, heart, mind and every behavior.

share these simple principles with others and calm envelops countless good souls. he lives around, in and through his chosen offspring perfectly and faithfully well.

progressing through **Our** spiritually sometimes uncertain world enlighten Yourself: there shall continuously remain only one absolute certainty, **God**, who transcends boundaries while unifying numerous hearts allowing love, kindness and patience, thus, continuous calmness and wonderfulness through each and every single individual living and doing his will rather than **Their** own upon his beautiful and plentiful earth.

need a personal prayer answered? ask **God** what to pray and then pray for Yours. length of time or duration remains only one second within your magnificent soul.

'I spoke for robert to join the prayer team within one of My countless churches for a reason: for Me to work through him and heal numerous. I told him verbatim what to pray and live within the Spirit with Me. the spiritual revolution is upon Us, and now, the time has come again for You to learn the process as well when You become qualified from Me.'

'You receive information that someone has a specific inequity. You silently ask Me if I will bless the individual, and I reply yes. then You ask Me to denounce satan from Their physical body and pray for God to heal Them. then ask if I will do this? I shall give My reply immediately. all remains well. You thank Me and I say You're welcome.'

'Healing and numerous other miracles shall occur when living in the Spirit and without negativity throughout your life. goodness remains directed from Me and I have a wonderful plan globally for humanism.'

through writer's continuous faith with **God**, all negative thought processes, feelings and electronic improprieties have dissipated to zero and these occurrences transpired for writing your blessed book. following four decades of anxiousness and other negative afflictions, your writer has finally received peace. thank **You God**. 'You're welcome.' God, shall continue blessing your calm and love through wonderful prayers: '**share My continuous hope, faith, love and peace within offspring whom desire receiving My favor.**'

a final question for **God**, 'have these miracles occurred because of your writer?'

'**Yes, within humanism: You have written where all good originations of Their healing, your prayers, thought processes and feelings derive.**'

'**My son, are You ready to become a history maker, teach spiritual truth and allow Me to heal who I choose?**'

You are the history maker: everything **You** desire occurs for your chosen.

'**You faithfully receive that I remain the solution from Our questions: You shall become revealed that we're the solution within My answer: revealing spiritual truth for humankind has been My desire for 5000 years: the future shall remain wonderful for countless more, as well.**'

'**As You reading, your writer remains aware of one percent of humanism and You have been revealed what I have spoken within his soul for You:**

I correlate, as well as, equate anything within your favored soul as well. remain aware, faithful and humble: all remains well with You from Me.'

'**Warth shall proceed better and better through these and future words spoken from Me through robert and numerous others, all** wars **shall cease and usher in My certainly calm presence throughout the earth.**'

'**Write corinthians 15:51-52**'

'Listen to a secret truth: We shall not all die, when the last trumpet sounds, We shall all be changed in an instant, as quickly as the blinking of an eye.'

'Write revelation 20.'

'Then I saw an angel coming down from heaven, holding in his hand the key to the abyss and a heavy chain. he seized the dragon, that ancient serpent that is, the devil or satan and chained him up for a thousand years. the angel threw him into the abyss, locked and sealed it so he could not deceive the nations any more until the thousand years were over. after that he must be set free for a little while.'

Write revelation 20:6

'Happy and greatly blessed are those whom are included in the first raising of the dead.' 'the first raising of the dead remains the numerous alive whom remained unaware of My absolute truth and become aware.'

'Humans knowing the truth are labeled postmillenarians, because they, thus, You shall teach the coming of lord Jesus centuries following the year 2000: a personal shift shall occur for those listening well.'

'The future shall proceed well through your faithful praise and prayers: many blessed offspring remain chosen and favored beyond measure.'

'The blasphemy remains negativity spoken through the writers of the bible and religious doctrines regarding Me, causing fear and anger. they were unaware. there remains a perfect reason, I have revealed everything within My Son and spoke for him to slate absolute truth for future generations who shall live well on earth.'

'There also remains the perfect reason You were revealed My mystery; live well favored and teach My certainty within many future offspring.'

'Many christians believe when revealed My mystery, Their rapture shall occur. first, why would You believe this untruth? second, I have a wonderful plan and whom I choose shall receive blessings from following slated suggestions into your hearts awareness of truth. My book remains profound for I remain profoundly good within You.'

'John, who had slated the book of revelation and following christians throughout history have received distortions within Their perspectives and perceptions causing fear, instability and uncertainty within humans. My book, God's offspring reveals what scientists, philosophers and spiritual humans have been seeking, the truth of everything living. a thousand years of peace shall occur for those I have chosen within Their souls, thus, hearts and minds because of heightened awareness of how to live with the good Spirit and I shall alleviate all inequities. these humans have learned the truth and shall live peacefully along My perfecting path while numerous unaware others receive frictions within Their consciousness and others around with certain instability. My gently profound spiritual revolution shall occur: heaven on earth.'

'Your final parable. I, have asked robert millions of questions throughout a lifetime and have given him throughout the previous seven years what I desire: every morning and throughout the day, he asks what My will is and does exactly how I instruct him. I taught him to pray for the denouncement of satan where I choose and then for himself, his son, family, neighborhood, edmond, oklahoma and texas, then all other states in America: he asks Me to bless Israel, australia, new zealand, asia, europe and western europe and specific cities whom I speak: then proceeds to the united states, canada, mexico and prays for Me working through humanism; drug cartels to be exposed and drug lords to be found and denounced in My time.'

'2009-13, My Son was asked to pray for God within individuals to overthrow brutal dictators or for Them to receive grim health: he was praying as he was receiving and thought he was hearing God's will because negative energies denounced within storms globally as well. within 2013 was the specific moment when he learned and now You become aware, all negativity within every human soul are from satan. read the underlined words within chapter 78, God's way again. upon this good juncture My Son received zero negative words or thoughts and I spoke: son, We shall no longer remain equated with what shall occur unwell upon earth, negative energy yields negative energy.'

'You shall refrain from speaking of Yourself My son: You shall ask and speak what I, the Spirit suggests within your heart/mind for others learning of My truth.'

'2012, My Son was told, pray for a specific city and country then badness occurred. this was when japan received a tsunami and massive chaos: My Son asked Me why? My writer learned the day before it occurred and this is when he learned in reference to himself: when robert is asked to pray for a specific place or person, they shall need prayers. I taught My writer to always ask Me to bless people and places and then pray for My desires. if You are unsure what I desire, ask and You shall receive the answer through a thought, word or vision. I have a wonderful plan for countless offspring globally. living is continual change: forever, I, am consistent calmness for all of My wonderful offspring and You living perfectly with love and peace through your loving and peaceful life: You and your family's lives shall modify well from implementing these spoken words from and with Me.'

'When I spoke through jesus, he was directed away from discussing old testament scripture because I spoke for him to teach love, as well as, denounce negativity spoken then and others to learn of My good: the seventh trump represents spiritual completeness of God's perfected plan.'

'I have gone further with My chosen and well favored current human. through the previous years, he was revealed why and what all of My writers of all religious doctrines globally were feeling and thinking: through millisecond communications from Me, he was taught truth regarding everything that remains relevant globally, from My desire: robert asks and receives My perfect will for others to learn very well.

through My time, humans I desire through him and You shall receive spiritual truth: I shall remain a God of all goodness through all wonderful offspring. for future reasons, your soul has received the most significantly simplified spiritual book throughout history: 2022 shall occur: numerous offspring shall receive enlightenment.'

'I shall intervene perfectly over My time and the spiritually chosen as well as elected shall receive My moral and physical transformation.'

'My new creation shall arrive perfectly for many, as well as, countless enlightened shall receive Their higher awareness and absolutely from Their higher awareness they shall receive a new relationship with Me.'

'Throughout history human vessels writing religious documents have received and distorted My continual good information over time and these interpretations have affected numerous following generations: this shall pass as well. within the future, My generations shall receive continual goodness because God's true words have been slated, thus, reveals your certainty and remains written for humans peacefulness.'

'You shall be chosen. I, God of the universe shall bless every individual reader further: I see through your eyes, feel through your heart and live well through your blessed soul. finally for You, God's offspring, believing and living spiritually favored remains My decision from perfected blessings directed through and within your graciously faith filled life. it is written: I am God, You are Mine and I have a wonderful plan that shall occur within Our favored decisions for peace on earth.'

'Why shall religious documents close when new chapter shall begin?'

Printed in the United States
By Bookmasters